THE MILLENNIALISM OF COTTON MATHER

An Historical and Theological Analysis

John S. Erwin

Studies in American Religion
Volume 45

The Edwin Mellen Press
Lewiston/Queenston/Lampeter

Library of Congress Cataloging-in-Publication Data

Erwin, John S. (John Stuart), 1954-
    The millennialism of Cotton Mather : an historical and theological analysis / John S. Erwin.
        p. cm. -- (Studies in American religion ; v. 45)
    Includes bibliographical references.
    ISBN 0-88946-645-9
    1. Mather, Cotton, 1663-1728--Contributions in millennialism.
2. Millennialism--History of doctrines. 3. Eschatology--History of doctrines. I. Title. II. Series.
BT891.E78 1990
236'.9--dc20

89-48625
CIP

This is volume 45 in the continuing series
Studies in American Religion
Volume 45 ISBN 0-88946-645-9
SAR Series ISBN 0-88946-992-X

A CIP catalog record for this book
is available from the British Library.

Copyright © 1990 The Edwin Mellen Press

All rights reserved. For information contact

The Edwin Mellen Press
Box 450
Lewiston, New York
USA 14092

The Edwin Mellen Press
Box 67
Queenston, Ontario
CANADA L0S 1L0

The Edwin Mellen Press, Ltd.
Lampeter, Dyfed, Wales
UNITED KINGDOM SA48 7DY

Printed in the United States of America

TABLE OF CONTENTS

Chapter 1
    Introduction 1

Chapter 2
    "pressing after the High Attainment of Religion" 26

Chapter 3
    Christus Victor: Jesus Christ's Second Coming 63

Chapter 4
    "The High Hope of Heaven" 91

Chapter 5
    "The Nishmath-Chajim" 116

Chapter 6
    "Horrible Enchantments and Possessions" 153

Chapter 7
    "The Torments of Hell or Christ's Grace" 175

Chapter 8
    "The Time is at Hand" 194

A BIBLIOGRAPHICAL ESSAY:
    Cotton Mather's Changing Image 216

INDEX 239

THE MILLENNIALISM OF COTTON MATHER

An Historical and Theological Analysis

Chapter 1

Introduction

COTTON MATHER (1663-1728) loved and studied scriptural prophecy. Within the framework of biblical prophecy, he focused upon "the doctrine of the millennium."[1] There are at least two reasons for studying Cotton Mather's millennialism. First, Mather is an historically significant figure. An increasingly large bibliography testifies to Cotton Mather's continued popularity as an historical figure whose theology, opinions, and pastoral ministry in colonial Boston has warranted close inspection by scholars for decades. The most recent biography, Kenneth Silverman's *The Life and Times of Cotton Mather* (New York: Harper & Row, 1984), is an adequate example of Mather's significance, not only as an American colonial whose Puritan family name has placed him prominently in the forefront of investigations into early American colonial religion, but also as a personality whose character still stimulates fresh research. Second, Mather's millennialism was boldly and clearly stated in both his public and private writings. His sermons, treatises, letters and

---

[1] Cotton Mather (hereafter cited as C. M.), *Parentator* (Boston, 1724), p. 64. Millennialism is based in theology and precisely in eschatology, the Christian doctrines concerned with the final end of man, and yet, more particularly, in apocalypticism, an even more confined cluster of ideas about the last things. In this study "apocalyptic" means the generic term and "millennial" that subgenus which assumes the second coming of Jesus Christ, the vindication of God's people, and the eventual reign of Christ on earth for a thousand years. Also, since "millennialism" is synonymous with "chiliasm," which comes from a Greek word meaning "a thousand," the two terms will be used interchangeably in this study.

unpublished manuscripts, as well as his diary, reveal an avid millennialist.

Cotton Mather's historical importance and his public and private theological expressions make him an ideal figure for examination into early American millennialism. For Mather, the millennium (taken from the Latin *mille*, meaning a thousand, and *annum*, meaning a year) meant the thousand-year reign of Jesus Christ with his saints after his return to earth but before the final judgment. The millennium was believed by him to be a time of peace and felicity. In one of his earliest writings, he spoke of himself as an ardent chiliast who held "impatient longings for the revolution of a golden age, wherein there shall be . . . a general peace or truce, throughout the whole world."[2] In 1720, Mather again records his interest in millennialism in a letter to a publisher, Mr. Baldwin. "Yett, but will you allow a Professor of Chiliasm to say," Mather proposes, "can anything be done to purpose until our Lord Himself attend with the Eagles of Heaven and makes his Descent unto us: Come, Lord Jesus, come quickly!"[3] While Mather's identification of himself with Christian millennialism was insistent during his adult years and consistent within his theological expressions, modern scholarship displays no such continuity with respect to millennial definitions and typologies.

Leonard Sweet, in his essay "Millennialism in America: Recent Studies," declared "there has been little conceptual consensus about the constitutive components of millennialism, breeding an infestatious

---

[2] C. M., *Military Duties* (Boston, 1687), p. 2.

[3] Cotton Mather's *Letters* (Folder #6, 1720-23), "1720 to Mr. Baldwin," at the American Antiquarian Society.

definitional imprecision that must be corrected before any major strides can be taken in interdisciplinary understanding and intelligible analysis."[4] Sweet decried the plethora of research devices used by the various disciplines of sociology, anthropology, and history to explain millennialism without recourse to dialogue to clarify the definitional malaise.

Definitions and typologies for millennialism abound. The most popular typology for millennialist interpreters has been the "pre" versus "post" categories. If one is a "premillennialist," he believes in Christ's coming before the thousand years of happiness. If one is a "postmillennialist," he believes in Christ's coming after the thousand years of bliss. These types are misleading, for the distinction between the two categories involves more than whether Christ returns before or after the millennium.

The paradise anticipated by the premillennialist is quite different than that expected by the postmillennialist, not only with respect to the time and manner with which the kingdom will be established but also with regard to the nature of the paradise and way Christ rules in it. The premillennialist affirms that Christ's return will be followed by a time of peace and justice before the end of the world during which time Jesus will rule. This kingdom is not to be established merely by the salvation of individual souls over a long period of time, but suddenly and by supernatural power. Satan is held in check during this golden period by Christ and his saints. This final resistance of evil is crushed by a militant Christ, and then the last judgment is held. Generally, premillennialists

---

[4]*Theological Studies*, Vol. 40, No. 3 (September, 1979), p. 523.

teach that the return of Christ will be preceded by wars, earthquakes, famine, the existence of Antichrist, a great apostasy, and a great tribulation for believers.[5]

Postmillennialists believe that the kingdom of God, or paradise, is elicited through Christian teaching and preaching which results in the world being gradually Christianized and experiencing a long period of righteousness and peace called the millennium. This millennium will not be essentially different from the present, and it slowly emerges while an ever-larger share of the world's population is Christianized. Evil is reduced to a minimum, but it is not eliminated as Christianity's spiritual and moral influence heightens. Numerous social, political, and economic issues are solved as the church gains larger importance during this new age. The millennium closes with the second coming of Jesus Christ, the resurrection of the dead, and the final judgment.[6]

The schematic division of millennialism into postmillennialism and premillennialism is highly unsatisfactory for investigating American colonial millennial expressions. I concur with one writer's recent observation that these categories are "largely inappropriate for seventeenth- and eighteenth-century apocalyptic thought because they imply too rigid a set of opposing assumptions."[7] Cotton Mather's

---

[5]Van A. Harvey, *A Handbook of Theological Terms* (New York: Macmillan, 1964), pp. 150-151.

[6]*Ibid.*, p. 151.

[7]Stephen Stein, ed., *The Works of Jonathan Edwards 5: Apocalyptic Writings* (New Haven: Yale University Press, 1977), pp. 5, 6 n.6.

millennialism illustrates the weakness of these typologies. While Mather is a premillennialist by the above definition, believing the earth's conflagration imminent and that Christ will return before the millennium begins, he also enthusiastically claimed that the Holy Spirit's angels were coming to spread the Gospel across New England, a postmillennial evangelization hope. Mather did not find it inconsistent to write hopefully of a coming "holy city in AMERICA" while being simultaneously anxious about New England's sinful, morally sleepy condition.[8] Apparently, for American colonial millennialism, there is needed a more sophisticated model than what the "pre" and "post" millennialistic types offer.

Sweet urged the millennial scholar to a more rigorous analysis by sharpening vocabulary and defining more precisely beliefs and behavior "which comprise the millennial phenomenon." The thrust of Sweet's contention concerning contemporary millennial scholarship's lack of definitional precision remains a serious charge and one which I will address using Cotton Mather's millennialism as a case in point to illustrate the advantages for research when one views Christian millennialism as mythology.

The study of Christian mythology has been gaining recognition within the last twenty-five years of this century. One of the reasons is the work of Carl Jung (1875-1961), a Swiss psychiatrist and colleague of Sigmund Freud. Jung recognized the theological significance of religious mythology as a way for dealing with sickness, catastrophe, and death.

---

[8]C. M., *Theopolis Americana* (Boston, 1710), p. 42.

"The religious myth," Jung wrote, "is one of man's greatest and most significant achievements, giving him the security and inner strength not to be crushed by the monstrousness of the universe."[9] But more recent scholarship has ventured beyond this correlation between human suffering and the Christian hope to view the entire Bible as a mythological expression.[10]

In the field of scriptural interpretation, the renowned German theologian, Rudolph Bultmann (1884-1976), advanced a theological method for biblical analysis which essentially claimed the scriptures as mythology. He called his hermeneutical method "de-mythologizing" the Bible. By "de-mythologizing" Bultmann meant that the Bible's content was mythological and therefore it expressed a certain understanding of human existence which affirmed that "the world and human life have their ground and their limits in a power which is beyond all that we can calculate or control."[11] To Bultmann, de-mythologizing was simply interpreting biblical mythology for the present generation. Millennial scholarship has ignored the methodological value residing in the perception that millennialism truly is mythological as Bultmann and Jung have implied through their research.

---

[9]Carl Jung, *The Collected Works of C. G. Jung, Vol. 5: Symbols of Transformation*, ed. Herbert Read, *et. al.* (New York: Pantheon, 1956), p. 231.

[10]See especially Rudolph Bultmann's groundbreaking work *Jesus Christ and Mythology* (New York: Charles Scribner's Sons, 1958).

[11]*Ibid.*, pp. 18-19.

A "myth" is defined as "a traditional or legendary story" and therefore contains the familiar elemental questions of who, what, when, where, and how.[12] Like a story, to understand Mather's perception of the millennium, I will examine the constitutive components that form the myth. The "who" of millennial mythology is Jesus Christ at his second coming to earth. The "what" of millennial mythology is paradise. The "when" of millennial mythology is prophetic prediction. The "where" of millennial mythology is seventeenth-century New England during the witchcraft outbreak in the 1690s. Millennial mythology's "how" is accomplished through salvation and judgment. As elements of the millennial myth, these categories form the content of Mather's millennialism and they may serve as a model for investigation into other Christian millennialists' chiliasm.

Cotton Mather wrote more about millennialism than any other colonial American. His unpublished manuscript "Triparadisus" is the longest treatise devoted to a millennial topic we have by an American author. Millennialism was essential to his thought. His public and private writings reveal a person deeply concerned with millennial themes: the date of Christ's return, how Christ will return, who will accompany Christ upon his return, the location of the "New Heavens and the New Earth," and how the soul will live in the new paradise. His millennialism influenced his theology by giving him a strong sense of hope for his personal future and the future of the world as being in God's hands. His

---

[12]*Random House Dictionary* (New York: Random House, 1973), p. 946.

theology influenced his millennialism by giving it purpose, direction, and a central person. His millennialism was based upon his understanding of the mission and ministry of Jesus Christ. Mather believed that God's ultimate purpose resulted in human history meaningfully ending with Jesus Christ as the victor over Satan's evil forces, while the millennium dawned precisely at the completion of this victory.[13]

The thousand years of peace and happiness resulting from Jesus' victory over Satan ended with a final conflagration. While the first conflagration purged the earth for the millennium to arrive, the second, or final, conflagration will witness Satan's legions finally defeated. With Satan's loss came Jesus' judgment over all souls, with the dead in Christ rising to eternally dwell in paradise and the unrepentant cast into hell for eternal torment.[14]

On the one hand, Mather affirmed that Jesus' return will be by surprise, "like a thief in the night," but on the other hand, he believed that the date could be predicted by properly interpreting contemporary events in light of prophetic passages.[15] Hence, Mather delved into a complex series of prophetic predictions which included 1697, 1716, and 1736 as dates when the first conflagration would arrive and the

---

[13]C. M. "Triparadisus." It is located at the American Antiquarian Society. Its length runs to 390 pages which are divided into three parts. The third part has twelve chapters.

[14]See pp. 7-10 of Chapter 1 of this study.

[15]See p. 69.

millennium would begin.[16]

The fact that two of these three dates carried no millennial significance after the years had passed did not leave Mather disgruntled with prophetic predictions; instead he merely began again to reexamine scriptural texts and align them with current events to make yet another prediction. This curious practice can be explained by the sincere desire Mather had to be a watchful Christian. To Mather, a watchful Christian was one who looked continually for the prophetic signs to be fulfilled and one who even prayed and longed for their fulfillment. The ambiguity surrounding his defense of the 1692 witchcraft trials at Salem was explained by his deepest wish for the millennium to begin and his observation that within these events the devil had unleashed his last fury upon New England. Mather was joyful that the millennium had begun because that meant the return of his savior Jesus Christ, but he could not celebrate this initial millennial stage because Satan's activity had come upon a neighboring community bringing it near destruction through the controversy aroused by the trials, deaths, and animosities elicited from the Salem ordeal. Yet, this episode and the venom directed Mather's way because of his marginal involvement in the trials, and the subsequent charges brought against him by Robert Calef, did not keep him from continuing his watchfulness for the millennium.

Mather's watchfulness extended into the natural realm as well as

---

[16]See pp. 135-149 of this study. He also relied heavily upon Joseph Mede, William Whiston, and Pierre Jurieu. See especially Robert Middlekauff, *The Mathers: Three Generations of Puritan Intellectuals, 1596-1728* (New York: Oxford University Press, 1971), pp. 327-345.

contemporary events; "it becomes us to look upon every Earthquake as a Pramonition of the Day," he wrote in 1727.[17] Earthquakes, fires, snowstorms, thunderstorms, and other natural "Curiosa" all joined together in Mather's thinking to form convincing evidence to him of a sovereign God who promised to return to establish his millennial kingdom.

The most compelling conclusion drawn from this study is that millennialism was an integral theological element in Mather's thought, not an enigma or curiosity. Robert Middlekauff called Mather's millennial obsession with a theory of the soul's immortality a "long flirtation." Yet, when placed within the context of his millennialism, Mather's belief in the Nishmath-Chajim becomes understandable as he wrestled with placing the science of his day in a scriptural framework.[18] Middlekauff claimed that there was "little of importance, or interest, . . . in the incredible stories Mather told in his last years about the world inhabited by spirits." Placed before the backdrop of millennialism Mather's predilection toward spiritual phenomena becomes an essential element of his theology, not something suggesting "the depths of Mather's growing anti-rationalism."[19] Millennialism gave Mather a superstructure that he fitted various puzzle pieces of life into to form a comprehensive whole. So integral did he believe millennialism to be to a right understanding of the universe, he

---

[17]C. M., *Boanerges* (Boston, 1727), pp. 26-27.

[18]See Chapter 4 of this study.

[19]Middlekauff, *op cit.*, pp. 318-319. For stories that Mather told about spirits, see "Triparadisus," "The Angel of Bethesda," and *Coheleth* (Boston, 1720).

placed enlightenment science into a millennialistic scheme, not vice versa. For Mather, millennialism did not reveal an anti-rationalistic inclination but a rational attempt at combining faith and science.

Other contemporary writers have misplaced or ignored Mather's millennialism. While Sacvan Bercovitch sought to support Puritan origins of the American self by using Mather's *Magnalia Christi Americana*, he failed to explain Mather's own millennial theory as a literal interpretation of Christ's return. However, in Bercovitch's defense, he does present an interesting question to be answered: "How much of the Puritan's vision of history is America's vision of itself?" Bercovitch's answer lies in the realm of the Romantic literary expressions of the early nineteenth century, but subsequent scholars have found it within Christian millennialism.[20]

James H. Moorhead summarized Protestantism's nineteenth-century answer to Bercovitch's query when he wrote that millennialism "provided a means whereby Protestants could reaffirm traditional eschatological symbols while simultaneously harnessing them to a distinctly modern vision of gradual secular improvement."[21] Millennialism, like a

---

[20] Sacvan Bercovitch, *The Puritan Origins of the American Self* (New Haven: Yale University Press, 1975), p. ix. See also Nathan Hatch, *The Sacred Cause of Liberty: Republican Thought and the Millennium in Revolutionary New England*, Yale University Press, 1977).

[21] James H. Moorhead, "Between Progress and Apocalypse: A Reassessment of Millennialism in American Religious Thought, 1800-1880," *The Journal of American History*, Vol. 71, No. 3, December 1984, p. 541.

chameleon, changes colors slightly to fit the surrounding circumstances. When one of Mather's children died, millennialism and its inherent hope for a better world served as one source for consolation to him. When the new science introduced a more sophisticated understanding of physiology than "humors," Mather applied the iatrochemical theory to his interpretation of the soul's immortality. When earthquake, fire, or flood brought terror to the people, Mather's ready response lay within his belief that the end time was near and that the millennium would come upon the earth's people by surprise, like a thief. When demon possession and other occult expressions like spectral evidence became noticeable in New England in the late 1600s, Mather interpreted them as a satanic outbreak, a terrible occurrence which signaled the millennium's initial stage. When Turks invaded Savoy and were defeated or when French Protestants suffered persecution in 1716, it was an indication to Mather that millennial events were unfolding and that its beginning was imminent. No contemporary event or personal experience was too small to be passed through his eschatological lens and viewed as a millennial happening.

Perry Miller could have just as easily been talking about millennialism when he described Emerson's interpretation of the presence of God in the soul and nature when he wrote that, "I am as guilty as Emerson himself if I treat ideas as a self-contained rhetoric, forgetting that they are, as we are now discovering, weapons, the weapons of classes and interests, a masquerade of power relations."[22] Millennialism was no

---

[22]Perry Miller, *Errand Into the Wilderness* (London: Harvard University Press, 1978), "From Edwards to Emerson," p. 198.

different for Cotton Mather. As an idea or a set of ideas, millennialism supported Mather's biblical understanding of life and life's meaning. Millennialism also enhanced his biblical interpretation of life's meaning by bringing a theological element into consideration. No matter what he faced in his personal life, the death of his father in 1724 or the loss of his beloved son "Creasy" at sea that same year, he hoped for, and trusted in, a better world in an afterlife with Christ. By 1724, he "daily look'd for" Christ's coming and he knew that all of the signs had been completed for the millennium's beginning.[23]

During Mather's adult years, millennialism's mythos--Jesus Christ's return, the soul's immortality, a final conflagration creating a "New Heavens and a New Earth," and prophetic prophecy--served his purposes as an historical framework for interpreting world, New England, and personal events. Some question may be left as to how his public writings, like his Sunday sermons, artillery sermons, and his election day sermons, can be grouped with his private reflections found within his diary since the audience was so different. However, to Mather, there was no such thing as "private" writings. All that he wrote he saw as an effort to bring his readers to holiness and salvation.

Kenneth Murdock, in his "Preface" to Cotton Mather's *Magnalia Christi Americana*, contended that all of Mather's writings must be considered as works coming from a minister who employed stylistic devices for the purpose of winning souls to Christ. "It is easy to imagine," Murdock wrote, "that when he settled himself in his study and began to

---

[23]C. M., *Diary II*, pp. 522, 740.

write anything, sermon or not, he heard echoing in his ears the sound of his own voice in the pulpit."[24] Murdock concluded that "Mather here was thinking primarily of his writings as a means of winning readers to holiness."[25] For Mather, there was no such idea as a secret or private writing. All things were written by him to glorify God or to glorify and reprimand Cotton Mather as an example for readers. To him, a saved soul was another soldier to fight with Christ on the millennial battle front against Satan.

Traditionally, Christian theology has called Jesus Christ's second coming to earth the "parousia," a transliteration of the Greek word meaning "advent" or "return."[26] The place of Christ's person and Christ's work in Mather's millennial scheme was as a victor. In the private realm of his study during devotions, Mather waxed eloquent about his desire to be united to a Christ whose final victory gloriously reflected not only the universal triumph of good over evil, but also a personal spiritual accomplishment for the individual believer. "I cannot express how much I find myself affected with that Word . . . I find my Soul rising and soaring to this; it shall not only be my greatest Glory to know, and serve

---

[24]C. M., *Magnalia Christi Americana*, ed. Kenneth B. Murdock (London: Harvard University Press, 1979, original 1703), p. 43.

[25]*Ibid.*

[26]"Parousia" is the transliteration from the Greek word which is the present participle of "ath," which means "to be near." See *Strong's Concordance of the Bible* (Nashville: Crusade, n.d.), "Greek Dictionary of the New Testament," p. 56.

and enjoy a Glorious CHRIST," he wrote in his diary, "but also His Glory shall be mine."[27] Hence, the protagonist in Mather's millennial mythology was Jesus Christ during his return to earth.

The "what" of Mather's millennial myth was paradise. Mather's interpretation of scripture led him to a threefold understanding of paradise. The first paradise was in the Garden of Eden where Adam and Eve dwelt until their fall from God's grace after eating the fruit from the tree of knowledge (Genesis 3). In this prelapsarian state, man had lived while "the Glorious God had finished his works of creation." Because Adam and Eve sinned by eating the forbidden fruit of the tree of knowledge, Mather sadly recognized that "poor mankind . . . lost the first Habitacion . . . lost the very knowledge as well as the comfort of that wonderful garden."[28] He concluded that after Noah's flood, there remained nothing for his interested contemporaries to see or understand of that first paradise. Besides, he reasoned, mankind's hopes rested not in the previous Garden of Eden or any return thereto, but in the second paradise, the place of departed souls. The second paradise gave comfort to the believer because it was the residence of immortal souls and "there the weary were at rest." Citing Psalm 124:7, Mather imagined that the second paradise allowed "Our Soul to Escape as a Bird out of the Snare of the Fowler" and that ultimately "our Soul will now be escaped from the

---

[27] C. M., *Diary*, ed. Worthington C. Ford (New York: Frederick Ungar Publishing, 1957), II, p. 731. (Hereafter cited as *Diary* with volume and page number given.)

[28] C. M., "Triparadisus," pt. I, pp. 1, 2.

Destroyer."²⁹ The "Destroyer" was for Mather Satan, Christ's archenemy.

However, the second paradise only temporarily housed the departed spirit. Eventually, when the millennium dawned, Mather considered the promise of scripture to point toward "a New Heavens and a New Earth" (II Peter 3:13). Consequently, the third paradise was the direct result of the millennium's arrival. After the first conflagration, earth was purged and the "New Heavens" was formed. The raised saints live with Christ for the thousand years in the third paradise until Satan's forces clash a second time with Christ. After the second conflagration, which defeats the Devil's legions, then Christ judges all souls, with the dead in Christ raised to eternally dwell in the third paradise and the unrepentant cast into hell for eternal torment.³⁰

The "when" of the millennial myth for Mather was prophetic prediction. Mather, like other New England millennialists, indulged in the fascinating occupation of millennial chronology.³¹ Mather's unpublished letter of 1703, "Problema Theologicum," held that a conclusive movement toward the end began with the passing of the Turkish "Second Wo." "Behold the Second Wo is passed away," speculated Mather, "then Quickly arrives the Second Coming of our Lord Jesus Christ." Mather

---

²⁹*Ibid.*, pt. II., pp. 36, 37.

³⁰*Ibid.*, pt. III., p. 1 and *passim*.

³¹For an excellent review of New England Clergymen's preoccupation with millennial speculation respecting chronology, see James W. Davidson, *The Logic of Millennial Thought: Eighteenth-Century New England* (New Haven: Yale University Press, 1977), pp. 37-80.

Introduction

reasoned that "the final Dispensations of Heaven towards the Turkish Empire" began "about the year 1697."[32] Basing his speculations upon the "Samaritan Pentateuch" and the Sabbatarian tradition which believed that the world would last six thousand years from its creation until God's final judgment, he claimed that "About the middle of the present century the world will want between Two and Three Hundred years of being Six Thousand Years Old; Tho' indeed by the Chronology of the Samaritan Pentateuch, it will be of that age in A.D. 1736." Mather found a good deal of satisfaction in these explicit prophetic predictions especially when he realized that ". . . the Time is to be Shortened for the Sake of the Elect." Even if he believed that mankind generally treated these prophetic matters too lightly, he gained assurance from the fact that "By this account, the Present Century should not remain long, before the Expiration of the Black Period; Yea, and it may be expired before Men make much observation of it."[33] Evidently, Mather's belief in Christ's imminent return informed his obsession with prophetic prediction and accounted for his lifelong interest with chronological theories by such men as Joseph Mede, Thomas Burnet, William Whiston, and Isaac Newton. Occasionally, though, the question of "when" the millennium will occur

---

[32] C. M., "Problema Theologicum" (1703), p. 56. The manuscript is at the American Antiquarian Society.

[33] *Ibid.*, p. 86. For a more thorough discussion of Mather's interest in millennial chronology, see Robert Middlekauff's *The Mathers: Three Generations of Puritan Intellectuals, 1596-1728* (Oxford University Press, 1971), pp. 340-349. He discusses Mather's interest in Whiston, Burnet, Mede and Newton.

crossed over into the realm of history and out of the speculative realm. In one notable instance, Mather feared that the millennium actually had begun in New England.

The 1692 Salem witchcraft ordeal represented for Mather the Devil's final wrath before he would be chained by Christ at the start of the millennium. The "where" of Mather's millennial mythology was New England in the last decade of the seventeenth century, and it was identified not only because of his scriptural interpretation of Revelation 12:12, "Rejoice then, O Heaven and you that dwell therein! But woe to you, O earth and sea, for the devil has come down to you in great wrath, because he knows that his time is short!" but also because of his personal experiences with energumens, possessed people like Margaret Rule, Mercy Short, and the Goodwin children.[34]

In *The Wonders of the Invisible World* (1693), a treatise written by Mather in response to the Salem trials, he wrote that "desparate and peculiar Attempts of the Devil" will be made upon the world when the time for Christ's appearance nears. God's anger with his people who turn to make a pact with Satan will usher in the final act of history for creation. "Great Wo proceeds from the Great WRATH," Mather warned, "with which the DEVIL, towards the end of his TIME, will make a

---

[34]For Mather's interest in energumens, see David Levin, *The Young Life of the Lord's Remembrancer, 1663-1703* (Cambridge: Harvard University Press, 1978), and for Mather's identification of the witchcraft affair with his millennialism, see Richard Weisman, *Witchcraft, Magic, and Religion in 17th-Century Massachusetts* (Amherst: The University of Massachusetts Press, 1984), pp. 130-131.

DESCENT upon a miserable World."[35] Mather really believed that witchcraft was practiced at Salem and that Satan's activity was only a harbinger of the last things before Christ's return to earth.

Other events or signs which precipitated the second coming of Jesus Christ were included in his millennial mythology. Personal conversion or salvation described "how" people became active participants on Christ's side during the millennial drama. Since the restoration of Israel was considered by Mather as one of the promised signs to be fulfilled before the millennium, Mather concerned himself with a Jewish national conversion. In 1699, Mather wrote *The Faith of the Fathers*, a Christian catechism designed "to prepare the Jewish Nation, for the coming of the Messiah." It was his belief that if the Jewish nation would but "Return to the Faith of the Old Testament," they would eventually come to the "Christian Religion."[36]

The evangelization of the Indian also carried for Mather millennial motivation. To him, every soul was valued by God; therefore, conversion to Jesus Christ preserved the spirit of each person for millennial participation. To Mather, the soul was saved from hell and for heaven. "My dear Indians, If you do forsake the wayes of the Lord Jesus Christ," he pleaded in an early work to the Indians, "I earnestly testify unto you, That you shall utterly perish. God will kill you with one Thunderstroke of His wrath after another. And in Hell, you shall cry out, I am

---

[35]*The Wonders of the Invisible World* (Boston, 1693), p. 42.

[36]*Diary* I, pp. 298-299.

tormented! I am tormented! for more years, than you now see Leaves upon the Trees." Nevertheless, Mather stridently urged the Indian to ponder the positive results of believing in Jesus Christ. "But, if you do follow the wayes of the Lord Jesus Christ, you will be Rich above those people that have Money, and all Riches." "At your Death," Mather, in typical chiliastic exhortation reasoned, "God will take your Souls to be among the Angels. The Lord Jesus Christ shall Raise you from the Dead unto everlasting Life, at the Day of Judgment."[37]

Likewise, blacks were considered by Mather as more than "meer Beasts of Burden" because they had "Immortal Souls in them" and were "of one Blood with the English." God was no respecter of race according to Mather. All souls potentially could reign with Christ during the millennium. Underpinned by an urgent millennial expectation, Mather gave away books and catechisms written for Negro conversion, wrote letters to important people to promote black Christianization, and asked the public to change its ill-treatment of slaves. ". . . there can be nothing more seasonable and reasonable than for us, to Consider whether our Conduct with relation to our African Slaves," he promoted, "be not one thing for which our God may have a Controversy with us."[38] The soul's

---

[37]Cited by Thomas J. Holmes, *Cotton Mather: A Bibliography* (Cambridge: Harvard University Press, 1940), I, p. 321.

[38]*Diary* II, p. 663, I, p. 598. Also see C. M.'s *The Negro Christianized: An Essay to excite and assist that Good Work; the Information of the Negroes in Christianity* (1706). Passage quoted is by Mather, and he is quoting Richard Baxter, *Christian Directory*, II, Chapter 14. Mather's activity on behalf of the Negro is apparent: "I not only write Letters, unto the most eminent Persons, in all the Islands, to promote the Design

initial response to God in Christ was one essential ingredient to explain how the millennial myth was completed, whether the soul was Jew, Negro, or Indian.

Besides his attention to a person's initial conversion to Christ, Mather also speculated about eternal salvation. What is the soul's immortality? Writing a treatise in 1728 entitled *The Comfortable Chambers*, a reference to the grave as a resting place for the physical body, Mather considered that God had added to our soul "a fine sort of Matter," which acted as a sense organ for it. To Mather, it was this "Instrument" which lived on eternally. ". . . thus the Spirit carries this Matter away with it," he believed, "when it can't continue Comfortably in the Body any longer."[39]

Mather gave a name to his theory of the soul. It was called by him the "Nishmath-Chajim," which in Hebrew means "breath of life" (Genesis 2;7). This theme appeared not only in his published "Curiosa," which listed items of scientific interest he sent to the Royal Society in London in 1722, but also as a chapter in his unpublished "Angel of Bethesda" (1724) and as a section in his second paradise of departed souls in "Triparadisus" (c. 1726), his most thorough millennial document. The Nishmath-Chajim disclosed a great deal about Mather's millennialism.

---

of Christianizing the Negroes; but I also apply myself unto Sir William Ashurst, and by him unto the Parliament, to procure and *Act of Parliament* for that Intention" (*Diary* I, p. 570-571). Also quoted in Sidney H. Rooy, *The Theology of Missions in the Puritan Tradition* (Grand Rapids: Eerdmans, 1965), p. 245.

[39]C. M., *The Comfortable Chambers* (Boston, 1728).

It explained the connectedness of the body to the soul, what happened to the soul at death, and how a soul could be united to Christ in a resurrected state at the establishment of the New Heavens and New Earth during the millennium.

Salvation, either initially at conversion or eternally with the soul's immortality, was merely a prelude, an event to be completed prior to God's great day of judgment according to Mather. Mather's millennial mythology rested upon a threefold understanding of God's judgment: afflictive, final, and eternal. Afflictive judgment was what Mather believed we experienced as God's providence in this life when there occurred disaster. A catastrophe, such as an earthquake, might signal the grand finale of history, or it may serve as a temporal judgmental warning. ". . . it becomes us," wrote Mather, "to look upon every Earthquake, as a Praemonition" of Christ's return.[40]

Mather perceived final judgment as a conflagration. Mather believed that a mighty fire would consume the earth and purge it for the millennium. "If I should make the cry, FIRE, FIRE! . . . I should be as much mocked, and be as little minded," considered Mather, "as Lot was in the Morning of the Day he went out of Sodom." Mather wanted to awaken the world to the imminency of the conflagration. The conflagration will come suddenly to an earth morally slumbering and "Like a thief in the night," while Christ's return will be accompanied by smoke and fire. In this first gigantic conflagration, Christ destroys

---

[40]C. M., *The Terror of the Lord* (Boston, 1727), p. 27. Also *Boanerges* (Boston, 1727), p. 41.

Antichrist, Satan incarnate, referred to in the book of Revelation (11:7, 19:19-21) and his legions, raises the saints living on earth to be with him above the fire, and gives them transformed bodies. After the fire ceases, Christ's saints rule the believing nations of the earth from the new heavens. The saved nations live for a millennium on an earth purged by the conflagration. The people of the believing nations maintain communication with the raised saints, as well as construct homes, plant gardens, and procreate during the thousand years.[41]

When the millennium ends, Satan leads Gog and Magog from Hell for a final rendezvous with Christ. A second conflagration consumes the Devil's minions and the final judgment results. Those who continued in sin during the millennium form the army of Gog and Magog and are to be cast into the lake of fire by Christ to be burned eternally, while the believers join the victorious Christ in the Third Heaven. Mather conceived of hell as a place for eternal judgment, where the sinner's soul suffered punishment. From this point of view, hell was privative; it separated the soul from Christ. Hell also was the place of active retribution; it inflicted punishment to ensure divine justice.[42]

Viewing millennialism as a mythology with its own constitutive

---

[41]C. M., *Ibid.*, p. 28.

[42]C. M., "Triparadisus," pts. VII, VIII, IX, X. See also *Things to be Look'd For* (Cambridge, 1691); *Perswasions From the Terror of the Lord* (Boston, 1711); *The World Alarm'd* (Boston, 1721); *Terra Beata* (Boston, 1726); "Biblia Americana" 2 Peter, Revelation, *passim*. For "Gog and Magog," see Mather's "Triparadisus" pt. X, "Where to find Gog and Magog," appended, 4 pp.).

parts of who, what, when, where, and how eliminates "infestatious definitional imprecision" and offers the millennial scholar a conceptual framework by which to investigate and analyze the subject. Examination of Jesus Christ's second coming, paradise, prophetic prediction, seventeenth-century New England's witchcraft episode, salvation and judgment as understood by Cotton Mather will be used to interpret his millennialism. Emphasis will be placed upon his millennial mythology's continuity.

Mather's millennialism was lifelong and consistent, with only variations of chiliasm coming in his fluctuating intensity and his prophetic forecasting.[43] Therefore, my method is thematical, not necessarily chronological, although the two methods need not be viewed as mutually exclusive. Biographical events in Mather's life and historical incidents in colonial New England's past will be used to buttress and give credence to the millennial component being investigated. The chronological method will only be explicitly used when a millennial element of Mather's has undergone a sharp change. For instance, prior to 1724 Mather believed that a national conversion of the Jews was a mandatory sign to be completed before the final millennium would erupt,[44] but after that date

---

[43]Robert Middlekauff's work, *The Mathers*, op. cit., views C. M.'s interest in millennialism as more disjunctive than I do. Mather's interest in the spirit world, according to Middlekauff, illustrates "the depths of Mather's growing anti-rationalism" (p. 319) whereas I believe this feature of Mather's Christianity undergirds his millennialism and is integral to his religious and intellectual expressions throughout his adult life.

[44]C. M., "Problema Theologicum" (1703).

he abandoned the Jewish salvation as a prerequisite for the millennium.[45] At this point, the chronological method will be the more useful mode of examination and will be used primarily to unravel Mather's reasons for this significant change in his millennial mythology.

The last ten years of Mather's life have been viewed as a time when he grew more anti-rational as he focused upon the "Prophetical Spirit" and prepared for "the Second Coming of Christ."[46] His millennial emphasis is placed in the context of his entire adult life, so that it may be seen as a constantly recurring theme within his personal reflections and public writings. Mather's millennialism is analyzed by looking at the constitutive elements of millennialism within the purview of a story: who, what, when, where, and how. These myth components translate into the following millennial aspects: Christ's second coming (Chapter 3), paradise (Chapter 4), the soul's immortality (Chapter 5), Mather's understanding of New England's seventeenth-century witchcraft episode as a millennial outbreak (Chapter 6), salvation and judgment (Chapter 7), and prophetic prediction (Chapter 8). Before examining these ideas, it is necessary to outline Mather's theology to begin to see millennialism's role in the broader context of his Christian thought and life.

---

[45]"Triparadisus," XI., "A National Conversion of the Jews." Mather's dropping the millennial sign of the conversion of the Jews is in opposition to his father Increase's beliefs on the matter. I think it is significant that Cotton changes his position in 1724, after his father's death.

[46]For the opinion that Mather grew more "anti-rational," see Middlekauff, *op. cit.*, p. 319.

Chapter 2

"pressing after the High Attainment of Religion"

COTTON MATHER'S intellectual and character formation rested extensively upon his connection to one of colonial New England's most influential families. In 1635, Richard Mather (1596-1669), Cotton's grandfather, arrived at Boston and answered a call to practice ministry at Dorchester's Congregational church. He stayed at Dorchester until his death, all the while contributing to the formation of Congregational polity in New England by writing major portions of the Cambridge Platform in 1648. This Platform declared that each church was autonomous but was related to other churches for fellowship and council. Each church was created by a church covenant linking the believers to one another and to Christ, the head of the Church. Pastors and deacons became the most important officials, and ordination was performed by neighboring ministers when a church wanted to ordain someone.[1]

Richard Mather died one of the most famous New England Puritans of his day. He was recognized for his translation of *The Whole Booke of Psalmes* (1640), a psalter designed for use by the colonial

---

[1]Perry Miller, *Orthodoxy in Massachusetts*, 1630-1650 (Cambridge: Harvard University Press, 1933), pp. 76-77. I have relied upon the excellent work of Richard Lovelace, *The American Pietism of Cotton Mather: Origins of American Evangelicalism* (Grand Rapids: Eerdmans, 1979), pp. 32-72, to prepare this material on Mather's theology. See also note 19.

churches, and as an active advocate of the "Half-Way Covenant," a plan which provided a method for those people who were unable to meet the prescribed tests for the original Congregational polity to become church members by a modified form.

His eldest son, Increase (1639-1723), graduated from Harvard in 1659, received his M.A. degree at Trinity College, Dublin, in 1658, and after serving several congregations in England, returned to Boston in 1661 alternately preaching at the new North Church and in Dorchester. He became teacher of the North Church in 1664 and remained in ministry there until his death in 1723. In 1662 he married John Cotton's daughter, uniting two of the main colonial New England families. Cotton Mather was the first child born to this marriage on February 12, 1663.

Cotton Mather's early life established a pattern for disciplined study of traditional Christian doctrine and classical languages. Eleven-year-old Cotton entered Harvard College in 1675 having already mastered Latin in oral and written fashion, studied the Greek New Testament and even made some progress in the study of Hebrew, all prior to his entrance into formal education. He graduated with a B.A. degree in 1678 after overcoming a bad stammer and his classmates' ridicule. Yet, in spite of peer-group activity which aimed at piercing Mather's pride in his forensic ability, Cotton excelled at his studies. It does not seem to be an exaggeration when the young Mather claimed to have read "Hundred of books" while at Harvard and kept a journal of his studies.² His lessons directed him away from the hazing by his fellow students. His excellence in pursuit of knowledge and the great expectations harbored for him as a precocious young man of a prominent Puritan family were summarized by President Urian Oakes on Commencement Day 1678:

> The next is called COTTONUS MATHERUS. What a name! I made a mistake, I confess; I should have said, what names! I shall say nothing of his reverend father, Overseer of the University most vigilant, since I wish not to praise him to his face. But if this youth bring back and represent the piety, learning, and graceful ingenuity, sound judgment, prudence and gravity of his reverend grandsires John Cotton and Richard Mather, he may be said to have done his part well. And I despair not that in this youth Cotton and Mather shall in fact as in name coalesce and revive!³

Despite the overwhelming pressure to conform to the Congregational ministry and join his father, Cotton resisted entering a pastoral career with a speech handicap, and he focused, instead, upon the practice of medicine. Working as a tutor while attending classes at

---

²Williston Walker, "The Services of the Mathers in New England Religious Development," *Papers of the American Society of Church History* V (1893), pp. 62-67.

³David Levin, *The Young Life of the Lord's Remembrancer, 1663-1703* (Cambridge: Harvard University Press, 1978), p. 55.

Harvard, he received the Master of Arts degree in 1681. At eighteen he stood prepared as a candidate for the ministry after conquering his speech problem and occasionally preaching to nearby congregations during the school year. He was promptly offered, upon graduation, a prestigious pastorate in New Haven, the church founded by John Davenport (1597-1670), but he preferred to remain as his father's assistant at the North Church in Boston, where he had previously served for a year. In 1683, the congregation called him to be an ordained minister, but he hesitated in accepting the offer because of his youthfulness and his sense of the awesome responsibilities in the pastorate.[4] The offer was repeated the next year and he accepted and was ordained in May 1685.

Mather was a conscientious pastor and a prolific worker in the life of the church. Evangelism to the outcasts of society; the poor, blacks, criminals, and Indians; the teaching of catechism to the young; the weekly duties of preaching, visitation, and studying; besides an occasional funeral oration or an election-day sermon--all formed part of the general pastoral labors performed by this Boston clergyman.

He was married in 1686 to Abigail Phillips, the daughter of a politician from Charlestown. She bore him nine children, five of whom died in childhood or infancy. She lived only until December 1702. In the sixteen years of marriage, Mather grew extremely fond of his "lovely Consort." Not able to withstand observing any longer Abigail's suffering, Mather separated himself from her during the closing hours of her year-

---

[4]*Diary* I, p. 53.

long illness. "With her then in my Hands, I solemnly and sincerely gave her up unto the Lord," he recorded in his diary, "and in token of my real RESIGNATION, I gently putt her out of my Hands, and laid away a most lovely Hand, resolving that I would never touch it any more! This was the hardest and perhaps the bravest Action, that ever I did."[5]

A good first marriage led Mather to expect the same marital concord a second time. A year after Abigail's death, Mather remarried, this time to Elizabeth Hubbard, a widow. He had six children by her, but only two lived beyond childhood. In 1713 she died, and in 1715 Mather married Lydia George, widow of John George of Boston. With his marriage to Lydia came tragedy, for she went insane, and to the severe tribulation this brought her husband was added the scandals of a wayward son. Increase Jr., born in 1699, or "Creasy" as he was affectionately called by his father, was publicly charged with bastardy in 1717 and was eventually lost at sea in 1724. Echoing King David's lament over the death of his son Absalom, Mather cried out in his diary: "Ah! My Son Increase! My Son! My Son! My Head is Waters, and my Eyes are a Fountain of Tears . . . I am overwhelmed!" His anguish temporarily waned when news arrived that the ship which was supposed to have been lost at sea actually docked in Newfoundland bringing his dear son back home to him. But Mather's hopes died with the news that "poor Creasy's" fate had actually been sealed with the early factual report, instead of the second false report of his ship's arrival in Newfoundland.

---

[5]*Ibid.*, p. 448.

Mather sadly dispelled the rumor, "T'was another Vessel."[6]

During his lifetime, Mather zealously supported the New England Way, and he plunged into the religious and political controversies of his day. In 1692, he championed the cause of Massachusetts' Royal Charter which his father, Increase, helped to obtain and in the same year was an innocent bystander in the notorious witchcraft affair.[7] Accused by his enemies for being largely responsible for the ordeal, and, although like the majority of his contemporaries he affirmed the reality of witches and published several works on the matter, Mather's efforts largely focused toward moderating the popular hysteria by cautioning the magistrates' use of "spectral evidence." Spectral evidence was testimony depicting supernatural visitations from a demonic creature who appeared in the shape of an accused witch. Even recently deceased persons may take the form of a specter and identify the individual who caused their death in a variant form of spectral testimony.[8] Obviously, spectral evidence remained practically impossible to substantiate since the specters were visible only to the person for whom the appearance was intended. Both Increase and Cotton Mather helped to eliminate the use of this type of spurious testimony.

---

[6]*Diary* II, pp. 753-760, indicates Mather's grief over the loss of Increase Jr.

[7]For Mather's support of his father in the controversy over Massachusetts' charter, see Levin, *op. cit.*, pp. 57-105.

[8]Paul Boyer and Stephen Nissenbaum, *Salem Possessed: The Social Origins of Witchcraft* (Cambridge: Harvard University Press, 1974), p. 18.

Simultaneous to the witchcraft controversy, the Massachusetts General Court exerted pressure on Increase Mather to take residency at Cambridge while he fulfilled responsibilities as Harvard College president. Since 1685 Increase had been president of Harvard College all the while serving Boston's Second Church as pastor. Supposedly, motivated by Elisha Cooke and other advocates of the old charter, the general court forced Mather to make a decision between the presidency or the pastorate. Increase decided to relinquish his presidency, and Samuel Willard was appointed to replace him in 1701. The loss of the position probably did not come as a tremendous blow to the elder Mather. His pastoral duties were of more immediate interest to him than the supervision of forty young men. But to Cotton the incident indicated a loss of his father's reputation. Also, during the period of this episode, November 1700, Robert Calef's *More Wonders of the Invisible World* arrived in Boston.

Robert Calef was a Boston merchant who had taken an interest in the witchcraft affair. Calef argued in his book that the trials in New England had been mismanaged and that the Puritan understanding of witchcraft was suspect. Furthermore, he believed that clergy meddlesomeness in judicial and political proceedings in the colony must be stopped. Most virulent was his attack upon the Mathers. He portrayed their involvement in the witchcraft outbreak as entirely self-serving and inappropriate.[9]

---

[9]Robert Calef, *More Wonders of the Invisible World: Or, The Wonders of the Invisible World Display'd in Five Parts* (London, 1700), excerpted in George Lincoln Burr, ed., *Narratives of the Witchcraft Cases, 1648-1706*

Calef was eventually arrested for libel by Increase, but he later dropped the charges after a conversation with the merchant. The book did not cause a large scandal except in the limited circle of Mather's enemies. The Mathers decided that ignoring Calef's work was the best policy, not realizing that the arguments would be revived during the inoculation controversy in the 1720s and among future generations of anti-Puritan writers.

Many trials filled Cotton Mather's public and private life. Like his father, whom he outlived by a mere five years and with whom he always closely identified, Mather gradually acknowledged that the political, economical, and social realities in New England life at the beginning of the eighteenth century were at odds with the first generation vision he so admired. In 1707, when Samuel Willard died, the Harvard presidency went to Jon Leverett instead of the younger Mather, leaving a bitter taste in Cotton for his alma mater. Harvard College progressively left the spiritual and intellectual standard Mather wished for it, and subsequently he severed his attachment to it and linked himself to the new college founded in New Haven in 1700. Mather's new relationship to the young college proved to be fruitful, for he secured for it an endowment and a name from a New England merchant, Elihu Yale (1648-1721). Apparently, out of appreciation for Mather's interest in the budding academic enterprise in Connecticut, Yale offered him the presidency in 1722 to succeed Timothy Cutler (1684-1765) who abdicated

---

(New York: Charles Scribner's Sons, 1914); reissued (New York: Barnes and Noble, 1968), pp. 342-371.

Congregationalism to join Episcopalian ranks. But his father's ill-health and the distasteful prospects of leaving his devoted church obliged him to decline the opportunity.[10]

Yet, in spite of bereavements, political disappointments, and pastoral duties, Mather wrote and studied constantly. He was an extraordinary man of letters and a virtual storehouse of knowledge. "There was scarcely any books written but he had somehow or other got sight of them," wrote Charles Chauncy (1705-1787), a ministerial contemporary of Mather's. "He was the greatest redeemer of time I ever knew."[11]

Mather held eclectic tastes in learning. Since his student days at Harvard, Mather showed interest in scientific questions. He read and purchased scientific books and more than once illustrated a surprisingly current knowledge of the latest discoveries in European and English laboratories. To Dr. John Woodward (1665-1728) of London, an eminent geologist and physician, Mather corresponded on such diverse subjects as fossils, hummingbirds, and medical cures. When given the task of seeking fossils for Woodward's collection, Mather bewailed the fact that "in an infant country" there existed a destitution of philosophers. This fact, coupled with his heavy work schedule, left Mather forming "the best

---

[10]See Kenneth B. Murdock, *Selections from Cotton Mather* (New York: Hafner, 1926), p. xviii.

[11]*Massachusetts Historical Society Proceedings*, xxxvii, p. 70. Also quoted in Murdock, *op. cit.*, p. xxviii, and Richard Lovelace, *The American Pietism of Cotton Mather: Origins of American Evangelicalism* (Grand Rapids: Eerdmans, 1979), p. 28.

projection" he could for the proposed collection.[12]

The letters he sent to the Royal Society, a London-based organization existing to promote scientific knowledge, were welcomed, and through its secretary, Dr. Woodward, it urged him to send more of his "observations on Natural Subjects." In 1713, at a meeting of the Council of the Society, one reads in the minutes, "Mr. Cotton Mather was proposed, balloted for, and approved to be a Member of the Society."[13] It was through his relationship to the Royal Society that he was exposed to the newest theories on smallpox inoculation which subsequently led him to support this theory in Boston during the 1721 outbreak. On one occasion, the opposition to his propagation of this new medical theory for preventing smallpox had reached such a fever pitch that a bomb was thrown through the window of his home with a note reading: "Cotton Mather, you Dog; Damn you: I'll inoculate you with this, with a pox to you."[14] Undaunted by this threat, he continued to support this medical method he had researched for years.

Besides his scientific interests, Mather also wrote prodigiously in many forms. Biography, history, essays, sermons, books of piety,

---

[12]Murdock, *op. cit.*, p. xx-xxi; also see Kenneth Silverman, *Selected Letters of Cotton Mather* (Baton Rouge: Louisiana State U. Press, 1971), pp. 107-110. Letters to Dr. Woodward found on pp. 110-118.

[13]See George L. Kittredge, "Cotton Mather's Election into the Royal Society," in *Publications of the Colonial Society of Massachusetts*, xiv, pp. 81-114.

[14]*Diary* II, p. 658 (November 14, 1721.)

theological treatises, and poetry are to be found among his works. In *The Christian Philosopher* he dabbles in science and natural philosophy; in his "Biblia Americana" he addresses a large compendium of material interpreting the Bible; in the *Psalterium Americanum* he attempts translating and adapting the Psalms for musical scores; in his "Angel of Bethesda" he surveys medical cures; and in his "Triparadisus" he completes a comprehensive millennial treatise supporting chiliasm. This list is not exhaustive, but it illustrates the vast range of Mather's writing and researching interests.

Activity filled Mather's life. In 1710, the University of Glasgow conferred on him the title of Doctor of Divinity, and from that time onward Mather wore a ring with a picture of a spreading tree upon it, inscribed "Glasskua Rigawit," meaning "Glasgow has watered it." It ever served to remind him of the exhortation to be fruitful. Even his dying words to his son Samuel in 1728 supported his life's motto, "Fruktuosis." In light of his tremendous activity and the volumes of his writings, Mather was a very fruitful tree. His fifteen unpublished manuscripts and four hundred and forty-four published works attest to his productivity. Benjamin Coleman (1673-1747), the pastor of the Brattle Street Church in Boston, who sometimes found himself at odds with Mather, wrote in Mather's funeral eulogy that "His works will indeed inform all that read of his great Knowledge, and singular Piety, his zeal for God, and Holiness and Truth; and his desire of the Salvation of precious Souls." Coleman then adds this interesting comment, "but it was Conversation and Acquaintance with him in his familiar and occasional Discourses and in private Communications; that discovered the vast compass of his Knowledge and the Projections of his Piety . . . here he excell'd, here he shone; being exceeding communicative, and bringing out of his Treasury things new and old, without measure. Here it was seen how his Wit, and Fancy, his Invention, his Quickness of thought and ready Apprehension were all consecrated to God, as well as his Heart, Will, and Affections."[15] Coleman's observations reveal Cotton Mather to have at least tried to parallel his public professions with his private relations. The veracity of Coleman's evaluation of Mather is underscored by the fact that this was not only a public statement, and therefore subject to a wide variety of personal critique, but it came from one for whom Mather lost little affection.[16]

Theology is one of the most exciting and ambitious of human endeavors. Essentially it is the technical ordering of the faith which a church confesses and teaches.[17] It goes beyond the normative expressions of faith in a community or person and goes toward ultimate questions of life and death, time and eternity, goodness and truth. Within its ambit

---

[15]Benjamin Coleman, *The Holy Walk of Blessed Enoch* (Boston, 1728), pp. 23-24.

[16]For Mather's antipathy toward Coleman (also spelled "Colman"), see *Diary* II, p. 809-810; especially did they temporarily part friendship over the Brattle Street Church affair; see Levin *op. cit.*, pp. 283, 290-291.

[17]See Gustaf Aulen, *The Faith of the Christian Church* (Philadelphia: Muhlenberg Press, 1948), pp. 3-22; and Karl Barth, *Dogmatics in Outline* (New York: Philosophical Library, 1949), pp. 9-14.

comes the difficult problems of nature, man, and God. Theology grapples with the human situation in its historical and universal totality. It purports to speak the truth about ultimate reality and about mankind's ultimate concerns. It calls for an historical grasp of the church's extensive involvement with major philosophical issues, requires an understanding of contemporary art, culture, and science, and presupposes a knowledge of the situation and nature of the people it addresses. Indeed, its boundaries are almost limitless.

Nevertheless, theology is controlled in specific ways: by doctrinal tradition, by the scriptural testimony, and by the living faith of the believers.[18] Yet, even here there are difficulties when scholars critique the biblical texts, when the tradition is subjected to new interpretations, and when people's popular faith is swayed by crosscurrents of changing morality and devotion. Theology, therefore, is the continuous attempt to relate the Christian faith to the conditions and needs of people. Cotton Mather made no less an effort for his day and age. He preserved the theological distinctives of Reformed orthodoxy: the sovereignty of God, justification by grace through faith in Christ and imputed by Christ's righteousness, sanctification through the directions of the Holy Spirit, belief in natural revelation, and original sin.[19]

---

[18] Sidney Ahlstrom, *Theology in America* (Indianapolis: Bobbs Merrill Co., 1967), p. 13.

[19] For an analysis of Mather's theology, and one which I am indebted to for my own investigation into the subject, see Lovelace *op. cit.*, pp. 32-72.

Mather's theology becomes most clear when he is vigorously defending it. In 1702, he drafted for the General Convention of Ministers at Boston a thorough defense of orthodox Calvinism. The paper was directed against the encroachment of English Arminianism, which stressed the ability of man to respond to divine grace and refuted the idea that God elected men to be damned. After citing against Arminianism the Thirty-Nine Articles, a collection of statements establishing the faith of The Church of England in 1563, Mather proceeded to assert the unregenerate will's bondage, justification by faith through the imputation of Christ's righteousness, unconditional election by God's mercy, the calling of the elect through irresistible grace, and man's total depravity through original sin.[20]

Mather staunchly defended the Reformed tradition, even the doctrine of predestination. "Indeed the Doctrine of PREDESTINATION hath its Mysteries, its Abstruce Difficulties, and Soaring Sublimities," he warned in his sermon on *Free Grace* (1706), "But for men to pretend therefore, that it should be Silenced and Smothered & Shut out of Sermons is for them to be . . . more Nice than Wise, more Cautious than they need be . . . We find, the Doctrine of PREDESTINATION Proposed by our Lord, and His Apostles, with a very frequent Inculcation; We find that it hath a wondrous Tendency to the Edification of the Faithful."[21] His belief in predestination rested squarely upon the practical

---

[20] C. M., *A Seasonable Testimony to the Glorious Doctrines* (Boston, 1702), cited in Lovelace *op. cit.*, p. 48.

[21] C. M., *Free Grace* (Boston, 1706), p. 2.

expression of faith which this doctrine elicited from the believer and his understanding of God's sovereignty.

Mather believed the religious life's center resided within the doctrine of God's sovereignty. Christian piety focused upon God through scripture, worship, and especially through prayer. In one of Mather's earliest sermons, he exhorted the listener to move away from self-centeredness by passively submitting to life's vicissitudes because "While we pray to live, we should account the Praises of God to be the Cheef End of our Life, in which Judgments of God are to be sought and used as our Help."[22] He believed that a God-centered life moved the faithful from selfishness, which subtracted from true worship because it negated God's providence and replaced it with self-concern, to an understanding of one's self as a creature of a glorious Creator. Elsewhere he encouraged those under harsh circumstances that "The Sovereignty of God, must be our Song in the Night." Man's creatureliness and temporal existence accounted for nothing more than life's brief span on earth dedicated to pleasing God. "Tis Enough, that be our Time never so Short," wrote Mather in *A Short Life* (1714), "the Infinite God, has had the Pleasure of Beholding the Man, whereof He is the Maker . . . This is End Enough to be assign'd for the whole Creation."[23] Such convictions indicated the essential place the doctrine of God's sovereignty held for Mather.

---

[22] C. M., *Small Offers* (Boston, 1689), p. 106.

[23] C. M., *A Short Life* (Boston, 1714), p. 18. Also cited in Lovelace *op. cit.*, p. 49.

While Mather generally agreed that all one possibly could do in response to God's sovereignty was pray for power to "be enabled to Look" to God, only God himself could grant this authority. One may, Mather realized, "as easily make Iron swim" as to look to the almighty "by any abilities of your own."[24] Yet, one might receive a direct promise from God that a specific desire be granted in the future. Mather received many such "particular faiths" in the course of his ministry. Not everyone obtained a particular faith when praying consistently; they occurred only sporadically, "but here and there, but now and then, unto those whom a Sovereign GOD shall Please to Favour with it."[25]

Despite the rarity of particular faiths, Mather relied upon them to direct his life. On one occasion when his "little Daughter Hannah" had taken a fever and was on the brink of death, Mather "pray'd and cry'd unto Heaven" for her. After resigning her life to the Lord, "the Lord raised" his "heart at last, unto something of a particular Faith, for its being restored unto mee." To Mather's amazement, "it came to pass accordingly."[26] Hannah's life was restored. Such success surrounding a "particular faith" led him to rely upon them as absolutely sure promises from God.

---

[24]C. M., *The Call of the Gospel* (Boston, 1686), p. 37. Also quoted in Middlekauff *op. cit.*, p. 234.

[25]C. M., *Parentator* (Boston, 1724), pp. 189-90.

[26]C. M., *Diary* I, pp. 258-59. Also see *Diary* I, pp. 40, 63, 206, 212, 327-328, 353; and II, 67, 83, 105, 561.

One of the major disappointments of Mather's young adulthood centered upon a particular faith's breakdown concerning his wife Abigail's prolonged illness. Abigail had been sick for months, during which time Mather fervently prayed for her release from sickness. He received a particular faith that she would survive the illness, but she did not live through the year. Mather was deeply discouraged with this turn of events in his prayer life. "Has not the Death of my Consort," he questioned in his diary, "that most astonishing Sting in it; a Miscarriage of a Particular Faith!" Steeped in grief by his wife's death and perplexed by the spiritual puzzle of a mistaken particular faith, he sadly reviewed those most recent events, "Truly, nothing has ever yett befallen me, that has come so near it." He desired, after reflecting upon this episode, that "It may be, the Lord will ere long enable me, to penetrate further into the Nature, Meaning, and Mystery of a Particular Faith. However, I have mett with enough to awaken in me a more exquisite Caution, than ever I had in my Life, concerning it."[27] When Abigail died in 1702, Mather thereafter exercised more careful use of language when describing his prayerful considerations on specific matters. He dropped the term "particular faith" and replaced it with "sacred faith," hoping to eliminate some of the absoluteness of those words of knowledge from God received in prayer. After 1702 the prayer promises were much less frequent.[28]

---

[27]*Diary* I, pp. 431-454. Quote is on pp. 453-454.

[28]*Diary* II, pp. 105-561.

If everyone did not reach the prayerful ecstasies of particular faiths, at least they could each seek Jesus Christ. Mather urged his congregation to be active in spiritual enterprises such as prayer, various services for the Lord in the church, and Bible reading, but he did not think any of these exercises would "prepare" the heart for Jesus Christ. Justification by grace through faith in Christ came, according to Mather, when the believer desired grace. "The Desire for Grace," he explained, "argues the Presence of Grace." Spiritual endeavors may sustain the believer in his quest for union with Christ, but they must not be construed to be faith itself. Mather emphasized this distinction by setting forth a pattern of conversion which began with the mind being reconstructed so the affections could follow. If one had the desire to be united with Christ, then one could assume that the rational faculty had already undergone rebirth and that the sensible faculty had subsequently followed. "A Desire, a Desire, to Fear the Name of GOD. If such a Desire be found in us," postulated Mather, "we shall be found among the True Servants of GOD; and His Ear will be attentive unto our Prayer. Verily as a Man Desireth in His Heart, so is He."[29] The believer then becomes Christ's servant and offers "consent" to a covenant with God. To Mather, "consent" meant "surrender." Believers were not to elevate their consent's importance, for in comparison to the Lord's mighty work rendered in Christ it was "a very poor one." In granting consent, the believer became

---

[29] *A Comforter of the Mourners* (Boston, 1704), p. 32; *Pia Desideria* (Boston, 1722); for an explanation of Mather's antipathy toward preparationists, see Middlekauff *op. cit.*, pp. 240-246.

a slave to Christ: "Coming into the Covenant of God, they then sign Indentures for the Service of the Savior."[30]

Justification by grace through faith in Christ based on Christ's imputed righteousness Mather supported as one of the Reformation's bulwarks. Specifically defending the Reformed doctrine of justification, Mather wrote in his *Everlasting Gospel* (1700) that "The righteousness of God is by faith in Jesus Christ," a perceived faith imputed through Jesus' own righteousness. "God never gives the Righteousness of the Lord Jesus Christ unto any man, without giving him Faith to Take the Gift of Righteousness." But he left no doubt where faith's genesis originated; it began with Jesus Christ's work, not the believer's effort. "Faith is the Instrument of our Justification," to Mather, and it was not to be confused with the instrument's originator, Jesus Christ. "Faith does not justify us, as it is a Work," purported Mather. "No, 'Tis Instrumentally and Relatively, and because it carries us unto Righteousness of our Lord Jesus Christ alone, for our Justification."[31]

Mather considered the believer's highest calling to be union with Jesus Christ, after one consented to the covenant of grace and recognized Christ's imputation of righteousness. Like Thomas a Kempis before him, Mather accented imitating Christ's life, a life which when rationally perceived presented knowledge for union, but not a saving knowledge. ". . . be very Really sensible of the Beauty and Sweetness that is in Him,"

---

[30]C. M., *Coelestinus* (Boston, 1723), pp. 7, 8.

[31]*Ibid.*, pp. 22-23. Also quoted in Middlekauff, *op. cit.*, p. 250.

Mather encouraged, "and like that woman once, we should feel Vertue going forth from Him unto our Souls; or, like Paul, find upon our selves the power of what is in our Lord."[32] Mather considered the Lord's power sufficient to bring the believer to holiness. Through the Holy Spirit's direction the faithful gradually reached sanctification. While for Mather, justification by grace through faith in Christ led eventually to imitating Christ, the actual effort toward imitation he called "sanctification." The believer must give his best efforts to conform to Christ. Mather even thought that "Without the Imitation of Christ, all thy Christianity is a meer Nonentity," and the believer's sanctification remained static.

Nonetheless, when the Holy Spirit accompanied the faithful in an intellectual fashion, then the soul received assurance of union with Christ. Mather called this kind of assurance "discursive," and he illustrated its weakness and explained that it contained "much of Darkness" in it. On a higher level, he professed an "Intuitive" assurance which broke "Directly" into the believer's soul with its "Mighty Light" bearing in upon the "Mind of the Believer a powerful persuasion of it, that he is a Child of GOD, and his GOD and Father will one day bring him to Inherit all Things."[33]

The Holy Spirit acted as a leavening agent for the Christian to

---

[32] C. M., *Addresses to Old Men and Young Men and Little Children* (Boston, 1690), pp. 7, 8.

[33] C. M., *Christianity to the Life* (Boston, 1702), p. 17. For a discussion of Mather's perspectives on imitating Christ, see Robert Middlekauff's "Piety and Intellect In Puritanism," *William and Mary Quarterly*, 3rd, Ser., (July, 1965), XXII, pp. 457-70.

gradually obtain holiness through union with Christ. The devoted believer gained assurance of "coming to dwell in the same Heavenly World, which those men of GOD are gone unto,"[34] by the actions of the spirit upon the individual soul. Those actions of the spirit, Mather claimed, originated within the Triune God. The vitality of the Christian's life depended upon God's sovereign action via the Holy Spirit, not their own willingness nor the holiness of their personal ministry. Mather observed that "The Success of the Ministry depends on the Gracious Influences of the Holy Spirit, that South-Wind blowing on the Garden."[35]

Separate from the Holy Spirit's activity, Mather allowed for God's natural revelation to sometimes occur through man's reason. He observed that every man had "a Faculty called Reason" and by the light given from this "Candle of the Lord" each person was able to "discern the Connection & Relation of Things to one another." The Lord planted in the human mind the ability to think and comprehend, so naturally when one activated this form of revelation, God became more comprehensible. Mather paralleled man's reason to the mind of God when he wrote that "We never Transgress any Law of Reason, but we do at the same time, Transgress the Law of God." He even identified the mind's comprehension with God's revelation. "The voice of Reason," Mather insisted, "is the Voice of God."[36] But in this instance Mather was not

---

[34]C. M., *Signatus* (Boston, 1727), pp. 14, 16, 20.

[35]C. M., *Coelestinus* (Boston, 1723), p. 68.

[36]C. M., *The Ambassadors Tears* (Boston, 1721), p. 13.

speaking of the exaltation of human reason that humanists and later Enlightenment Deists practiced, but of what occurred when a sovereign God ruled a Christian's every faculty. For Mather saw that mankind's rationality, like every other human aspect, carried original corruption from the Fall and suffered from a depraved nature. He questioned whether "There is hardly any one thing in the World, the Essence whereof we can perfectly comprehend. But then to the natural Imbecility of REASON, and the moral Depravations of it, by our Fall from God, and the Ascendent which a corrupt and vicious Will has obtained over it," he wondered, "how much ought this Consideration to warn us against the Conduct of an unhumbled Understanding in things relating to the Kingdom of God?"[37] Man's reason granted anyone an avenue to God, and yet it did not completely or without qualifications reveal the deity.

Mather affirmed the positive accomplishments of reason even while maintaining its essentially depraved condition. But he also pondered its considerable natural shortcomings. "There are Mysteries in Religion, which we know not now but we may know hereafter. Those Men are strangers to Christianity," he suggested, "who are so Vain, as to write, Christian Religion, that is against Reason . . . Nevertheless, there are Truths that go beyond Reason; Truths that soar above Reason; Truths which the faculties of our feeble Reason cannot see into, especially as our Fall from God has enfeebled and impaired our Faculties."[38] Yet,

---

[37] C. M., *A Man of Reason* (Boston, 1718), pp. 1, 3, 7.

[38] C. M., *The Christian Philosopher* (London, 1721), p. 114.

reason did not consume all of Mather's inclination toward natural revelation; the external world such as stars, sun, moon, animals, seasonal changes, and plants all were included in his fascination with God as a Creator who placed his image in all that he created.

God's wonderful works appeared to Mather as an extravagant tapestry outlining the universe's breadth and depth. The distances between the stars, even the stars' number, Mather thought defied calculation because they were "like the Sand of the sea, innumerable." The universe's vastness encompassed the earth's small circumference lending majesty to the master's handiwork and leaving Mather feeling his world was but a "Pin's point" when compared "with the Mighty Universe." He sometimes found more immediate material for God's natural revelation in the plant and animal world around him. He speculated that there were "above six Thousand Plants" on earth, a large number, but hardly to be equal to the numerous varieties of living creatures. What, he wondered, "might then be said upon the Hundred and fifty Quadrupeds, the Hundred and fifty Volatils, the five and twenty Reptiles, besides the vast multitudes of Aquatils, added unto the rich variety of Gems and Minerals in our World?" Indeed, Mather answered his own question, for he acknowledged nature's magnificence, the extent of its beauty, and professed it to be God's natural revelation to man. To him, the believer's confession of faith was sustained by God's natural works in the world, but the unbeliever's ground for lack of belief in God crumbled before nature's evidence. Mather whimsically professed, after a long list of God's natural works, that "There is not a Fly, but what may confute an Atheist."[39]

Even if the Christian could take consolation in God's natural revelation, it was a tenuous satisfaction. The Christian's justification, sanctification, and reason Mather explained as tinctured by original sin. The doctrine of mankind's original sin existed as a central construction in his theology. No matter how arduously the Christian faithfully practiced the means of grace, attending worship, taking Holy Communion, studying scripture, or how assured the believer felt united in Christ for his/her own salvation, Mather witnessed sin's infiltration. "The very best of our Performances are Defective, are Defiled," he wrote, "let us do our very Best, some Sin will still cleave unto it."[40]

Essentially Mather viewed original sin as a pattern established "from our First Parents," a "Habitual Inclination to Do Evil." Our first parents' sin disposed us toward evil leaving us a "poisoned Nature." The only response to such corruption of mankind's nature was to turn to a savior, who, according to Mather, was "The Blessed JESUS," a person in whom "alone we have the Relief of all Evil Habits."[41] The Christian endured a lifelong struggle between sinful desires and the Holy Spirit's actions. Despite being "Renewed by the Grace of God," Mather

---

[39] C. M., *Utilia* (Boston, 1716), pp. 260-61.

[40] *The Wonderful Works of God Commemorated* (Boston, 1690), pp. 25-27. Also quoted in Middlekauff, *op. cit.*, pp. 282-283.

[41] C. M., *A Good Character* (Boston, 1723), p. 10; *Utilia* (Boston, 1716), p. 175; and *Advice from the Watch-Tower* (Boston, 1713), p. 6.

suspected many people may have Indwelling Sin." He concluded that "In some Regenerate Souls the struggles between the Spirit and the Flesh are so dubiously managed, that one will have much ado to say, which overcomes."[42] To Mather, man's nature, whether regenerated or not, was totally and originally depraved by sin. A Christian lived in the tension between Christ's gift of grace which offered justification and sanctification by the direction of the Holy Spirit for the believer and the temptations of a soul naturally inclined toward evil.

Mather's theology was simple and reductionist. He reduced the Christian faith to what he considered to be the essential doctrines. His interest in communicating the Christian faith to children, blacks, criminals, Jews, and Indians motivated him to this doctrinal simplification. A scholar recently depicted Mather's pursuit toward a Christian core of beliefs as evidence of being "in a sense the first 'fundamentalist' and the first major ecumenist in American church history."[43] Mather maintained the theological distinctives of Reformed Calvinism by his emphasis upon a sovereign God, justification by grace through faith in Christ, sanctification by the Holy Spirit's direction, natural revelation through nature and reason, and original sin.

Why is Mather's millennialism important for understanding American colonial culture? One of the major contributions of this study

---

[42]C. M., *Utilia* (Boston, 1716), p. 175.

[43]Richard Lovelace, *The American Pietism of Cotton Mather: Origins of American Evangelicalism* (Grand Rapids: Eerdmans), pp. 59-62. The quote is on p. 62.

is that it illustrates how pervasive Mather's millennialism is to his thought and life. His millennialism is not on the fringe of his life but is central to understanding his theology and his explanation for the episodes that make up his turbulent colonial experience. Mather, as well as other colonial clergymen, interpreted to their congregations the vicissitudes of life through a millennial framework. Millennialism, as a point of reference, served as a rationale for explaining catastrophe by fire, earthquake, or storm and by giving meaning to history and hope for the future by presenting Christ's return as God's promise. In this respect, Mather was not unusual in his millennialism. He, like his colleagues and his ancestors, appreciated Christ's return as an answer to the question of "Why is life meaningful?" To Mather, and other millennialists, life was meaningful when lived expecting Christ's immediate return.

Mather's continuity with the New England millennialism was stronger than his discontinuity. Like other New England millennialists of the seventeenth century, such as John Cotton, Samuel Sewall, John Eliot, and his own father, Increase Mather, Cotton theologized about many typical millennial themes. Prophetic prediction, the role of the Indians and the Jews in the millennium, weather occurrences and natural disasters, all pointed to Christ's imminent return and revealed God's judgment on New England's people. Like the radical Fifth Monarchy Men, such as Thomas Venner, who were active in both New England and old England, Mather expected and hoped for Christ's sudden return--"like a thief in the night." But unlike the Fifth Monarchy Men, he refrained from believing that any activity on the part of God's people, especially violence, would hasten to establish "King Jesus" over earthly kings.[44]

John Cotton (1584-1652), Mather's maternal grandfather, studied prophetic signs and believed in the closeness of the last days. Each of John Cotton's works, *The Church's Resurrection* and *The Pouring of the Seven Vials*, argued that Jesus' return "hastens fast" and that New England's people "may live to see it."[45] Mather likewise believed adamantly in Christ's imminent return to earth. In 1692 Mather wrote *A Midnight Cry* to startle readers and listeners to prepare their souls for Jesus' immediate return. "We are to watch by a constant Expectation of, and Preparation for, the COMING of our Lord," he contended, and "We should always be expecting that Glorious Revolution."[46] Besides this sense of immediacy for Jesus to establish his millennial kingdom, Mather shared with his fellow colonial millennialists a concern for the conversion of all people but especially the Jews and Indians who were to play a particular role as subjects whose evangelization marked the dawn of the millennium according to the millennialists' interpretation of the signs.

---

[44]See James F. Maclear, "New England and the Fifth Monarchy: The Quest for the Millennium in Early New England Puritanism," *William and Mary Quarterly*, 3rd series, 32 (1975), pp. 223-60.

[45]*The Churches Resurrection or the Opening of the Fifth and Sixth Verses of the 20th Chapter of the Revelation* (London, 1642), p. 30. Also see Larzer Ziff's *The Career of John Cotton: Puritanism and the American Experience* (Princeton: Princeton University Press, 1962).

[46]*A Midnight Cry* (Boston, 1692), p. 22.

John Eliot (1604-1690), a Puritan occupied primarily with the Indians' conversion to Christianity in seventeenth-century Essex County, Massachusetts, also directed his attention toward the natives' citizenship in the heavenly city. In *The Christian Commonwealth*, Eliot proposes that all people, but particularly those colonies, need to "follow the Lord, and accomplish His Word, aim at the fulfiling of His ends and design, denying themselves" in order that "they may advance Christ Jesus in the throne, and let Him reign over them."[47] Mather echoed this interest in the Indian role for the millennium by involving himself in The New England Company, an organization whose sole activity was Christianizing natives and by publishing two works in 1702 which underlined his convictions.

In the *Magnalia Christi Americana*, Cotton Mather extolled the virtues of Eliot's efforts toward converting the Indians for the millennium. Also in *An Advice to the Churches of the Faithful*, Mather appealed to Christians "for regular intercession for the revival of the churches and the conversion of Jews, Muslims, and pagans."[48] In each work Mather implicitly granted the Jewish and Indian conversions as necessary signs before the millennium. Other contemporary millennialists, like Mather,

---

[47]*The Christian Commonwealth* (London, 1659); reprinted in the Massachusetts Historical Society *Collections*, 3rd series, vol. 9 (Boston, 1846), p. 130. James Holstun's *A Rational Millennium* (New York: Oxford University Press, 1987) explains Eliot's millennialism in terms of his evangelization of the Indians. See especially pp. 102-165.

[48]*Magnalia Christi Americana* (London, 1702); *An Advice to the Churches of the Faithful* (Boston, 1702).

combined themes and argued for the advance of the millennium. Judge Samuel Sewall (1652-1730), a friend of the Mathers, in one instance, explained that the signs for the pouring of the sixth vial had been completed and therefore he believed the exact location for the heavenly city could be cited. But it was the combination of several signs that led Sewall to this conclusion. As late as 1710, in *Theopolis Americana*, Mather hoped for the long-awaited millennium to develop in the colonies, but its theme attracted the individual listeners to their own condition before God, not to a dramatic millennial prediction for New England's future.

Both the themes of the millennium's immediacy and the conversion of the Jews occupied Sewall's millennialism. In his work *Phenomena quadaem Apocalyptica*, Sewall combined the Turkish woe and the Jewish national conversion as elements within the sixth vial to be completed before the millennium. After ascertaining the successful completion of the signs of the sixth vial, Sewall pinpointed Mexico as the site for the New Jerusalem.[49] While in this latter detail Cotton Mather did not concur, in general, until the 1720s, Mather still believed a Jewish national conversion to be prerequisite to Christ's return.

Increase Mather, Cotton's father, vigorously believed in Jesus' literal return. Gradually, from his earliest years as a minister at the Second Church in Boston to his final days living with his son Cotton,

---

[49]Cited in James W. Davidson's *The Logic of Millennial Thought: Eighteenth-Century New England* (New Haven: Yale University Press, 1977), pp. 66-67.

Increase studied the millennium.

Increase suggested that by 1709 Jewish national conversion was under way. Wars, revolutions, famine, and pestilence in Europe pointed to the Antichrist's reign and his terrible fury. When the Turkish Empire crumbled under the Russians' persistent advances into the Caucasus in 1689, when Danzig suffered the loss of 40,000 people from the plague in 1709, and when 100 Jews in Hamburg converted to Christianity, he asked rhetorically whether this evidence sufficiently fulfilled the initial signs for the millennium. "May this be," he questioned, "the first Fruits of a greater harvest shortly to follow?"[50] Cotton was just as sure as his father that his own generation would experience the millennium. But the millennium Cotton dreamed of did not include all of the people of the colonies or New England. He firmly believed that the first generation of New Englanders, and now himself, had been sent on a special mission by God to lead his own and his father's generation out of their years of confusion and into a new era inaugurating Christ's coming and the establishment of the New Jerusalem.

Mather's early preaching promised a glorious future for New England's elect. But outside of the elect, numerous forces were at work to thwart God's plan. Yet, he confidently believed that God's people in New England would triumph. He boldly proclaimed to his people: "We

---

[50]*Faith and Fervancy in Prayer* (Boston, 1710), p. 99. See also his *The Mystery of Israel's Salvation* (London, 1669); *A Dissertation Concerning the Future Conversion of the Jewish Nation* (London, 1709); and *A Dissertation Wherein the Strage Doctrine* (Boston, 1708); and *Meditations on the Glory of the Heavenly World* (Boston, 1711).

shall soon Enjoy Halcyon Days with all the Vultures of Hell Trodden under our Feet."⁵¹ That period he spoke about was the millennium. He optimistically thought New England's future resided in a role as the New Jerusalem.

Until the 1720s, Mather primarily preached a millennial theme of national salvation to his own third generation of New Englanders. He looked upon the second generation's decline as difficult years when "all Debauchery was coming in among us like a mightly Flood. . . . We were in a Sea of Fire miserably scorched and scalded, and yet it was mingled with Ice . . . there was no getting out."⁵² As signs of millennial hope, Mather looked around him at contemporary events. In 1688, when the Glorious Revolution had ended the reign of the Roman Catholic king, James II in England, and when Governor Andros was overthrown in New England, the Boston clergyman took these historical events as initial signs of "the Dawnings of that day."⁵³

---

⁵¹*Wonders of the Invisible World* (Boston, 1692), p. 14. Also quoted in Emory Elliott's *Power and the Pulpit in Puritan New England* (Princeton: Princeton University Press, 1975), p. 189.

⁵²*The Wonderful Works of God Commemorated* (Boston, 1690), p. 43. Other works by Mather which support the optimism he held for the third generation and the second generation's declension are: *Addresses to Old Men, Young Men, and Little Children* (Boston, 1690); *Balsamum Vulnerarium* (Boston, 1692); *Call of the Gospel* (Boston, 1686); *The Serviceable Man* (Boston, 1690); *Small Offers toward the Service of the Tabernacle in the Wilderness* (Boston, 1689); also see Elliott, *op. cit.*, pp. 187-200.

⁵³*Ibid.*, p. 4.

"pressing after the High Attainment of Religion" 57

Previous to the 1720s, Mather looked at the other nations of the world and did not find any of them as virtuous as New England. Decay and vice permeated other countries, pulling religion down to an ebbtide. Only New England, to him, "enjoys these Dews of Heaven when the rest of the World is dry" for "they alone . . . have known [Christ's love] above all the Families of the Earth."[54] Evidently, both his eschatological view of history and the political crises of the last half of the seventeenth century in New England informed his national millennialism.

Historians usually have identified the declension with the jeremiad. While Sacvan Bercovitch argued in *The American Jeremiad* that Perry Miller took the jeremiad's message too much at face value and failed to recognize adequately the form's essential optimism, he finally came to the same conclusion: the purpose and the effect of the jeremiad was "to direct an imperiled people of God toward the fulfillment of their destiny, to guide them individually toward salvation, and collectively toward the American city of God."[55] Yet, even during the years when Cotton Mather

---

[54]*Call of the Gospel* (Boston, 1686), p. 24.

[55]Sacvan Bercovitch, *The American Jeremiad* (Madison: The University of Wisconsin Press, 1978), p. 9. For the view that Mather's millennialism was a product of political crises, see Perry Miller, *The New England Mind: From Colony to Province* (Cambridge, Mass.: Harvard University Press, 1953), pp. 185-190. For an understanding of Mather's millennialism being rooted in his eschatology, see Bercovitch, "Cotton Mather," in *Major Writers of Early American Literature* (Madison: The University of Wisconsin Press, 1972), pp. 93-149; and Mason I. Lowance, "Typology and the New England Way: Cotton Mather and the Exegesis of Biblical Types," *Early American Literature*, 4 (1969), pp. 15-37.

maintained an exclusive position toward New England's millennial role within his jeremiads, whether from the political crises or from his eschatology, he also was concerned with the individual's salvation. The individual who accepted Christ and joined the church became a candidate as one of the elect for a millennial role. For example, he encouraged his listeners to "run away from your old masters. Come away poor souls, come away from your land of Captivity." Continuing to use the image of the servant and the master for the individual enslaved by sin, Mather urged his congregation to escape sin's tyranny: "Look upon the grim face of the Patrons under which you groan; say to them all, 'Farewell, you malicious, you bloody, you sordid Masters, Farewell; We hope you shall never have any of our Service more."[56]

Collective and individual millennial aspects interested Mather throughout his life, but by his later years (1720s), his focus was more individualistic. Mather's nationalistic salvation waned as the place of the individual's soul before God took precedence. Why after years of support for New England's errand did his nationalistic millennialism fade? It was more a shift in degree than kind. It was not so much that Mather abandoned the New England Way and the errand in the wilderness as much as he felt a priority for the individual's soul.

At least two reasons account for Mather's shift away from collective millennialism and toward individual millennialism. First, Mather himself was aging and sensed acutely his own soul's status before God.

---

[56]*Small Offers toward the Service of the Tabernacle in the Wilderness* (Boston, 1689), pp. 23-24. Also quoted in Elliott, *op. cit.*, p. 197.

He said to a friend in reference to the completion of his work "Triparadisus" that he not only was writing about the nearness of the last days when Christ returned, but also he was "hastening toward Paradise."[57] Mather directed his interest in immortality to a study of the soul. Although throughout his adult life he held rigorous daily prayer and study vigils to commune with God, by 1722 until his death in 1727, he was preoccupied with the soul's immortality. The "Nishmath-Chajim," which appeared in three different manuscripts from 1722-1726 (*Curiosa* to the Royal Society in 1722, "Angel of Bethseda," 1724, and "Triparadisus," 1726), united body and soul into a theological theory to explain the soul's immortality, and it illustrated his emphasis upon the individual's salvation for the millennium.

A second reason for Mather's shift toward an emphasis upon the individual's soul and away from New England's place in the millennial drama combined various social and theological elements. A traditional view of the Puritans espoused by historians was that the third generation of Mather's had witnessed a decline in the morals and in the impious habits of the second generation. Typically referred to as "the declension," this period, roughly 1640-1690, was portrayed as a time of commercial expansion, steady immigration, both intercolonial and transatlantic, and a movement away from the New England Way.[58]

---

[57]*Diary II*, p. 811.

[58]There are many works illustrating this position, but the ones most germane to this study are: Perry Miller, *The New England Mind: The Seventeenth Century* (Cambridge: Belknap Press, 1936) and *The New England Mind: From Colony to Province* (Cambridge: Harvard University

Recent scholarship has criticized the declension theory upon the grounds that it is not historically accurate as an evaluation of the second generation's religious life in colonial America. One writer has called it "the illusion of decline."[59] But Cotton Mather did not have the advantage of retrospect upon his father's generation, and he perceived that it was not as moral or as pious as the first generation.[60] Yet, scholars have found an abundance of evidence indicating that instead of decline, the colonies experienced "proliferation and growth" in their religious life.[61] If religion in general did not decline in colonial America by the eighteenth century, then why were the ministers in New England, like Reverend Cotton Mather, lamenting apostasy? The general practice of religion was not being decried by eighteenth-century ministers in New England, but a falling away from a specific religion--the New England Way. The New

---

Press, 1953) and his essay, "Errand into the Wilderness," *Errand into the Wilderness* (Cambridge: Belknap Press, 1956); and Sacvan Bercovitch, *The American Jeremiad* (Madison: The University of Wisconsin Press, 1978).

[59]Patricia Bonomi, *Under the Cope of Heaven* (New York: Oxford University Press, 1986), p. 7. Others who have critiqued this theory are: David Hall, *The Faithful Shepherd* (Chapel Hill: The University of North Carolina Press, 1972); David E. Shi, *The Simple Life: Plain Living and High Thinking in American Culture* (New York: Oxford University Press, 1985); Keith W. F. Stavely, *Puritan Legacies: Paradise Lost and the New England Tradition, 1630-1890* (Ithaca: Cornell University Press, 1987).

[60]See above note 9.

[61]Bonomi, *op. cit.*, p. 6.

England Way preached by first-generation ministers to the colonies included a utopian vision. For example, in John Winthrop's words, it was the duty of the first planter "to raise a bulwarke against the kingdom of Antichrist which the Jesuits labor to rear up in all of the places of the world."[62]

But the higher the expectations set by the first generation for adhering to such a "bulwarke" only left the potential disillusionment greater for those who would follow the first generation. By the time the third generation took the reins of leadership, doctrinal compromise was in place--most graphically illustrated by the Half-Way Covenant (1662).

Cotton Mather's own contradictions show the inherent difficulties of maintaining the Puritan version of Calvinism into the third generation in colonial New England. In his *Magnalia,* Mather claimed that religion "brought forth prosperity, and the daughter destroyed the mother." Within the matrix of colonial bounty could be found the reason for decline in New England's Christian observance. At the same time Mather complained of New England's prosperity taking away from religious habits, he resided on Hanover Street, Boston, in a three-story dwelling decorated with lavish ornamentation and classic pilasters, more befitting "a merchant prince than a minister." He even defended the use of periwigs from his pulpit in 1691, proclaiming that it was wrong "to be so zealous against this innocent fashion, taken up and used by the best of men." His good friend, Judge Sewall, thought the position to support the wearing of periwigs unthinkable and replied, "I expected not to hear a

---

[62]"General Observations," *Winthrop Papers II,* p. 114.

vindication of Periwigs in Boston Pulpit by Mr. Mather."[63] Like Perry Miller suggested in both volumes of *The New England Mind*, Mather was an example of, and fought against, Calvinism's decline in New England.

Less and less Mather perceived of New England as a national entity while he perceptually veered toward the individual before God as his main millennial theme. In "Triparadisus" he is more concerned with the individual believer as a millennial agent than he is a national conversion of the colonies in general or New England in particular. The reason for this shift is his observance of a change from the intentions of the original Puritans to his own generation. The first planters he viewed as devout Calvinists dedicated to creating a theocracy in the wilderness. By the time his own generation obtained leadership, he witnessed the people drifting more toward this worldly, rather than other worldly, affairs. Even while Mather illustrated this change with his defense of periwigs and the ornate structure of his home, he believed he was defending and explicating the New England Way essentials through his ministry--and one essential was the hope inherent in Christ's immediate return.

---

[63]The quotes are found in David E. Shi, *op. cit.*, p. 21.

Chapter 3

Christus Victor: Jesus Christ's Second Coming

COTTON MATHER viewed Jesus' consummation of history at the millennium's dawn as a special act in the process of God's conflict and ultimate victory over Satan's forces. Jesus Christ as "Christus Victor" struggles against and triumphs over the world's evil powers; "the tyrants' under which mankind is in bondage and suffering, and in Him God reconciles the world to Himself."[1] Christ's millennial victory completed the personal achievement the Christian experienced when their savior aided the individual believer to thwart temptation and overcome sin in their daily life. Mather knew sin could be resisted by "Acknowledgment of a Risen Saviour" and that the "Saviour will bless this Method of Resisting the Devil . . . by causing him . . . to Flee from You."[2]

For Mather, personal triumph over the devil came through meditation, imitation of Christ, and by the agency of angels. The devotional practice he encouraged led the individual to obtain righteousness by Christ's grace and to experience a foretaste of Christ's triumph at the millennium's dawn. For example, a soul overwhelmed with "The most filthy leprosy; all sorts of Maladies and Abominations, A

---

[1] The term "Christus Victor" was used by Gustaf Aulen in his book *Christus Victor* (New York: MacMillan, 1969, 1931) to describe the classic view of Jesus' atonement (p. 4ff).

[2] C. M., *Reason Satisfied* (Boston, 1712), p. 30.

Merciful SAVIOUR," believed Mather, "still says 'Come to me, and I will not cast thee out.'" A sinful life did not necessarily eliminate the person from Christ's grace. "Satan may tell you, 'The Day of Grace is over with you.' Yet, Oh! Despair not . . . Satan may tell you 'You have Sinned Unpardonably,' Yet, Oh! Despair not."[3]

Besides the personal victory Jesus achieved in the believer's soul, as a prelude to the millennial triumph, there simultaneously existed the cosmic battle against Satan's minions which the Church must participate in by unifying its efforts. Mather supported ecumenical enterprises which focused upon Jesus, while bewailing the meager christocentrism he found within global Christianity. "I make no Doubt of it," Mather assured his listeners, "That the almost Epidemical Extinction of True Christianity, or what is little short of it, in the Nations that profess it, is very much owing to the inexcusable Impiety of overlooking a Glorious CHRIST."[4] Yet, personal and ecumenical efforts prompted by Christ's spirit in this life culminated in Jesus' universal victory over evil when he comes in authority and with power judging the world and establishing the New Heavens and the New Earth. Mather envisioned that a world morally asleep will see the millennium's dawn when Jesus comes "as a Thief in the Night."[5] The component of surprise which surrounds Christ's

---

[3] C. M., *Utilia* (Boston, 1716), p. 13, 51.

[4] C. M., *Manuductio ad Ministering* (Boston, 1726), p. 94.

[5] C. M., "Biblia Americana," (n.p.): I Thessalonians 5:2, II Peter 3:10, Revelation 3:3, 16:15.

anticipated second coming for Mather, as well as the personal and universal aspects of Christ's victory over evil, comprise the elements herein examined in Mather's christology as it informs his millennialism.

For a convenient method of assessing Mather's christology and exhibiting its millennialistic focus, an analysis will be formed under the headings of three typical Christian views of the atonement that have recurred in Christian theology: The Moral Influence Theory, the Penal Substitutionary Theory, and the Classical Theory.[6] The first two christological theories will be investigated briefly since they do not influence Mather's millennialism as extensively as the classical theory. Mather's understanding of the classical theory will be discussed with respect to angels, ecumenism, and the aspect of surprise in his millennialism.

THE MORAL INFLUENCE THEORY[7]

Little emphasis can reasonably be expected from Mather on the power of Christ's example in drawing humanity into salvation in light of his focus upon man's utter inability to raise himself toward a sovereign

---

[6]See H. R. Mackintosh, *The Doctrine of the Person of Jesus Christ* (Edinburgh: T & T Clark, 1972, 1912), pp. 1-4. Also see Aulen, *op. cit.*, pp. 1-35 ff. "Atonement" in Christian theology refers to the restoration of the broken relationship between God and man that was accomplished in the life and death of Jesus Christ.

[7]The Moral Influence theory is often identified with Abelard (1079-1142). It stresses the importance of God's satisfaction being met through the sacrificial love in the life and passion of Christ on the cross, an event which grasps the imagination and moves the heart to a desire for union with Christ. Aulen, *op. cit.*, pp. 95-97.

God. But, in fact, we find a considerable concentration upon Christ as a model. Christ is the one who, in his life, death, resurrection, and second coming, is the "vital principle" sent by the Father to guide the believer along the road to salvation and millennial triumph; he is the revealer of true holiness without which no man shall see the Lord. It is this "Principle inclining the Soul, to Fear God, and Prize Christ, and hate all Sin, and sleight this World," that prompts Mather to encourage the Christian to "do all the Good we can to all about us, and Look and Long for the Glories of the Heavenly World."[8] This vital principle aids the Christian to conform to Christ and overcome temptation. "We are by our Baptism obliged unto a conformity unto the Death of our Buried JESUS," Mather noted in a sermon based upon Romans 6:3, 4, "and unto His Rising again; unto His Death in our dying to Sin; unto His Rising again in our living to GOD." He witnessed the virtue of Christ's life drawing the believer to God and preparing him for death to self, "that it may no longer be I that live, but CHRIST living in me."[9]

Christ's holiness repeatedly appeared as a motif in Mather's writings encouraging the Christian into a deeper spiritual relationship with God. However, this union with Christ never reached perfection for the individual according to Mather. The believer always fell short of Christ's divine glory. Unlike John Wesley (1703-1791), who exhorted his listeners to imitation of Christ unto perfection, Mather saw the goal of Christ's

---

[8] C. M., *Winter Piety* (Boston, 1712), p. 29.

[9] C. M., *Baptismal Piety* (Boston, 1727), pp. 5-7.

imitation as the ability to overcome sin and temptation through grace. Jesus' holiness was well beyond the grasp of the individual. "Our Lord Jesus Christ is that Holy One who may say: 'To whom will ye liken me, or shall I be equal?'"[10]

Elsewhere, Mather established the importance of setting a devotional routine which focused upon Christ's example. "Let it be our Custome often to Think upon the Example of our Holy JESUS. Often, set the Exemplary JESUS before our Eyes."[11] The routine Mather called the believer to practice instilled meditationary forms for imitation. Like Thomas a Kempis (1380-1471), he invited the Christian to meditate upon Christ for the purpose of imitating Jesus' life, a life which transcended creedal formulations. "It is not the Recitation of a Creed," Mather wrote, "but the Imitation of a Christ, that will make a Christian."[12]

Mather saw trust in Christ's authority growing as awareness of sin crept into a person's mind. The believer was helpless without faith in Christ as power to triumph over sin. With reference to this process from unbelieving to imitation of Christ, Mather asserted that "First the Foundation must be Laid Low enough. The goodness of One who is a Good Man, begins with a deep Apprehension and Acknowledgment of his Badness . . . 'Tis a Regeneration that makes a Good Man . . . Having

---

[10] C. M., *Christianity to Life* (Boston, 1702), p. 9. See also p. 10 for his invitation to imitate, yet fall short of equality with Christ, ". . . be holy like He was Holy" (p. 12).

[11] C. M., *Advice from the Watch Tower* (Boston, 1713), p. 20.

[12] C. M., *Utilia* (Boston, 1716), p. 153.

dug this Low for the Foundation, we must then see to it that there be the Rock in the Foundation. What I mean is, a Faith which brings us into an Union with our SAVIOUR . . . Our SAVIOUR has told us John XV 5: 'Without me, you can do nothing.'"[13] Christ's life then was the model that Mather understood one must imitate. Yet, Jesus' example was a possibility only for those who were justified by faith in Christ's merits and received Christ as a savior. Mather's point was that union with Christ is only a real possibility after a faith relationship was established, and this new covenant led the Christian to follow Christ.

Mather drew the moral influence theory of Christ firmly into his picture of the Christian life, yet it formed only part of his christological portrait. While union with Christ in this life led to a genuine daily piety and ultimately to sainthood, the person of Jesus Christ called for more than just devotional rigor to appreciate and participate in his Lordship. Mather viewed Christ's sacrifice on the cross as a debt paid for the cost of mankind's original sin. Hence, God's reconciliation to humanity through Christ was not merely accomplished by the believer's imitation of the savior, but also by Jesus' ransom or substitution for mankind's sins before a just God.

---

[13]C. M., *Benedictus* (Boston, 1715), pp. 5, 6, 16. Quoted in Lovelace, *op. cit.*, p. 166.

THE PENAL SUBSTITUTIONARY THEORY[14]

The penal substitutionary theory outlined Christ's crucifixion as the satisfier of humanity's guilt and sin. The one who died as the sacrifice to satisfy the divine wrath and to provide forgiveness by the infinite value of his sacrifice satisfied God's justice. We hear overtones of Anselm (1033-1109), as Mather stated the problem man faced: "Yea, our Mighty Saviour Himself, counted the very Blood of God, and Life of God a fit Ransome for the Salvation of the Church; and shall not we then reckon on the Church and People of God a fit subject for the best of our sorry Services?"[15] The understanding that Christ paid a penalty for mankind's debt to God formed an essential ingredient in Mather's christology, although not a frequent one. When he did refer to the penal substitution theory, it often coalesced with an affirmation to imitate Christ. Such was the case when Mather challenged Christians to have "Christ in the Heart," or else there was no "Hope of Coming to Glory . . . He purchased a share in His Victory for all that believe on Him."[16] Christ's purchase

---

[14]The Penal Substitutionary theory of the atonement is identified with Anselm of Canterbury (1033-1109). The structure of this theory is juridical. Man's disobedience is regarded as nothing less than an affront to the infinite majesty of God. Such an affront requires an infinite satisfaction; God himself must offer it, although in the form of a man, since it is on man's behalf. God becomes man in order to satisfy his offended honor. Jesus is substituted for man and pays man's penalty to God as God.

[15]C. M., *The Present State of New England* (Boston, 1690), p. 21.

[16]C. M., *Christianity to Life* (Boston, 1702), p. 42.

price was over Satan and sin upon the cross.

Mather depicted Christ's supreme sacrifice most diligently in his diary where contemplation reached its zenith for him. "Now I strive until I find the Holy One working in my own Soul. . . . Thus disposed, I beg with Agony for the Pardon, which my SAVIOUR so disposed, has with His precious Blood purchased for me."[17] Meditation upon Christ's paying the sinner's debt at Calvary resulted in Mather again directing Christians upon the necessity of imitating Christ." To gain the greater Assurance of this Life," he wrote, "I find, that the Blood of my SAVIOUR is running warm in the Veins of my Soul; quickening of me to mighty Anhelations, after an Imitation of Him . . . yea, an universal Conformity unto Him. An infallible Token that this precious Blood has been applied unto me."[18]

When Mather conveyed the sinner's debt as paid by Christ's sacrifice, the legal order moved the believer from the system of merit and the covenant of works into the covenant of grace which was established by Christ's death. Covenant theology provided a conceptual framework for almost all Puritan theologians from William Perkins (1558-1602) to Jonathan Edwards (1703-1758) and existed in the background within most of Mather's writings. Mather followed a dual covenant theology which emphasized the believer's passivity for salvation and his activity in witnessing. For instance, Mather wrote in *The Greatest Concern* (1765, 1707) that "Indeed there is Nothing to be done by us, thro' Christ who

---

[17]*Diary* II, p. 575.

[18]*Ibid.*, p. 576.

strengthen us. More plainly. Our Blessedness now cometh not unto us, on the Terms of a Covenant of Works."[19] To him, the Christian passively received his salvation by Christ's action, but good works still held a position of esteem within his theology. After Christians received the benefits of Christ's substitutionary act, then the new believer revealed Christ through his witness. Believers were to do good so that "the Great GOD and His CHRIST may be more Known and Serv'd in the World" and because the new Christian's nature inclined him toward the good.[20]

The covenant of works primarily served as the initial condition under which one functions in the world. For Mather, God was a free sovereign and related himself to humanity under successive covenants. Under the first, the covenant of works, God subjected mankind to the law of his justice so that, as a result of humanity's separation from him, people were revealed as condemned under original sin's bondage. In this first covenant, the law was seen as God's instrument for bringing everyone to a knowledge of their guilt and recognition of their total need for mercy. Within this revelation of guilt and mankind's need for God's mercy, the covenant of works fulfilled its task and pointed people on to the covenant of grace which God provided by giving his son as the satisfaction for humanity's guilt.

Mather discovered reassurance in his observation that God's wrath only vindicated itself upon the unrepentant. A sense of contrition before

---

[19]pp. 10, 11.

[20]C. M., *Bonifacius* (Boston, 1710), p. 23.

God and an awareness of his own filthiness and "Foolishness" drove him "unto the great Sacrifice of a Glorious CHRIST" for his "Atonement." Yet, Mather's forgiveness before God also relinquished his congregation and family from suffering on his account. "One of the Supplications, which I saw unspeakable Reason, this Day," he acknowledged in his diary, "with unspeakable Ardor to insist upon was, that the Wrath of God may not for my Sin, break forth either against my Children, or against my People. I am afraid, I am afraid, lest my Sin may expose them, to the terrible Strokes of Heaven."[21]

These covenantal terms reveal Mather's treatment of Christ as mediator. Christ was the Son of God who became man in order to mediate the new covenant between God and man by acting as the representative of the human race and paying the debt for man's sins. It was while treating Christ's work as the mediator that Mather found it necessary to discuss Christ's deity and twofold nature. As the mediator of the new covenant and the bearer of God's righteousness, he must be seen as both God and man. "This God man is become the Mediator between GOD and Man."[22] Here Mather spoke of Christ as the representative of man, not in the metaphysical sense of being bound together with humanity by a common substance nor in the psychological sense of being united with the believer in some hidden stream of consciousness, but in the sense of a covenant established by a sovereign

---

[21]*Diary* I, pp. 558-559.

[22]C. M., *Eternal Salvation* (Boston, 1720), p. 10.

divine act in which Christ satisfied the requirements of the old covenant under which mankind was bound in order to present a new covenant of grace in which the elect may enter. Mather saw all people as "dead in sin" in the First Adam, and therefore subject to God's wrath but as "made alive unto God" by the Second Adam, and therefore subject to his mercy.[23]

In faith, Mather relied upon the merit of Christ's atonement. Christians were no longer to be judged according to a legal code. The believer was to strive to live in unbroken conscious dependence upon Christ now that he was ransomed from God's wrath.[24] The covenant of works was still important to Christians for it illustrated the promises God was willing to fulfill, but it no longer judged them, for now they lived in the covenant of grace in faith in Christ's substitutionary atonement.

THE CLASSICAL THEORY[25]

The classical theory of Christ's atonement is truly eschatological. Mather's millennialism hinged upon the perceived struggle of Christ against the demonic evil powers that individually and corporately enslaved

---

[23]C. M., "Biblia Americana," I Corinthians Chapter 15, *Diary II*, p. 284.

[24]*Diary II*, p. 731. Also see *Christianity to Life, op. cit.*, pp. 12, 23.

[25]The classical theory of Christ's atonement was identified by Aulen in *Christus Victor, op. cit.*, pp. 4 ff. It emphasizes the universal struggle between good and evil exemplified by Christ's victory over Satan through the power over the crucifixion by Jesus' resurrection. Mather adhered closely to the classical theory in his apocalyptical expressions, especially when delineating Christ's second coming to launch the millennium.

humanity. Jesus' victory over those spiritual powers constituted the millennium's climax. Christus Victor triumphed over the world's evil powers, and mankind found glory and atonement in reconciliation before God. The classical theory is dualistic, but not in the sense of metaphysical dualism between the infinite and the finite or between spirit and matter, nor even in the sense of the absolute dualism between Good and Evil typical of the Zoroastrian and Manichean teaching, in which Evil is treated as an eternal principle opposed to Good. It is dualistic in the scriptural sense; the opposition between the Divine Love and the rebellion of created wills against Him. This dualism is an altogether radical opposition, but it is not an absolute dualism. In the scriptural view evil does not have an eternal existence. Therefore, Mather, in classical theory terms, asserts that evil is ultimately conquered by Christ at the end of the millennium and is not an idea, action, or person with eternal consequences.[26]

---

[26]See Mather's "Triparadisus," pt. III; *Diary II*, pp. 66, 243, 245, 348; and Aulen, *op. cit.*, pp. 4-7. Manichaeism arose in the third century in the eastern part of the Roman Empire. It absorbed Christian elements as it moved westward. The founder of Manichaeism was Mani, a member of a distinguished Magian family. Mani's problem was the conflict between good and evil. His answer was to posit two original principles: light and darkness. In the long conflict between these two principles, a portion of the light became imprisoned in the darkness. In order to retain this light, the power of darkness created man in whom darkness and light were combined. Man, then, from the beginning was the victim of two antagonistic principles which struggled within him for mastery. To relieve this deplorable condition, Christ was to draw all the particles of light to himself. The office of the Holy Spirit, or the Paraclete, is filled by Mani. The extreme dualism of this system forced extreme asceticism. Matter is entirely bad, and the soul must be entirely

Christus Victor: Jesus Christ's Second Coming

On September 13, 1686, Mather explicitly outlined the cosmic battle between Christ and Satan in his artillery sermon *Military Duties*. Paralleling the "souldier's" responsibility to stop the attacks of a "swarthy Generation of Philistines . . . the Indian Natives," to the "Warr with the Flesh, the World, and the Devil" which man is "prest unto," Mather comforted his audience with the thought that there was to be an angelic escort whenever anyone died in battle. "And so the Holy Angels," he exclaimed, "may at the first Arrival of your disengaged Souls into the Spiritual World, welcome them with the Salutation which an Angel gave to Gideon, 'The Lord is with Thee, thou Mighty man of Valour.'"[27] The cosmic struggle dramatized the angels' agency in aiding Christ to accomplish the millennial victory in classical christology. A fervent belief in angels accompanied Mather's millennialism. Cotton Mather inherited from his father, Increase, a thoroughgoing interest in angels which influenced his chiliasm.[28]

Mather's own angelology is found within his numerous treatises and especially in his diary. In 1697, in *Humiliations follow'd with Deliverances*, he encouraged believers to turn all burdens over to Jesus whom he called

---

free. Manichaeism was influenced by Zoroastrianism.
    Zoroastrianism began in sixth-century Persia under the guidance of the religious teacher Zoroaster. Zoroastrianism centers its beliefs upon a supreme deity, Ahura Mazda, and in a cosmic struggle between a spirit of good, Spenta Mainyu, and a spirit of evil, Angra Mainyu.

[27]C. M., *Military Duties* (Boston, 1686), pp. 44, 32.

[28]Increase Mather, *Angelographia* (Boston, 1696).

"the Great Angel of the Covenant."[29] Besides being referred to as an angel by Mather, Christ also led an army of angels that were at his constant command.[30] Christ's millennial victory was believed by Mather to be secured by the angels, among whom Christ was the chief. "Here is the SAVIOUR, who being the Lord of Angels and having all power given unto Him," Mather declared, "orders our whole State . . . takes our Departed Spirits into His Custody . . . Reunites us unto God."[31]

The first references made to angels within his diary were recorded immediately after his ordination into the pastoral ministry. The section of the ordination service called "The Charge" referred to the attendance of angels during that service. It reads: "Whereas you upon whom wee impose our Hands, are called to the Work of the Ministry, and to the Office of a Pastor in this Church of Christ, wee charge you before God and the Lord Jesus Christ and in the Presence of elect Angels, that you take heed to the Ministry. . . ."[32] Cotton's father, Increase, composed "The Charge," and it was read as part of the ordination service in the Second Church at Boston in May 1685. According to the outline of the liturgy, Mather, if he kept his "charge," would be given "a Place among His Holy Angels that stand by, and are Witnesses of this Dayes-

---

[29](Boston, 1697), p. 38.

[30]C. M., *Christianus per Ignem* (Boston, 1702), p. 135: "There are Angels . . . under the Command of the Lord Jesus Christ."

[31]C. M., *The Salvation of the Soul* (Boston, 1720), p. 10.

[32]*Diary I*, p. 99.

Solemnity. . . ."³³

Mather's diary explains such concepts of angelology as good and bad angels, guardian angels, angelic assistance in the ministry, and the key role of angels in Christ's second coming.

In 1692, with the advent of the Salem Village witchcraft ordeal, Mather defined the outbreak as an "assault of the evil Angels upon the Countrey" which affirmed the classic theory's emphasis upon the heavenly drama acted out by Satan on the one hand, as an outcast archangel, and Christ on the other hand, "the Lord of Angels" who eventually conquers all the demonic forces at the millennium's end. A "Divel" in Mather's nomenclature was simply another name for "evil angels," whose lifespan was restricted by millennial chronological bounds.³⁴ Mather's belief in the imminency of Christ's thousand-year reign led him to carefully observe any angelic activity, evil or good, which gestured toward the final days before Jesus' return. In his own home it took the form of the Lord's "Good Angel" visiting his wife's room while she experienced labor before childbirth or the "Good Angel of the Lord" expressing the assurance that his son will recover from an illness.³⁵

Personal contact with angels frequently occurred in his daily spiritual exercises. He not only advocated an ultra sense of angelic guardianship by claiming that the Lord sent to each person their own

---

³³*Ibid.*

³⁴*Ibid.*, pp. 156, 178.

³⁵pp. 307, 348.

angel, but he also had, on at least two occasions, a direct communication with an angel.[36]

Recorded on the first leaf of his diary for the year 1685, written on the inner side of the cover as a lengthy Latin paragraph, Mather described a phenomenal event in his young life:

> A strange and memorable thing. After outpourings of prayer, with the utmost fervour and fasting, there appeared an Angel, whose face shone like the noonday sun. His features were those of a man, and beardless; his head was encircled with a splendid tiara; on his shoulders were wings; his garments were white and shining; his robe reached to his ankles; and on his loins was a belt not unlike the girdles of the peoples of the East. And this Angel said that he was sent by the Lord Jesus to bear a clear answer to the prayers of a certain youth, and to bear back his words in reply. Many things this Angel said which it is not fit to set down here. But among other things not to be forgotten he declared that the fate of this youth should be to find full expression for what in him was best: and this he said in the words of the prophet Ezekiel (Ezekiel 31:3, 4, 5, 7, and 9) . . . And in particular this Angel spoke of the influence his branches should have, and of the books this youth should

---

[36]For examples of Mather's appeal to angelic guardianship, see his *Diary I* pp. 119; 188, 209, and 249. Also see p. 234 for another angelic visitation while Mather "was in the Spirit," October, 1697.

> write and publish, not only in America but in Europe. And he added certain special prophecies of the great works this youth should do for the church of Christ in the revolutions that are now in hand. Lord Jesus! What is the meaning of this marvel? From the wiles of the Devil, I beseech thee, deliver and defend Thy most unworthy servant.[37]

This extraordinary experience reveals two observations about Mather. First, and most obvious, the twenty-two year old Mather discovered through this splendid presence his Christian destiny. It would be his fate to achieve complete fulfillment for what was best in him. The Lord's emissary satisfied his yearnings which he had so longed to hear about his potential accomplishments from the early days of his youth at Harvard and as a member of a prominent Puritan, New England family. The high expectations his family held for him had now received divine sanction. Second, this incident influenced the rest of his life. Theologically and spiritually, Mather never really separated his devotional communication with angels from his recorded interpretations of scripture, catechisms, sermons, or treatises. Indeed, he periodically gave the angels credit for his vast literary achievements. He believed they actually assisted him in his Christian endeavors. "The Ministry of the Holy Angels" impressed

---

[37]Translation from Wendell, *op. cit.*, pp. 47, 48.

Mather to seek special favor from God to excel in his own ministry.[38]

He advised his son in his spiritual autobiography, *Paterna*, that from the angels he had received "marvellous and amazing Favours" and that they directed his studies, assisted in his pastoral duties, prevented "Wrong Steps," supplied his wants, and comforted him against "Temptations." He desired his son to believe in the efficacy of the angels, and he understood his testimony as a witness against what he called "Sadducism," a theological position which denied the resurrection of Jesus and discounted angelical phenomena. Mather considered himself to have an "infallible Demonstration of the Existence and Agency of those Heavenly Spirits" during his lifetime. One example that he shared within his autobiography illustrated the direct effect angels had on his ministry.

An army squadron had returned from an expedition to the West Indies and had beached on a nearby island during a Sunday. Mather was solicited to preach a sermon to this group. "I rashly undertook it; but while I was in his Excellencies Barge, I was taken so very Sick, that my Friends would needs carry me back again. I was well as soon as I came home; and the Admiral afterwards told me, It was well for me, that I

---

[38]*Diary I*, pp. 99, 119, 136, 156, 178, good angels, 162, 167, 188, 201, 209; 224, 249, 255, 267, 396, vision of angel 234, general, 222, 223, 224, 226, my angel, 232, 233, 234, 237, 366, 240, 247, 249, 254-55, 267, 270, 279, 280-81, 307, 348, 399, 343,344, 353, 374, 378, 396; 411, 414, 425, 441, 446, 450, 478-79, 482, 497, 520, 536, 577, 581, 594. *Diary II* pp. 6, 8, 40, 60, 67, 114, 130, 140-41, 190, 200, 209, 224, 241, 334, 399, 365, 371, 372, 376, 392, 395, 396, 398, 449, 453; 470; 474, 487, 488, 520-21, 525, 535, 570, 577, 578, 580, 584, 587, 590, 609, 619, 621, 652, 659, 696, 758, 800, 812.

went no further. For ye Army have newly suffered a fearful Desolation, by a Sickness more Infectious & more Destructive than ye Plague itself; and had I gone, and Conversed among so Infectious a Company, it would have probably cost me my life . . . I have cause to think, It was a Good Angel, which then struck me Sick & So Sav'd my Life."[39]

A lifelong fascination with angelology explained for Mather many unusual circumstances. Even thirty-three years after the direct visitation from an angel, Mather still sought through prayer, fasting, and contemplation the heavenly assistance offered him by angels. In March 1718, he felt compelled to find further enjoyment through the ministrations granted to him from God's angels. "After this, and after suitable and affectuous Meditations on the ANGELS of God, I did on my Knees, glorify Him, as the Creator of those wonderful Creatures." He continued his thoughts with a reference to Christ's leadership over the activity of the angels. "I considered my admirable SAVIOUR, the Son of God incarnate in my blessed JESUS, as now on the Throne of God," he recorded, "as having all these mighty ANGELS under His Dominion." After further consideration on the "Ministry of the mighty Angels" to societies, individuals, and the personal benefits his family received from them, he concluded with an ecstatic millennial expectation: "I then also entreated, that the holy ANGELS, may make their Descent, and the Kingdom of the Heavens come on, wherein they shall possess the

---

[39] C. M., *Paterna, op. cit.*, pp. 122, 125, 136.

Children of men, and preach the everlasting Gospel unto the Nations."[40] To Mather, Jesus Christ's millennial victory will begin with the increased activity of the angels on behalf of believers and will be consummated by their joint efforts. He described the millennial dawn in classic christological terms as a grand descent of Christ and his angelical army. "For our Saviour will come accompanied," he expected, "with His Holy Angels."[41]

While the angels worked for the personal enhancement of each believer, the believer himself could encourage Christian unity among the brethren. For his own part, Mather's efforts toward ecumenism reflected his intense millennialism.[42] Mather included only those brothers and sisters of the Reformed faith, particularly the English, in his ecumenism, but he did not restrict this select group by ecclesiology. Mather urged all believers to converse with one another whether Congregational, Presbyterian, "and EPISCOPAL too when Piety is otherwise visible. . . ." His ecumenical goal focused upon bringing the elect together in order to witness to the visible union of the saints who will join with Christ at the millennium's dawn. Positively stated, his ecumenism served to prepare the earthly church for its millennial transformation. Negatively stated, the Christians' "Blessed Union" prevented Satan from prolonging the

---

[40]*Diary II*, pp. 520-23.

[41]C. M., "Biblia Americana," Matthew chapter 24.

[42]C. M., *Paterna, op. cit.*, pp. 122, 125, 136.

anticipated second coming.[43]

Cotton's father, Increase, traveled to London in 1689 to present Massachusetts' case for a new charter. While there, Increase also served as a neutral in the debates between Presbyterians and Congregationalists who were eager to come together on fundamental theological issues but needed help from someone they could respect. Increase represented Nonconformity. Although Increase's presence did not initiate the conversations over religious toleration among Englishmen, he did serve as a bridge to join together separate ranks at that time. The Toleration Act passed Parliament May 24, 1689. By July 1690 Matthew Mead, a Congregational minister, and John Howe, a Presbyterian minister, led a group of representatives of the two denominations in London to form a common fund for the aid of impoverished churches. In October, Cambridge, Boston, and adjacent town ministers assembled at Harvard College to form the "Cambridge Association." Cotton Mather represented these events as proof of reconciled differences among Independents and Presbyterians in both England and New England.[44]

On April 6, 1691, Howe, Mead, and Increase Mather (who was still in London) composed *The Heads of Agreement*, which traced fifty years of Puritan history by accenting harmonies between Presbyterians and Independents while dispelling differences. They encouraged each group to relinquish suspicions and jealousies and become "UNITED

---

[43]C. M., *Blessed Unions* (Boston, 1692), pp. 72-79.

[44]Perry Miller, *The New England Mind: From Colony to Province* (Harvard University Press: London, 1953), pp. 168-172.

BRETHREN." When a copy of the agreement reached Cotton Mather in Boston, he enthusiastically responded to the ecumenical statement by dedicating a sermon, *Blessed Unions*, to Howe, Mead, and his father.

Mather's most direct ecumenical statement occurred in *Blessed Unions* (1692). He challenged Christians to examine their motivations which sharpened doctrinal differences and supported rampant denominationalism. Instead of imposing "Christian Doctrine" upon the "understandings of men," Mather asked each person to "make the fairest construction of all Actions, and Lovingly take everything by the Best Handle." When Christian love revealed the love of Christ, then the party spirit diminished. "A Samaritan sort of crabbedness, churlishness, frowardness, towards all that are not in everything just jumping with us," Mather foresaw, "Tis not the Spirit of the Gospel." He reasoned that "We must beware how we Monopolize all Godliness to our own Little Party . . . Where-ever we can see . . . any thing of Christ, let it be dear to us."[45]

Mather attempted throughout the spring of 1692 to convince his congregation to accept a covenant ceremony as a symbol of "awakening" and support of the newly created union between Congregationalists and Presbyterians. By returning to God, Mather considered New England fulfilling her millennial role.

Ultimately for Mather, Christian unity depended upon more than a mere intangible spiritual union. It meant Christians visibly united in order to illustrate the saints number and power prior to the millennial

---

[45]*Ibid.*, pp. 72-79.

siege taken upon Christ's return to earth. "It is not enough that we have Invisible Union with all the Saints of God; but we must have a Visible Union, too, or such an one as our context mentions, 'That the World may Believe,' at the Contemplation and Invitation of it."[46] Mather called for more specific ecumenical action, but outside of suggesting more communication, he did not indicate what other steps toward unity denominations should take. But he did have a goal in mind for his ecumenism.

Christian ecumenism's goal resided for Mather in God's kingdom being finally established on a new earth. He harbored no illusions that the kingdom evolved by man's volition or effort. The millennial kingdom was strictly initiated and consummated by God through Christ. Although not having any causative power, ecumenism's witness strengthened Christians for the coming of Christ. Mather thought that it was only through Christ that Christians could unite. He testified to the biblical basis for ecumenism as a millennial prelude by focusing upon verse seven, chapter fifteen in Paul's letter to the Romans, "Receive ye one another, as CHRIST also has Received us into the Glory of GOD." He believed that those whom Christians judged to be received into Christ's glory "in the Heavenly World" ought to be received into Christian fellowship during the present time.[47] A premillennial revival was expected by Mather where Reformed groups buried their differences and united in expectation for

---

[46]p. 41.

[47]C. M., *Piety & Equity, United* (Boston, 1717), pp. 26-28.

Christ's return.

As a premillennial revival, ecumenism coincided with Mather's emphasis upon "vital PIETY."[48] He defined piety as "The Life of God in the Soul of Man" and claimed that it contained potential revolutionary power but was encumbered by apostasy until "the Term allotted by the Great Lord of Time" expired its efforts. He expected a final reformation before the millennial dawn. "But there is a Time not far off, . . . when these Impressions from God on the Spirits of Men," he contemplated, "will be under a more Effectual Direction, disentangling and disengaging them from the Follies which many Sectaries have been left unto; and this Panting and Heaving Tendency to Reformation will bear down all before it; and nothing shall obstruct the KINGDOM OF GOD from appearing in an universal Reign of Holiness and Righteousness among the Nations."[49] All demonic attempts to destroy the millennial kingdom through the sectarian spirit will be ended. Satan's activity only temporarily restricted the church's victory in Christ. Mather considered "The House of God Haunted with Evil Spirits" when Satan's "Bolts of Contention" embroiled and enraged God's people.[50]

---

[48]Lovelace, *op. cit.*, pp. 251-281; Middlekauff, *op. cit.*, pp. 228-230. Lovelace identifies Mather's piety as the chief basis for Christian unity and also acknowledges the impact of Mather's millennialism upon his ecumenism (pp. 269-271).

[49]C. M., *Things to be More Thought Upon* (Boston, 1713), pp. 86-87. Quoted in Lovelace, *op. cit.*, pp. 270-271.

[50]C. M., *Agricola* (Boston, 1727), p. 66.

Although the union between Congregationalists and Presbyterians deteriorated in England, in New England Mather encouraged unity in religious essentials.[51] While he wished for uniformity, he knew that realistically he must cultivate unity. In 1702, ten years after the "BLESSED UNION," he confessed "I never much admired, the violent pressing of Uniformity; but there may be Unity without Uniformity."[52] laid the groundwork for the millennium's beginning while it maintained a defense against the Devil's wiles. The sectarian spirit Mather viewed as a Devil's project that "almost ruined" Christianity "Because the Strength of their Spirits is all spent in the Concerns of some little Party."[53] Fearing God, seeking forgiveness, bridling their tongues, or imitating Christ served no purpose if one gave obeisance to sectarianism.[54] Mather's ecumenism invited the believers to look toward the "Vitals of Christianity" which he outlined as "fear of the Lord," washing "their Hearts from all wicked Lusts," keeping "their Tongues from Evil" and walking "as the Lord Jesus Christ walked."[55] It is evident here that Mather's christology informed his

---

[51]For a brief history of the English deterioration of the agreement, see Perry Miller, *The New England Mind: From Colony to Province* (Cambridge, Mass.: Harvard U. Press, 1954), pp. 248-268.

[52]C. M., *Christians Per Ignem* (Boston, 1702), p. 151.

[53]C. M., *The Armour of Christianity* (Boston, 1704), pp. 168-170. Also see his *Batteries upon the Kingdom of the Devil* (London, 1695).

[54]C. M., *Christianity to the Life* (Boston, 1702), p. 15.

[55]*Ibid.*

ecumenism and consequently prepared Christians for the protracted struggle of good against evil during the believer's lifetime. Underlying the time of waiting for the millennium's dawn was a sense of expectancy for Christ's return. Yet, this waiting was not a passive waiting, as witnessed by Mather's interest in Christian unity. Nevertheless, a tone of anticipation, even surprise, ensued from Mather's millennial expectation, a surprise which accepted the suddenness of Christ's return.

In 1692, Mather wrote *A Midnight Cry* as an urgent, preemptory, and dramatic message to startle his listeners to attend to their soul's condition prior to Christ's return. "We are to watch by a constant Expectation of, and Preparation for, the COMING of our Lord . . . We should always be expecting that Glorious Revolution," Mather contended, "wherein our Lord Jesus Christ will both dispose the Devils of the Air, making of it a New Heaven, filled with the New Jerusalem of his Raised Saints; and also by a terrible Conflagration make a New Earth, whereon the Escaped Nations are to walk in the Light of that Holy City."[56] While one could possibly believe in the suddenness of Christ's return and not accept its immediacy, Mather faithfully affirmed both the surprise element and the nearness of Jesus' coming again. "THE TIME OF THE END, seems just going to lay its Arrest upon us; and we are doubtless very near the Last Hours of that Wicked One," he exclaimed, yet hastened to add, "whom our Lord shall Destroy with the Brightness of His Coming."[57]

---

[56] C. M., *A Midnight Cry* (Boston, 1692), pp. 22-23.

[57] *Ibid.*, p. 24.

Mather's millennial imagination focused upon the scriptural image of the thief who comes stealthily in the night hours. He anticipated Christ's coming as a surprise.[58] During his adult years he never wavered on this millennial point. A few short months before his death, Boston experienced one of its worst earthquakes. On October 29, 1727, New England felt "a most awful Trembling of the Earth, which did heave and shake so as to Rocque the Houses. . . ."[59] Mather wrote *Boanerges* in answer to the spiritual questions that surrounded such a devastating disaster for Puritans whose sovereign God gave such effects as providential evidence. The theme of immediacy was displayed throughout the text, but Mather moved beyond mere repetition of a sense "That His Coming will be with all possible Surprize upon the World; like that of a Thief in the Night, wholly unlook'd for . . ." to make a subtle distinction about "the Signs concerning Christ's return." Mather did not believe that the signs were meant so much for signals to precede Christ's coming as they were for actually demonstrating to people "How Things will be at His coming." He thought that after every earthquake there was a renewing and "enforcing of the promised Signs" and that God "puts us in mind, of what He is going to do upon a World that has His Curse lying upon it." In reference to God's judgment through Christ at the end of the millennium, Mather understood that "it becomes us to look upon

---

[58] See Mather's "Biblia Americana," Matthew 24:43, Luke 12:39, I Thessalonians 5:2, 5:4, II Peter 3:10, Revelation 3:3, 16:15. See note 5 in this chapter.

[59] C. M., *Boanerges* (Boston, 1727), p. 1.

every Earthquake as a Praemonition of the Day."[60]

Such admonitions underscored Mather's interest in increasing vital piety among united Christians preparing for the time when suddenly they will ascend as saints with a savior who victoriously assails evil, both in the present, by personal forgiveness for sins, and in the near future, as the Victor over Satan at the millennium's dawn.[61]

---

[60]*Ibid.*, pp. 26-27.

[61]For other references to Christ's millennial victory over Satan, see Mather's "Biblia Americana," Revelation Chapter 4, and Matthew 24; *Paterna, op. cit.*, pp. 98-99; *Theopolis Americana* (Boston, 1710), pp. 43, 50, and 51; and "Problema Theologicum" (written in 1605), pp. 4-5.

Chapter 4

"The High Hope of Heaven"

COTTON MATHER'S christology described the millennium's main character, a victorious Christ, but his millennialism also propelled him into a speculative realm. Where will the saints and Christ reside? Where will the soul exist after death? What was paradise? What are the conditions in paradise? Mather's biblical studies led him to understand a threefold paradise: the Garden of Eden, the place of departed souls, and a "New Heavens and a New Earth" established at the millennium as paradise.

The primary text for exhibiting Mather's paradisaical speculations was "Triparadisus," a treatise which he worked on occasionally until 1726. The last few years of his life were spent completing this treatise for possible publication. He wrote to his friend Thomas Prince (1687-1758) in January, 1725-26: "I am hastening unto the Work of my *Triparadisus*. But perhaps making more Haste unto the Paradise of God."[1] He died two years later, but not before he completed his manuscript about paradise.

"Triparadisus" is a rich theological discourse filled with interesting philosophical conjectures centered upon God's "SACRED GEOGRAPHY" in three paradises. The manuscript was divided into

---

[1] C. M., *Diary II*, p. 811. See also Thomas J. Holmes, *Cotton Mather: A Bibliography of His Works* (Cambridge: Harvard University Press, 1940), p. 1124.

three sections:

    I. The paradise of the old world (the Garden of Eden)

    II. The paradise of departed spirits

    III. The paradise of the New Earth (the millennial kingdom)[2]

By far the greatest space among the three sections was given to the third paradise (290 pp.), contrasted with the first paradise (28 pp.) and the second paradise (62 pp.). Such a measurement of emphasis used by Mather for his threefold paradise will be borrowed to balance this chapter's description of his heavenly speculations. Each paradise will be described, but the emphasis will be on Mather's third millennial paradise.

I. The First Paradise: The Garden of Eden

The first paradise Mather described as "The paradise of the Old World," known in the biblical record as the Garden of Eden. He believed that God had placed in a specific time in ancient mankind's past, the first parents in a "garden of delights" full of beauty and fertility. His detailed description of this earthly paradise began with some introductory remarks. He then traced the four ends of the compass, west, north, south, and east of Eden to pinpoint the Garden in the "SACRED GEOGRAPHY." He ended this section with the hope that Jesus Christ will help all people to attain the second paradise of departed souls.[3]

Mather's idea for "Triparadisus" came from a manuscript he had in his hands at one time. Samuel Lee, an English divine who spent some

---

    [2]Holmes, *op. cit.*, p. 1305. The third section is subdivided into 12 chapters.

    [3]C. M., "Triparadisus," Pt. I., pp. 1-28.

time in New England later in his life, had begun a treatise called "Triparadisus." But he advanced only as far as the first terrestrial paradise, the Garden of Eden. Mather had in his possession Lee's manuscript for a few hours, during which time he "carefully epitomized it."[4] Since that timely event, Lee's treatise was lost. Mather rewarded Lee's work in his "Biblia Americana" by including a section in his commentary on the book of Genesis concerning "The Situation of the Terrestrial Paradise," which he credited Lee for writing. Essentially, the four compass directions surrounding Eden described in the first part in "Triparadisus" is the same as "The Situation for the Terrestrial Paradise" in Mather's "Biblia Americana." Yet, Mather deemed a synopsis of previous scholarship important to establish the interest in finding the "Seat of Paradise," and for placing his conjectures in context.[5]

The lengthy argument Cotton Mather made for placing Eden in a specific geographical region drew him into a scholarly debate which fell into polarized positions. Either Eden was in Armenia, near the origins of the Tigris and Euphrates rivers, or it was in Babylon, near the Persian Gulf. The rationale of this first section in "Triparadisus" he directed toward proving that the Garden of Eden was located near Armenia and that it was an island, an interesting addition to the biblical interpretations previously given for Genesis chapter 2. Mather compared this journey to

---

[4]*Ibid.*, p. 4.

[5]*Ibid.* On page 6 Mather identifies "Triparadisus" as originally a city in Syria on the Orontes River. The city was known for its beauty. It was possibly present-day Damascus.

locate the Edenic paradise to the quest for the Philosopher's Stone. Although never identified, the search for the Philosopher's Stone, Mather contended, reaped great results through the "notable experiments" conducted by the people who made the search. The compensation for his "quest for Paradise," he asserted, came from the "notable Illustrations upon the SACRED GEOGRAPHY," which his efforts produced.[6]

While Mather's own quest for geographically identifying the Edenic paradise found him citing ancient writers like Pliny, Ptolomy, and Strabo, most material used in his argument came directly from biblical evidence persuasively presented by his knowledge of ancient Hebrew and Greek.[7] He began his study by depicting the broad references in scripture to Eden, in order to place it in its general vicinity. From Genesis chapter 2:8-10, Mather constructed his case: "The Lord God planted a Garden Eastward in Eden - And a River went out of Eden, to water the Garden; and from thence it was parted & became into four Heads."[8]

"Kedemah" Mather identified as the country which lay to the west of Eden. By carefully plotting the proper location for Kedemah, Mather

---

[6]*Ibid.* The places Mather quotes from Lee's treatise which previous Edenic scholars had identified as Eden were Caspian Sea, Terra del Fuego, Banks of Ganges, Island of Ceylon, parts of Asia, ancient Mesopotamia, Assyria, and Persia.

[7]For citations on Pliny, Strabo, and Ptolomy, see the pages 6, 9 and 12. Mather also cites such diverse writers as Sir Walter Rawleigh and Samuel Purchas to undergird his argument for an Edenic island. *Ibid.*, p. 19.

[8]"Triparadisus," Pt. I, p. 7.

"The High Hope of Heaven" 95

concluded that he then could accurately place Eden. Kedemah was "a Territory in & near Aramnaharaim, or Syria . . . that is, Mesopotamia, or, Armenia."[9] By coming down on the Armenian side of the Edenic placement argument, as opposed to the Babylonian location, Mather proved himself to be a judicious exponent of biblical language exegesis, as well as an adept reader of the classical geographers. Conscious that the burden of proof for an Armenian Eden rested upon his geographical argument, Mather proceeded to review the four compass directions around the Edenic paradise.

Kedemah, the west side of paradise, was known for Job's occupation of the ancient land and the resting of Noah's ark on Mt. Ararat.[10] Also, a heathen people lived "all along the Banks of Uphrates, as far as Haran, where dwelt Laban, and of those poor Star-gazers, who composed (as is judged), his Talismanical gods of certain metals, imprinted in the Lion, or Scorpion . . .,"[11] which were stolen by his daughter Rachel who married Jacob, a man later named "Israel," the father of the Hebrew people. Besides being the center of these biblical stories, Kedemah received the first planting effort after the flood where

---

[9]*Ibid.* For other scriptural references cited by Mather for "Kedemah," see Genesis 25:15, Genesis 16:12, Genesis 25:6, Genesis 37:25, Judges 7:24, Genesis 37:41, Jeremiah 49:28, Ezekiel 47:16, Isaiah 60:6, and Genesis 36:36.

[10]"Triparadisus," pp. 12, 13.

[11]*Ibid.*, p. 12.

the posterity of Shem settled.[12] Mather perpetuates a distinction between the actual "Garden of Eden" and the country of Eden. The country of Eden he placed in "the principal part, if not the whole of Mesopotamia, between the two famous Rivers of Tigris and Uphrates: The same Country which the Arabians call Algerive."[13]

To assist in the location of Eden's garden, Mather traveled to the north side of the country of Eden. "Famous Rivers ran down the Mountainous Crags in the North of Assyria and Mesopotamia, and imparted innumerable Exellencies to the Transcendent and Illustrious Country which was of old called Voluptas, the Country of Eden, or, Delight: and by the Greeks, and Adonis." Of the two rivers, Tigris and Euphrates, he argued for the Tigris being the river mentioned in Genesis, chapter 2 as the main river running through the Garden of Eden where the ancient city of Cholcis was near the headwaters, "where the Golden Fleece, as the Poets remarkably tell us was kept by a Dragon."[14]

Next, Mather moved to the east side of Eden which "Moses acquaints us (Gen. III. 24.) there were Cherubims placed with Flaming Swords, to keep the way of the Tree of Life." One millennial implication coming from Eden's east side was Mather's identifying the angels' flaming swords with the sulphurous lakes in the region cited in Plutarch's life of Alexander the Great. Supporting his millennial claim that the earth will

---

[12]p. 14.

[13]p. 14.

[14]p. 14.

be destroyed by fire in a final conflagration, he supposed the fires to still continue burning "and are apt on the Least occasion, to Enkindle."[15] After identifying this land as the same land which went by the title "Nod" in scripture, where Cain dwelt after slaying his brother Abel (Gen. 4:16), Mather ended his geographical description of Eden by defining its circumference along Eden's southern edge.

Eden's southern edge, according to Mather's interpretation of Genesis chapter two, divided into four "head Waters; Pison, Gihon, Hiddekel, and the Euphrates." The Pison or "Fish-ful River," lived up to its name. Mather cited Pliny's reference to eels thirty feet long "to be caught in this River" as evidence of its prosperous fishing.[16] It surrounded Havilah, a land abundant in gold, precious stones like onyx, ophir, and pearls. And the name of the second river was Gihon meaning "the bursting," which encompassed Ethiopia. Many an interpreter believed and still believe this to be the African Cush, hence identifying this river as the present day Nile.[17] Mather recognized Ethiopia as an Arabian Ethiopia and astutely detected the name "Kush" in the words "Caucasus" and "Caspian," and looked for the site of Eden about the sources of the Tigris in Armenia. The Gihon he considered to be the leading stream

---

[15]p. 15.

[16]p. 16.

[17]See *The Pulpit Commentary*, Vol. I., p. 45 (Grand Rapids: Eerdmans, 1950).

flowing into the Caspian or "the Lakes of Chaldea."[18] The Hiddekel, named for "a Dart" because of its swiftness, ran through Assyria. Mather purported this river to be the Tigris. In the present language of the Persians it is designated "tir," which signifies an arrow. It is styled in Aramaic "diglath" or "diglah." He fixed the fourth river as the Euphrates or "the fruitful" from an unused root, "parath" referring to the sweet taste of its waters (Jeremiah 2:18).[19]

Concluding his description of the four rivers in Eden, Mather places the garden on an island. He appealed not only to his already meticulous biblical exegesis, but also mentioned Sir Walter Rawleigh's testimony taken out of *Masius*, an epistle of "the Nestorian Bishops who live at or near the place," and "the Accounts of Travellers" in Purchas, who "asserted that the true ancient Garden of Eden was in the island of Gozoria."[20] He believed that the language from Genesis 2:8 "may intimate that Paradise was a Locus Circumseptus, walled with Water,"[21] and that God eventually will "in the Latter Dayes" deliver the ancient island of Adam "into some wonderful circumstances not yett comprehended."[22] He dramatically concluded that the terrestrial paradise cannot be found.

---

[18]"Triparadisus," Pt. I, p. 18.

[19]*Ibid.*, pp. 18-23.

[20]p. 19

[21]p. 19.

[22]p. 20.

After the flood it disappeared from the world. "Like a great milestone [sic] thrown down into the sea," Mather wrote, "it is gone."

Two ideas apparently prompted Mather to write this extensive geographical discourse on Eden. First, his penchant for thoroughness motivated him to carefully trace the geographical description he outlined from Samuel Lee's treatise on "Triparadisus." By adopting the same millennial interest in following God's establishment of paradises from the first garden to the millennial new heavens and new earth, he naturally had to describe the existence and location of Eden. Secondly, and more importantly, Mather viewed this opening section as the foundation for his millennial expectation for a future paradise. By proving God created a first terrestrial paradise, Mather later persuasively argued for God once again creating a paradise, only this last time it will be through Jesus Christ's direct intervention to defeat the Devil's forces and give the saints a place to dwell. Like a lawyer's brief, Mather built his case for the last and most comprehensive section of his millennial treatise.

Before reviewing Mather's last paradise, a second paradise was detailed by him. As beautiful and enchanting as the original Eden was for Adam and Eve, he knew that God had prepared "a Better Thing for His People." "There is a PARADISE" he foresaw as "infinitely more Desireable," a place for all departed souls.

II. *The Second Paradise: The Place of Departed Spirits*

The second paradise Mather described as that place where "immortal souls of the righteous are subject, between their expiration and the Resurrection. . . ."[23] Presupposing a belief in the soul's immortality, he posited a second paradise's existence where the soul migrated, assisted by angels, to dwell with the Lord immediately after death. The second paradise served as an intermediate state, filled with many rich blessings due to the Lord's presence, but not yet the perfection of the believer's blessedness. That perfection only came with the new heavens and the new earth. Again, scripture formed the nexus of his argument, but he also ushered in evidence from classical writers like Plato and Aristotle for the soul's immortality, as well as the reformer, John Calvin.[24]

At the point where the spirit was separated from the body and dwelt in the second paradise, resurrection of the soul, according to Mather, had not yet taken place for the believer. The soul was still subject to Adam and Eve's original sin. The curse remained to taint even the celestial experience in this paradise. "While our spirits are in paradise," Mather claimed, "there is an External part of us yett remaining under ye curse." He concluded that "As long as we are in the state of the dead the curse is not wholly taken off."[25] He referred to the resurrection of the soul as "the perfection of blessedness" for the believer. Yet, the question remained as to what happened to all the saints and

---

[23]"Triparadisus," Pt. II, p. 1.

[24]See below pp. 116 ff. for a discussion of Mather's theology of the soul's immortality. Also see "Triparadisus," Pt. II, pp. 2-25, for an explanation of his theory.

[25]"Triparadisus," Pt. II, p. 27.

patriarchs who died previous to Christ. Were the saints already perfected in blessedness?

Mather foresaw the necessity for those who died in Christ since the time of the Lord's resurrection and those who died previous to Christ's resurrection who held to the promises of Israel's God, to be joined together at one time, "at the Resurrection of the Dead." To him, "The Saints, which are dead before us (Heb. XI. 40) will not be made perfect without us."[26] This grand heavenly reunion of departed souls takes place only when the Lord appears as a millennial conqueror. Mather cited various scriptural texts to illustrate that even in the second paradise, the soul of each individual still hopes for its ultimate salvation in Christ. The just reward that God gives to them that fear his name will finally be granted when "the Last Trumpet shall bring on the time of the Dead, that they shall be judged," appropriately promised in Revelation 11:18.[27] Then each believer will receive the glory long expected and waited for in this life, and in the existence in the second paradise for departed souls.

In other words, the second paradise for departed souls acted as a receptacle of spirits. It doesn't contain all the good things Christ promised to his followers, but one is filled with joy and hope for complete salvation at the resurrection of the dead.

But what other conditions characterized this in-between state? Cotton Mather did not resist further speculation concerning the status of

---

[26]*Ibid.*, p. 28.

[27]*Ibid.*, p. 28.

the separate souls in this heavenly world. Referring to Revelation 6:11, Mather predicted "White Robes are given to them" that abide in the second paradise. He believed the white apparel implied worship of God and "an Holy priesthood."[28] He continued his argument for celestial worship in the second paradise by citing the "Ancients" as sources. Quoting a reference by another author to the "Chaldaic Oracle," he says "The Chaldees give the soul Two Clothings. The One Spiritual Body, weaved out of that which is subject to sense: The other, a Thinner material, not subject unto ye touch. . . ."[29] Even the Jews in their Book of Zohar, a Kabbalistical writing dealing with mystical theological elements in Hebraic thought,[30] conjectured that this clothing will be either light or fire. "The Bodies of the Jews shall be clothed with the Light of God," Mather quoted from the Zohar, and consequently transferred this Jewish mysticism into his Christian millennialism. The essential and final reference for the soul's clothing in paradise illustrated Christ's transfiguration.

The transfiguration, when Jesus' appearance became glorious in the presence of three disciples on a mountaintop (Matthew 17:1-9, Mark 9:2-10, Luke 9:28-36, and II Peter 1:16-21), for early Christians, typically

---

[28]p. 37.

[29]p. 38.

[30]For an understanding of Jewish cabala, see Gershom Scholem, *Major Trends in Jewish Mysticism* (New York: Schocken Books, 1941).

described paradise and verified the second coming of Jesus Christ.[31] For Mather, the same luminosity brilliantly displayed at the Mount of Transfiguration before Peter, James, and John also will be evident in each believer in a paradisaical afterlife. Furthermore, the first parents' sin in the garden paradise caused the luminous garments to vanish from them. This was how Mather explained the shame and fear of Adam and Eve before a glorious God after their sin. Their "Nakedness" actually was the loss of the "luminous garments." These garments will be reclaimed in the second paradise and they represented the perfection of holiness to which the believer has arrived. Thematically, the heavenly clothing described by Mather as lost by the first parents and regained in a heavenly paradise, linked part one and part two of his treatise. Predictably, he saw the final restoration of mankind in Jesus' millennial triumph. The redemptive action of Christ on earth only partially completed humankind's restoration represented by Adam and Eve's fall. Not until the immortal souls unite with a victorious Christ and the resurrection of the dead takes place at the time of the new heavens and the new earth did Mather believe the redemptive process ended. Hence, the three parts; the garden, the place of departed souls, and the new heavens and new earth formed a logical progression for identifying his millennialistic locations.[32]

A second element in the place of departed souls Mather described was the blessing each believer received. He called this "the Sweetest

---

[31]See *The Interpreter's Dictionary of the Bible* (Nashville: Abingdon, 1962), ed., G. A. Buttrick, et. al., pp. 686-87.

[32]"Triparadisus," Pt. II, p. 39.

Fruit of Paradise." Mather based this blessing upon Philippians 1:23, "To depart and live with CHRIST, which is far better than to live in the Flesh," and II Corinthians 5:8, "To be present with the Lord, when Absent from the Body." As significant as this blessing is for the residents of the second paradise, the question remains as to how may Christ's appearing bring the final perfection in holiness when he appears to the believers immediately upon their death. He responded to this query by seeing the initial contact with the Lord in the second paradise as merely a visitation. Christ's visitation in the faithful soul's apartment became a fixed point for further contemplation. Christ's appearance in the second paradise, although not the Third Heaven described by the Apostle Paul as the primary place of the Lord's residence, still pleasantly directed the believer to worship with thanksgiving, joy, and hope. The final appearance of Christ was different in degree, not in kind, from this earlier visitation.[33]

Sections five, six, and seven dealt with the final aspect of Mather's second paradise. These sections are composed of biographical accounts of people who have either communicated with someone who had died, come back from death themselves to tell of their experience, or had a deathbed ecstasy supporting the belief in an afterlife.[34] These "Praelibations of Paradise" Mather believed to have substantiated his speculations about the existence of this place of departed souls. His

---

[33]*Ibid.*, pp. 41-42.

[34]pp. 43-62.

theory collaborated with these accounts to give a persuasive crescendo mounting toward his third and most elaborate exposition of paradise, the millennial kingdom of the new heavens and the new earth. Yet, some observations concerning these accounts is in order. The eighteenth-century New Englander interested in this treatise would also have believed in the spirit world. Why then did Mather usher this evidence forward? Apparently, not only to convince the reader that there existed a spirit world, but also to describe what kind of spirit world it was and how it fit into Christian millennialism. Mather argued that conversations with the dead, life after life experiences, and deathbed ecstasies are not difficult to understand when viewed as the occasional activities of a spirit world waiting for the millennium. Most of these occurrences aided the faithful toward a smooth transition into the second paradise and edified the believers who remained on earth to finish out their days knowing that their own glorious crossing into the place of departed souls will someday arrive.[35]

For Mather this case-study approach came as close as he was able to prove the existence of an afterlife. Today, in such specialized studies as logic, law, and science, the words, "conclusion," "evidence," and "proof," are technical terms and have more sophisticated meanings than they did in eighteenth-century New England. His method was a limitation of a then currently accepted mode of scientific or logical thought. When

---

[35]For a contemporary attempt at explaining near-death experiences, see *Life After Life* by Raymond A. Moody (New York: Bantam Books, 1975).

grappling with spiritual matters, we suffer the same inability to construct a proof climate. Possibly the only recourse we have, even today, is a case-history, a personal experience account.[36]

III. The New Heavens and the New Earth: The Millennial Kingdom

The third section was by far the most detailed description Mather gave of any paradise. Part three of "Triparadisus" was divided into eleven sections. Two sections concern us here, sections nine and ten, "The New Heavens Opened" and "The New Earth Surveyed."[37]

Cotton Mather in "The New Heavens Opened" painstakingly described the grandeur found in the biblical description of the millennial heaven. The people who populate the new heaven will be raised from the dead. Their resurrected bodies will be "Embodied Spirits." Basing his account upon Revelation, chapter twenty-one, Mather emphasized material aspects witnessed in the city. Mather criticized people who may hold to a mere spiritual understanding of the new heaven by claiming it to be "a Material City." "The city is material," he wrote, "because it will be inhabited by 'Bodies.'"[38]

Mather's argument stands as a monument against "Sadducism," a seventeenth-century word signifying atheism. A growing literature in the

---

[36]"Triparadisus," Pt. III, pp. 1-143. For an analysis of Mather's belief in the conflagration as an element of millennial judgment, see chapter 7.

[37]*Ibid.*, p. 2.

[38]Kenneth Silverman, *The Life and Times of Cotton Mather* (New York: Harper and Row, 1984), p. 92.

1680s targeted Sadducism as the archenemy of Christianity.[39] To Mather, "spirit" meant something beyond transcendency. Spiritual entities were also substantive. Citing Tertullian's *Third Book against Marcion*, Mather related the story of the appearance of the New Jerusalem to the "Primitive Christians." "About the year CXCVIII, there was a wonderful Appearance over Judea," he wrote, "beheld with Astonishments for Forty Mornings together. It appeared still in the Morning," Tertullian said, "but as the Forenoons come on it became Invisible."[40] Even though Mather himself is impressed with this Christian legend, he encouraged his reader to not become engrossed with "Grandiose Fancy," or "Idle Notions." Instead, sound biblical exegesis was needed to explain the "substance" of this heavenly place.

Mather believed that the New Jerusalem was to be "ye Reverse" of the old city of Babylon. Babylon symbolized the decadence of presumptuous power before an almighty God. "Nebuchadnezzar," the Babylonian king under whose rule the fabulous city was constructed, brought in people from every nation to inhabit this "Wonder of the World." The city's walls were "eighty seven feet thick" and "three hundred feet high."[41] Yet, this fortress was a mere shadow compared to the future heavenly city. Babylon became "an Eternal Desolation," but "ye New Jerusalem" will be a "Victorious Declaration" illustrating the

---

[39]"Triparadisus," Pt. III, section 9, p. 3.

[40]*Ibid.*, p. 4.

[41]p. 5.

power and authority of God.⁴²

In the New Jerusalem there will be perfect happiness for all of God's saints. Mather longingly looked to the millennial consummation as a time of eternal blessedness. No more death, tears, crying, or pain will exist in the heavenly city. The Raised Saints' condition will be one in which the "Self will be entirely denounced." They will not be the same as God but will be "Divine Beings" who retain their "individuation." By "individuation" Mather meant that the Raised Saints will have some kind of feature which will identify them as they were in their earthly habitat.⁴³

The lost image of God forsaken by the original Adam is reclaimed by the second Adam, Jesus Christ. Jesus, as humankind's redeemer, Mather claimed will restore the "Beatific Vision" in the human soul through "perfection of Holiness." The perfection of holiness is attained by Jesus' power. Jesus unites the spirit to the body through the "Resurrection of the Dead" for the Saints, by transforming their bodies "like unto his own glorious body."⁴⁴ Mather avoided any specific description of the nature of this heavenly body, except to say that it "shall have some conformity to the Old Humane Figure" and "a wonderful accession of New Qualities, agreeable to an Heavenly World." To him, the Christian sacraments of the Lord's Supper and Baptism when they enact washing and feeding of the body, and yet simultaneously witness to

---

⁴²pp. 5-9.

⁴³p. 14.

⁴⁴pp. 15-18.

a spiritual union with Christ, actually prefigures the heavenly state of the Raised Saint. The body in this spiritual state Mather considered a "Luminous Body" perfected and cleansed and "Salted by the Garments of Light." There will exist for the resurrected body no sickness, nor corruption. In this sense Mather foresaw the Raised Saints as "Angelical," taking on the attributes of the Angels, including the ability to transcend space by flying.[45]

Mather considered the Raised Saints likely candidates to fulfill God's work. To him the employments of the redeemed were summarized in two words "teach and rule." The Saints will reign over the earth and have authority over the cities as well as judge the world. The people who remain on the New Earth to inhabit it will be the subjects of the Saints. The Saints "will be the Angels of the World to Come." Just as the angels in the present are messengers, Mather explained the transportation of the dead inhabitants of the New Earth, after their spirits had been transformed, to be carried on by the Raised Saints to the New Heaven.[46] The Raised Saints fulfilled the millennial messenger role that angels had performed on earth previously.

Males and females will not exist in the New Heavens. "There will be no Different Sexes," Mather wrote, "in the Holy City." Women will be equal to men and men will be equal to the angels. Mather confirmed the asexuality of the Raised Saints by citing Jesus' words, "Ye Raised Marry

---

[45]pp. 19-29.

[46]pp. 31-32.

not, nor are given in marriage." After an explanation of the development of the embryo in comparison to the growth of woman from the rib of the first Adam, he concluded that the mystical union which existed between Christ as the groom and the Church as his bride will be consummated in the millennial era with the result that members will be "of His Flesh; of His Bones."[47]

Mather foresaw a glorious advancement for women in the millennial kingdom. "The Female Sex may think they have cause to complain of us, that we stunt them so much in their Education and abridge them of many points wherein they might be serviceable." Yet, he quickly added, "But ye Handmaids of the Lord, a REDEEMER who was once born of a Woman, intends unknown Dignities for you, and will make a use of you beyond what we yett know. . . ."[48] Interestingly, the implication is that he was quite aware of the discrepancies offered between the sexes in his own time. Male dominance will subside in the Holy City. After he mentioned the role of women performing instrumental and vocal music in the temple for the ancient Hebrews, he declared that females will lose their name "Woman" in their "marriage to ye Son of God."[49]

Mather's closing thoughts on the New Heavens are directed toward an assertion that they will occupy a particular place, based upon his

---

[47]p. 32.

[48]p. 33.

[49]p. 34.

interpretation of a Hebrew word which he renders "a definite place." He declares that the New Heavens will be "in the place where the Stars appear to us" and that "the New Earth" will be "the lower part of the Heavenly Countrey to be Look'd for."[50]

In section ten, "The New Earth Surveyed," Mather speculated as to whether the entire earth will be destroyed, or some of it. "Some have imagined," he wrote, "that the Old State of the Earth will not be so much altered by ye Conflagration, but that there may in ye Ruins be Left some Remembrances of them." He believed that "The Land of Canaan will be the spot on earth which will survive the conflagration." He concluded that "we are at a Loss how this Imagination will stand before the Fire of those oracles which works that are therein shall be BURNT up; And ALL these things shall be Dissolved."[51]

After basing this conclusion upon early church fathers such as Cyril of Jerusalem and Cyril of Alexandria, Mather summarized these writings predicting that at the very least the earth will be changed enough to be called "A New Creation." He believed God's power capable of making the necessary requisites for a new earth. Citing Acts 2:21, he claimed a "Restitution of ALL THINGS when Christ returns." The earth will once again be in a state of paradise "Like the Garden of Eden." The earth will be refined into a holy and heavenly place.[52]

---

[50]pp. 35-37.

[51]p. 39.

[52]pp. 40-41.

Mather addressed the question of who will inhabit the new earth. The wicked will be dispatched with the conflagration, and the Raised Saints will be in the New Heavens. He insisted it must be filled with a "sinless people," inhabitants who will build houses, plant vineyards, and have offspring, where there will be no dying. How does this occur? Mather conceived of the conflagration destroying the wicked, hence he postulated that the "Saved Nations" will not be consumed by the conflagration because they will be "caught up to meet the Lord in the air and then returned again to populate the New Earth. They will be delivered from the wrath to come and the Flames of a World on Fire." An "Aerial place of Safety" will exist for the people still on earth during the conflagration who are the saved in Christ.[53]

The New Earth bodies will not have died and there will be no graves from which to raise them. Accordingly, they retain the conditions of the flesh, without sinning. "Ye Changed Ones will on the New Earth have some Circumstances of the Animal Oeconomy, which the Raised Ones will forever have done withal." The sexes will be retained by those people caught up to escape the terrible conflagration, and children will be a pleasant result of this condition.[54]

By "Animal Oeconomy" Mather meant that the people of the New Earth would still perform physical activity and functions. Yet, traditionally, Christianity attributed the flesh to sin. Mather denied the

---

[53]pp. 42-43.

[54]p. 49.

existence of sin in the New Earth. The major transformation occurring for the individual left on earth was the purification of the soul granted by Christ's return. He related a story about his youth. Several of his Christian friends discussed the kingdom of God. Mather introduced the question "What shall we think about the state of the New Earth with relation to Sin?" A "Grave Old Man" replied, "What! The Spouse of CHRIST have the Foul Disease? Never Tell me that!" The man's response impressed Mather and he never relinquished his sentiment toward a sinless people inhabiting the New Earth. He bluntly states his position in section ten: "If Sin be there, the Devil is there."[55] Since Satan is defeated, there will be no sin for the "Changed Saints" of the New Earth.

The New Earth responded to this sinless state where the curse of Adam is absent by regaining its Edenic fecundity. There will be "Healing Waters" and plenty of "corn" and "wine" for all people. No sickness, no physicians will exist there. Mather joyfully summarized the bountiful condition of the New Earth by exclaiming it "will be a True Eutopia!"

Mather concluded section ten of "Triparadisus" with a closing comment about the query "Where will you find Gog and Magog appear in Jewish eschatology as leading the final, but abortive assault of the powers of the world upon the kingdom of God?"[56] Mather understood the question to be too specific and he compared it to asking if the

---

[55]pp. 56-60.

[56]*Dictionary of the Bible*, ed., James Hastings (New York: Scribners & Sons, 1963), pp. 338-339.

"Raised Saints" will have teeth.

One of Mather's friends, Judge Samuel Sewall of Boston, once debated with Paul Dudley about the body's condition when resurrected. Dudley claimed that "the Belly should not be raised, because he knew of no use for it." Yet, Sewall responded that since Christ was perfect and had a stomach, so would the saints. Sewall capped his position by asserting that Jesus had redeemed his belly as well as his soul.[57]

Mather did not indulge in his friends' kind of eschatological speculation. But sometimes he strained to bring his millennialism into a consistent whole. Nonetheless, he stated that after a period of one thousand years there "shall be an unaccountable attempt from Hell against the New Jerusalem" in the New Earth. But the attempt will be stopped with help from the New Heavens. Antichrist will be destroyed. Mather considered Joseph Mede (1586-1638), a popular millennial interpreter, to be misguided in his claim that the American Hemisphere will escape the conflagration and the Devil will convince Americans to invade other regions of the New Earth."[58]

Although Mather's millennial interests had taken him into an investigation of the "Sacred Geography," the hope of heaven also prompted him to examine the individual soul's meaning. Within the area of Christian theology the soul's immortality posed a considerable obstacle to millennialists. Most of them took for granted the soul's eternal station

---

[57]"Triparadisus," Pt. III, pp. 66-68.

[58]Perry Miller, *The New England Mind: The Seventeenth Century* (London: Harvard University Press, 1939), pp. 463-491.

as a precept of faith, but Mather explored the question with his usual thoroughness.

Chapter 5

"The Nishmath-Chajim"

Christianity's various forms have all depicted an end to the world. Mankind's judgment, Christians believed, will be by a creator who carried a ledger of good and ill performed by every person. New England's Puritan founders reflected this abiding concern that the end might be near.[1] The seventeenth century, earmarked by the migration to America and the English Civil War as deeply unsettling experiences, challenged men to consider the final resolution of human affairs. In the New World, death drew its carnage from wars, such as the Pequot War (1637) and King Philip's War (1676), as well as that most dreaded disease smallpox. Cotton Mather's own preoccupation with death increased his millennial hope for a thousand year reign with Christ and guided him to formulate a chiliastic theology detailing the soul's immortality; both its future resurrected state and its earthly efficacy for healing disease. Mather believed in the hope of a future state in another world. "An Hope not only that our Spirits at their Departure from our Bodies will be lodg'd in sweet Mansions of Rest under the Custody of our Great Saviour," he wrote in *A Soul Well-Anchored* (Boston, 1712), "but also that by a Resurrection from the Dead, He will restore our Bodies to our Spirits marvelously altered from what now they are, and bring us to dwell with

---

[1]Perry Miller, *The New England Mind: The Seventeenth Century* (London: Harvard University Press, 1939), pp. 463-491.

Him in the Full Joyes of His Holy City. . . ." Mather relied for this millennial hope upon Jewish mystical writings known as "Cabala," the Cambridge Platonists' scholarship, particularly Henry More (1614-1687), Rene Descartes' (1596-1650) mechanistic philosophy, and Jean Baptiste van Helmont's chemical theories (1577-1644), to bolster what he believed to be a scriptural and millennial necessity--the soul's immortality.

"It is indeed impossible to imagine our own death," wrote the famous Viennese psychiatrist Sigmund Freud, as he considered the aftermath of World War I, "and whenever we attempt to do so we can perceive that we are in fact still present as spectators. Hence . . . at bottom no one believes in his own death, or, to put the same thing another way, in the unconscious every one of us is convinced of his own immortality."[2] The dilemma we face when considering the finiteness of our own existence, the unpredictableness surrounding death, some philosophers have described as the primary source, or, at the least, the very wellspring of religion. From this primordial beginning the religions of the world have attempted to explain the mysterious and to posit categories lending meaning to speculative theories, such as "soul," "spirit," and "immortality," while generally concluding it is the work of divine will.[3]

---

[2]Sigmund Freud, *Standard Edition of the Complete Psychological Works of Sigmund Freud*, ed., James Strachey (London: The Hogarth Press, 1957), vol. 14, p. 289.

[3]E. 0. James, *Prehistoric Religion* (New York: Praeger, 1957), pp. 23-30.

Despite Copernicus's work, elaborated and expanded by Brahe, Kepler, Galileo, and others, seventeenth-century Englishmen still viewed the world as part of a systematic and meaningful universe governed by God's created overarching scheme. "It was natural that the findings of the new science should seem to threaten the security of people who had imagined that they inhabited the center of the universe," observed G. R. Cragg, "and equally natural that they should attack those who disturbed their peace of mind."[4] The new science's heliocentricity did not sway Christians to a less than temporal placement of the world in the center of God's magnificently and perfectly created universe. All things existed for them in hierarchical fashion, beginning with man at the pinnacle. Yet, this earthly kingdom was not a paradise, not since four thousand years before Christ's birth when Adam and Eve rejected God in the Garden of Eden. As a kingdom under siege by evil forces, those who succumbed to Satan could expect their just reward. Hell supposedly smoldered in the earth's center. Reports issued from "Aetna in Italy, Hecla in Island, Saint Patricks hole in Ireland, or that formidable burning Mountayne by the American Mexico . . .," wrote the staid encyclopedist David Person, "that there are complaints and mourning voices to bee heard through by the vents and Chimneyes of hell, as they give out." Strict dichotomies, like that which existed between good and evil, prevailed in the Englishman's mindset. Preoccupied with ghosts and witches, divine portents such as earthquakes, droughts, plagues and comets, inundated with astrological

---

[4]G. R. Cragg, *From Puritanism to the Age of Reason* (Cambridge: Cambridge University Press, 1966), p. 91.

and magical responses to the spiritual forces permeating the countryside, the English-speaking people joined supernatural convictions to their religious beliefs.[5]

Coupled with the supernatural explanations given to daily phenomena, the people of the seventeenth century suffered persistent physical hardship. Beggars wandered the streets and roadways, while poverty and misery exerted extreme deprivation upon the common folk. From the early sixteenth to the mid-seventeenth century, London was free for barely a decade of the bubonic plague. More than one out of six inhabitants died from this pestilence in the city during some years. Entire villages were destroyed by it. The small parish in Cheshire in 1625 was literally erased by an epidemic. When the last adult became infected, he dug his own grave and buried himself, apparently because the remaining survivors were children incapable of transferring his body from the home.[6]

Even the English nobleman's life expectancy by 1675 barely reached thirty years. Yet, as noblemen they did not die of starvation. The less fortunate simply did not have enough food to go around, and the nutritional value of that which they did have was questionable. Distribution of food lacked the consistent marketability we enjoy today. Some domestic animals became larder for the table, as observed by the

---

[5]David Person, *Varieties: or, A Surveigh of Rare and Excellent Matters* (London, 1635), bk. five, pp. 81-82. Also quoted in Stannard, *op. cit.*, p. 37.

[6]Carl Bridenbaugh, *Vexed and Troubled Englishmen, 1590-1642* (New York: Oxford University Press, 1968), p. 376.

1623 report from Lincolnshire that "dog's flesh is a dainty dish, and found . . . in many houses."[7]

The world that gave birth to the Puritan saw divine purpose, perfection and design in nature's details; it accepted the everyday existence of demons and witches and challenged them with astrology and magic; it helplessly received disease's scourge, starvation and neglect. From this deprivational existence sprang the Puritan's hope, a deep-rooted expectation for Christ's Second Coming. The scriptural interpretations simply confirmed what they observed all around them; that the millennium was at hand. They believed themselves on the vanguard of a movement to bring Christendom into God's kingdom. Driven by an urge to reform their life, they sought to bring England and eventually New England under heaven's wing. As Thomas Cartwright, a venerable sixteenth-century Puritan divine, suggested as early as 1572, theirs was not a mission of "innovation but renovation, and the doctrine not new but renewed."[8] This zealous commitment for reform displayed individual as well as national tendencies. Surrounded by mortality's evidence, the Puritans adhered to the traditional Christian doctrine of the soul's immortality. But this doctrine evolved from the realities the Puritans faced in Old and New England, and those realities were tinctured by an

---

[7]Peter Laslett, *The World We Have Lost: England Before the Industrial Age* (New York: Scribner's, 1965), p. 117.

[8]Thomas Cartwright, *A Reply to an Answer Made of Master Doctor Whitgift Agaynst the Admonition to the Parliament* (London, 1572), p. 1. Also quoted in Stannard, *op. cit.*, p. 28.

existential concern for one's own death, or as one author phrased it, "deathbed anxiety."[9]

New England offered no different climate for theological reflection or physiological disease than old England. The most infamous killer in New England was smallpox. The devastating smallpox epidemic in 1677-78 combined with the natural death rate to kill more than one-fifth Boston's entire population. "Boston buring-places," [sic] witnessed the young Cotton Mather, who by 1722 would fight smallpox by supporting inoculation, "never filled so fast." Continuing his reflections upon the epidemic in Boston, the young Mather wrote to his maternal grandfather, John Cotton: "It is easy to tell the time when we did not have the bells tolling for burials on a Sabbath morning by sunrise; to have 7 buried on a Sabbath day night, after Meeting. To have coffins crossing each other as they have been carried in the street ... To attempt a Bill of Mortality, and number the very spires of grace in a Burying Place seem to have a parity of difficulty and in accomplishment."[10]

---

[9]Stannard, p. 83.

[10]Cotton Mather to John Cotton, November 1678, in Massachusetts Historical Society *Collections*, 4th Series, VIII (1868), 383-384; contemporary estimates concerning the toll of the epidemic were made by Increase Mather and John Foster in Thomas Thatcher, *A Brief Rule to Guide the Common People* (Boston, 1678). Also see John B. Blake, *Public Health in the Town of Boston, 1630-1822* (Cambridge, Mass.: Harvard University Press, 1959), p. 20; for an estimate of the population in Boston during the epidemic, see Carl Bridenbaugh, *Cities in the Wilderness: Urban Life in America, 1625-1742* (New York: Capricorn Books, 1964, originally published in 1936), pp. 6, 87. Also quoted in Stannard, pp. 53-54.

By May 1678 hundreds had died as the Massachusetts government and the town hurriedly passed legislation projected to hold down the deadly infection's spread. Those who had survived the disease could not circulate with others for specified periods of time, while others were directed not to hang out bedding or clothes near the roadways or in their yards. In eighteen months, it was as though, proportionate to New York City's current population, over a million and a half of its people died. In one day, September 30, 1677, thirty people died, equivalent to more than sixty thousand present-day New Yorkers.[11]

Two years earlier New England endured King Philip's War (1675-76) in which greater casualties were inflicted in proportion to the population than any subsequent war in American history, not even counting the enormous Native Americans' number dead.[12] Surrounded by these realities, death permeated the New England Puritan's consciousness. Samuel Sewall, a contemporary of Mather's, fathered fourteen children,

---

[11]Boston Record Commissioners, *Report*, VII, 119. Cited in Blake, *Public Health*, p. 19; see also Bridenbaugh, *Cities in the Wilderness*, p. 87, and Stannard, p. 61.

[12]Douglas Edward Leach, *Flintlock and Tomahawk: New England in King Philip's War* (New York: Norton, 1958), p. 243. Between 1620 and 1720 more than twenty-five percent of the Native American population was lost in wars with white settlers: Sherburne F. Cook, "Interracial Warfare and Population Decline Among the New England Indians," *Ethnohistory* 20 (1973), pp. 1-24. On the general topic of conflict among white settlers and the Native Americans depicted in a specific massacre in New England, see "Captain Myles Standish's Military Role in Plymouth," John S. Erwin, *Historical Journal of Massachusetts*, (January, 1985), pp. 1-13.

one of which was stillborn, several died as infants, and several more as young adults. It is no wonder that Sewall dreamed his daughter had mysteriously disappeared after he had taken her "in a little closet to pray with her," or that he suffered from recurring dreams that his wife or children had died. Cotton Mather, himself, lived to see seven babies die shortly after delivery, one died at two years of age and six survived into adulthood, five of whom died in their twenties. Mather had continual "Apprehension" over the thought that his sole surviving son, Samuel, "will dy in its infancy."[13]

For Mather, death also held a theological thrust. "A prudent man," Mather wrote, "will Dy Daily; and this is one Thing in our doing too: Tis to live Daily under the power of such Impressions, as we shall have upon us, when we come to Dy . . . Every Time the Clock Strikes, it may Strike upon our Hearts, to think, thus I am one Hour nearer to my last! But, O mark what I say; That Hour is probably Nearer to None than to such as Least Think of it."[14]

From young adulthood to his later years, Mather displayed an obsession with death. In 1701, writing *Death Made Easie & Happy*, he pleaded for the reader to remember constantly "that he is to die shortly, Let us look upon everything as a sort of Death's Head set before us, with

---

[13]*The Diary of Samuel Sewall, 1674-1729*, ed. M. Halsey Thomas (New York: Farrar, Straus & Giroux, 1973), vol. I, p. 592; "Diary of Cotton Mather," Massachusetts Historical Society *Collections*, 7th series (Boston, 1911), VII, pp. 380-82.

[14]C. M., *The Thoughts of a Dying Man* (Boston, 1697), pp. 38-39.

a Memento mortis written upon it."[15] He believed that a perpetual awareness of one's own death kept one alert to the spiritual benefits of the present.

Giving a lecture on *Seasonable Thoughts Upon Mortality* in Boston January 24, 1711, Mather based his remarks on Job 24:19, "Drought and Heat consume the snow waters; so doth the grave those who have sinned." After a description of the heavy snowfall in New England, he compared the melting of the snow to the passing of life. Going beyond this metaphor, he planted a reminder that "The Lively Thoughts of Death, will have a singular Tendency to make us Lively Saints; they tend to keep alive all Serious and Practical Religion." Not content to give his reader a moment's rest, Mather made an interesting demographical statement: "In a few years there will be, Not one of them left! They that have made Nice Remarks, our Bills of Mortality, will tell you; That one half of those that are Born, don't live Seventeen years: That about Forty of an hundred, are found Alive, at Sixteen years: That about Ten out of an hundred, at Forty-Six; but Six, at Fifty Six; but Three at Sixty-Six; but One at Seventy-Six." The application for such a dire picture of human existence was centered upon Mather's millennial hope.

"There shall be a New Earth, wherein - shall dwell Righteousness; there shall be none but Righteous Ones," Mather wrote, "And when the Seventh Apocalyptical Trumpet Sounds, which may new be (God knows How Quickly!) it brings on that Revolution; Rev. XI. 18. To Destroy them which corrupt the Earth." A belief in the millennium, for Mather,

---

[15] C. M., *Death Made Easie & Happy* (London, 1701), p. 94.

carried the two-edged sword of judgment and redemption for mankind's soul. A prerequisite for hell or heaven was immortality. But the soul's immortality was conditioned by its nature, which according to Mather "is unspeakably depraved."[16]

When Jeremiah Fenwick of Boston, who had in November 1716 killed Ralph Moxtershed, a ropemaker, and then, subsequently, chose Reverend Mather to preach his gallow's sermon, Mather expounded upon "The Terrors of Hell demonstrated." "The Destruction of the Soul as well as the body, in HELL," considered Mather, "is a Thing so much more Formidable than any Death," and ultimately brings "us to fear God." Mather believed that the only way a person could overcome the depraved nature of the soul centered upon a spiritual union to Jesus Christ.[17]

Preaching a wedding service in 1728, Mather related the marital ceremony which unites a man and a woman to the believer's marriage to Christ. The condition of this world often lacked the religious equipment to usher one to spiritual union with Christ. "Our corrupt Nature is thereby initiated unto Rebellion," he wrote, "rather than animated unto obedience, and the Evil Principle gains the Force of a Law upon us." The law Mather refers to is the law of sin, which Calvinists traditionally attributed to man's nature. The most one can hope for is a soul residing in a state of happiness, in other words, salvation's assurance rested for

---

[16] C. M., *Seasonable Thoughts upon Mortality* (Boston, 1711), pp. 7, 15, 24. For his comment on the soul being depraved, see his *A Treacle Fetch'd out of a Viper* (Boston, 1707), p. 4.

[17] C. M., *The Valley of Hinnom* (Boston, 1717), p. 4.

Mather in the mystical marriage of the believer to Christ. "A Soul Married unto a Jesus Raised from the Dead," he asserted, "is an Happy Soul."[18]

Underlying death's supposed spiritual edification for Mather resided a basic fear toward life's culmination. If the believer, according to him, did not come to an assurance of one's own salvation, then "the Terror of Death alone would be enough to kill them! They would Chatter like a Crane or a Swallow, and mourne like a Dove, going to be pulled out of their Nest, and cry out, Lord, This Hour is what I am not ready for!"[19] It is important to progress past this state of fear and enter in union with Christ. Ultimate acceptance of one's own death, for Mather, only came after meditating upon death's consequences. "It was not folly in some of the Ancients," he wrote in 1726, "to assign the Contemplation of Death, as the main Foundation, and Exercise of their Philosophy; And the Young Man will arrive to more Understanding than the Ancients; who does practice upon it."[20] Indeed, Mather followed his own advice and he did not restrict it to young men. Occasionally, when children died unexpectedly, he forcefully urged his listeners during the funeral sermon to consider death's impact upon their spiritual condition. When fourteen-year-old Richard Hobby was squashed to death under a

---

[18]C. M., *The Mystical Marriage* (Boston, 1728), pp. 2, 4. Also *Agricola* (Boston, 1727), 150.

[19]C. M., *Euthanasia* (Boston, 1723), p. 5.

[20]C. M., *Manuductio ad Ministerium* (Boston, 1726), p. 3.

tipped cart, Mather captured the opportunity to preach and quickly thereafter publish *Perswasions from the Terror of the Lord* (Boston, 1711). Mather claimed that the young as well as the old will one day have to face their maker, a common Christian theme. But, he pushed this to the point of the bizarre when he contrasted the playground to the graveyard, maintained the child's equal awareness of both, and summarized his argument with this dreadful warning to the child at play: "Yea, you may be at Play one Hour; Dead, Dead the next."[21] While priming the spiritual pump for the Puritans at the time of death may seem like an emotionally wrenching experience to us, sometimes the net result ultimately reflected for them acceptance of personal death.

Katharin Mather's death, Cotton's daughter, clearly illustrates a common deathbed paradigm. Mather's own "lovely Katy" exuded such tranquility at her death that even "some who had Read and Heard much, said, they never Saw till now." Mather noted that her assurance "was not a Rash Perswasion. She was desirous to have the matter Disputed unto the uttermost. How pathetically would she say, Oh that my portion may be among the wise Virgins! But, in this time, often she would say unto her Father, Is my Soul safe? Will my Saviour accept me?"[22] Mather counseled Katy that God would ultimately accept her. All through "the

---

[21]p. 35. Also quoted in "The Printed Funeral Sermons of Cotton Mather," William D. Andrews, *Early American Literature*, vol. 5, no. 2, Fall, 1970, p. 34.

[22]C. M., *Victorina* (Boston, 1717), pp. 73-78. The quote is taken from "An Account of Mrs. Katharin Mather, By Another Hand," following the printed sermon text by Mather.

Storms which had sometimes disquieted her Soul" he witnessed his daughter's battle to overcome death's rage to gain eventual peace. Finally, on December 12, "In the Night she seemed entering into the last Agonies of Death. And felt then some Returns of Darkness upon her. In which she expressed herself afraid of Dying, afraid whether her Saviour would accept her," which allowed her father one last chance to reassure her.[23] Mather's desire to give her "Essayes to strengthen her in her Agonies" ended triumphantly. He sublimely recorded: "my lovely Daughter Katharin expired gloriously."[24]

Death, for Mather, hopefully glorified God. He welcomed death for more than just relieving the person of this life's pain and disease. The death he encouraged others to think upon, and he yearned for, led him into questioning the soul's form when it entered immortality. "Our Appearance in this World is brought to an End," he postulated, "But what then becomes of us?" In answer to his own query, Mather resorted to a much used comparison between the death of a human being and the hatching of a bird's egg and the subsequent experiment in flying for the young. At the point of death we are merely entering another world which we will reach by flying. As the bird pecked away at the shell which enclosed it, so time passed for the human being until "the Shell breaks,

---

[23]*Ibid.*

[24]*Diary of Cotton Mather*, ed. Worthington C. Ford (New York: Ungar Press, 1957), vol. II, p. 388. Hereafter cited as *Diary*. For most other quotations from the diary, I will give the volume and page numbers and the date in parentheses at the conclusion of the note.

and the Bird then does fly away." Mather believed, "Our Death is the breaking of the Shell." The soul's immortality was claimed by him with little apparent doubt. As a Christian, Mather posited God's justice upon the inevitability of the soul living eternally so as to render a proper judgment for the person to be either saved in a millennial heaven or damned in an everlasting hell.[25] The millennial drama was the larger production wherein the soul danced its immortal number. The saints, Mather claimed, joined a glorious Christ, the corporeal form left behind, to rule on the New Earth for a millennium. Consequently, death, on both the communal and personal levels, graphically revealed to Mather the Christian hope in a future millennial reign. But to reach the point where the issue of death resulted in a thorough chiliasm, as the mature years of his life revealed, Mather earlier faced the actuality of his own death.

In September 1686, at the age of twenty-three, Mather "dreamt that in a Room with other Gentlemen there was my friend Mr. Shepard of Charlestown, whom yett in my sleep, I knew to bee dead." Perceiving the deathly state of Shepard's body, Mather tried to avoid him by "contriving to slip out of the Room." But before he can make his escape, "Hee nimbly coming up with mee, took mee by the Hand, and said, 'Syr, you need not bee so shie of mee, for you shall quickly bee as I am, and where I am.'" Following this advance by Shepard in his dream, Mather

---

[25]C. M., *The Soul Upon the Wing* (Boston, 1733), p. 10. For an enlightening discussion of this common metaphor, see Allan I. Ludwig, *Graven Images: New England Stonecarving and its Symbols, 1650-1815* (Middletown, Conn.: Wesleyan Press, 1966), pp. 214-216.

related that he was struck with "a Fit of my Ephialtes, which almost killed mee." "Ephialtes" was the term Mather used to describe a dream condition similar to a nightmare. Immediately upon awaking from the dream, Mather contracted a cold and fever. The illness was not surprising, for he intimately connected his physical health to his soul's condition. But the cure was revealing. It illustrated Mather's intense and persistent fear of death while he concurrently held to a belief in death's ecstatic release when the body turned to dust and the soul obtained immortality during the conclusion of the millennial scheme. Mather believed that through the illness's course "the Lord overcame for mee, the Fears of Death." This high claim was further supported by his having sensed the soul's quintessential victory as he "apprehended not such Ghastliness therein, as heretofore." With death's terror momentarily subsided, he concluded with a Puritan benediction, ". . . I felt in my own Soul, the Foretastes and Earnests of life eternal."[26] Although the thousand-year reign of the saints with Christ lay sometime in the near future, Mather had experienced an abiding trust and hope that he would one day join their ranks.

---

[26]*Diary*, Vol. I, p. 130 (September, 1686). Mather had numerous instances of being directed through dreams, especially around the issue of death. For example, in September 1713 (*Diary*, vol. II, p. 241), Mather tells of having a dream where he is given a text to preach from the scriptures. "I proceeded and all fell out, unto good Acceptance among the People of God." He had the dream-sermon published. "The Subject is the most important in the World . . . A brief Essay to awaken in a Dying Man . . . a proper and lively Concern for, A Good State after Death." It was printed by T. Green, for D. Henchman, 1713.

On Saturday, September 28, 1700, fourteen years almost to the day that Mather saw Reverend Shepard in his dreams, he felt again "strongly accosted in my Sleep, with a Dream of this Importance." An "old Man" stood before him while he heard the words, "take notice of this old man, speak to him, do for him!" The very next day Mather saw the old man of his dream at the public sermon, a place he believed unusual for the old man to attend. One day later he met the old man in the street, but this time Mather greeted him by saying, "I am glad for to see you still in this World; I pray God prepare you for another! I suppose it won't be long before you are called away; Can I do you no Service!" The next day the old man came to the Reverend's home looking for advice. Mather proceeded to instruct him "how to prepare for Death." After giving him a book, *Grace Triumphant*, and some money, Mather sent the old man away. Seven weeks passed, during which time the old man visited Mather to receive more instruction. The old man "dyed suddenly" at the end of this period "a regenerate Man."[27] Mather relished his own, Katharin's, and the old man's successes over the fear of death. Yet, his passion for overcoming death's terror went beyond a sense of duty and on to saving a lost soul for the Lord. One event, even as dramatic as his "Ephialtes" were, could not serve to salve a lifetime's anxiety. The ultimate unction for deathbed anxiety resided in his fervent devotional life. As a minister,

---

[27]*Diary*, Vol. I, pp. 372-373 (September, 1700). For a suggestive essay on Mather as a diarist, see Lawrence Alan Rosenwald, "Cotton Mather as Diarist," *Prospects*, ed. by Jack Salzman (Cambridge, Mass.: Cambridge University Press, 1983), pp. 129-161, especially pp. 145-146 on the death of Mather's wife, Abigail.

Mather considered it an obligation to single out suitable subjects to consider for devotions. With characteristic organization, Mather began to "methodize" his "nocturnal Recollections." The pressing question of his own death haunted Mather during these evening devotional queries. "Have I lived this Day under a deep Sense of Mortalitie and Eternitie; and as a Stranger in the World?" he asked himself.[28] The issue of death gradually served for Mather more and more as a reflective catalyst, which stirred him toward spiritual contemplation and lifted him momentarily beyond the pain, suffering, and disease which filled everyday life.

The soul's millennial victory also held instructional value for him. Consideration given to the form and substance of the soul composed part of the evening self-examinations Mather practiced. He affirmed a scriptural understanding of mankind which divided the anatomy into three parts: spirit, soul, and body. He claimed "The Oracles of God, make a Distribution of Man, into three Parts" and that "The Spirit is the rational Mind . . . The Soul, is a vital Flame, . . . The Body, is the obvious Receptacle and Habitation of these wonderful Agents."[29]

Mather's theology tended to maximize the organic connectedness of this physical trilogy of spirit, soul, and body. Ursula King, in her recent study of Teilhard de Chardin, considered that ". . . Christian theology . . . has the tendency to give the word mystical (in mystical body, mystical union) a minimum of organic or physical meaning'. This is due

---

[28]*Diary*, Vol. I, p. 74 (September, 1683).

[29]*Ibid.*, p. 526 (1705).

to the very common mistake," she continued, "of regarding the spiritual as an attenuation of the material, whereas it is in fact the material carried beyond itself: it is super-material."[30] Mather also linked closely the body and soul while appreciating them as separate entities.

He represented death as the unnatural separation of soul and body. "The Union between the Soul and Body is a very Strong Union," Mather affirmed, but, "The Dissolution of the Vital Tye between the Soul & Body is an Unnatural Thing." Actually, for him, death wrenched the soul and body asunder. Pain is the result as death drew close. "It is considerable Torture, we feel, before the Silver Cord be loosed," Mather speculated, "And then, what the Pangs of Death are; or, what the Dying feel in their Last Agonies; no Words can declare; none return to declare." The separation only temporarily existed, according to Mather, between the body and soul after death. "Our Body and Spirit upon the Dissolution made of the Union between them, when we Dye, continue in a state of Separation," Mather claimed, "till the Resurrection of the Dead."[31] Mather reasoned that our bodies dwell in the chambers of the grave, while our soul goes to paradise, or the third heaven, awaiting the moment when God will blow the millennial trumpet and restore the body and soul by setting "this Principle to work again," so all may be "Children

---

[30]Ursula King, *Towards a New Mysticism* (New York: Seabury Press, 1980), p. 68.

[31]C. M., *The Comfortable Chambers* (Boston, 1728), p. 4.

of the Resurrection."[32]

Later in his life, the "Principle" which Mather believed was exercised to reunite the soul and body was explained in more detail. In "Coheleth," an essay he wrote as "instruction for a son," Mather desired to lay before his readers the basic facts of the Christian faith, which he called "those Incontestible Sentiments of Religion." First and foremost, among religious sentiments, lay the obvious existence of the soul. "I am Apprehensive of this," wrote Mather, "That there is in me a SOUL, which is of a Spiritual & Intellectual Nature, and which does Think, and has a Conscience of God and what is True and what is Just; and which does perform operations, with Reflex Acts as well as Direct ones' which the Brutal World cannot attain unto."[33] The soul, as an entity for Mather, existed organically separate from the mind and body and held a unique nature as the divine spark within man. He thought that a "lively Image" of God had been "grafted" into man's soul by which the creator communicated ideas to the creature. "There is nothing in this world more clear to me than this;" Mather asserted, "That I have in me a Principle, which does not merely receive ideas (as a Looking-Glass may images,) but also perceive them, and make Remarks upon them; and has a certainty of itself, and what is done in itself . . ." Such objectivity residing in the soul appeared to carry the connotation that a creature, i.e., the soul, existed within a creature, i.e., a human being. The "Principle" has the

---

[32]*Ibid.*, p. 10.

[33]C. M., *Coheleth* (Boston, 1720), p. 2, 3.

stamp of God upon it, therefore, as Mather wrote, it has "immense capacity of Sentiment; and can take in all the Ideas that the glorious God shall please to send to it: An Indivisible Being, and get what can Embrace and Contain the Universe." Mather's universal principle, which functioned with man's soul, not only served as a receptacle for communication with God, but also was the essential consideration in perceiving its own immortal nature. To him the universal principle could not be destroyed. "The Spiritual and Intelligent Nature of my Soul," he argued, "puts it beyond all Doubt unto me that it is Immortal; and the Death which comes on the Ruin of the Commerce between my Heart and my Brain, and will make havoc of my Body, cannot in the least prey upon my SOUL." Mather believed, identical to classical Platonic thought, and in harmony with Jewish mysticism, that the soul was in a state of trial upon earth and that upon death it returned to God who had left his impression upon it and granted it eternal life after the return of Christ. For Mather then, the existence of God's principle in man was a fact which substantiated the soul's immortality within the millennialistic drama, but how it actually worked remained a mystery and was "beyond the search & reach of our Philosophy."[34]

The death that Mather longed to overcome, by union with Christ and self-examination, led him into an investigation of the physical and millennial meaning of immortality. What composed the soul's substance? Where does the soul reside in man? The saints, as Mather understood scripture, eventually joined Christ, leaving the corporeal body behind.

---

[34]*Ibid.*, p. 5.

But what kind of spiritual transformation took place to allow the soul to prevail over the physical body when the millennium dawns? As a prelude, death was understood to begin a process which ended in the soul's immortality. But this traditional Christian interpretation left unsatisfied his thirst for further understanding. Speculative by nature and eclectic in his taste, Mather investigated the Jewish mystical writings known as Kabbalah (Mather cited it as "Cabala"). From this esoteric collection he borrowed the title from a section of sayings, "Nishmath-Chajim," which in the Hebrew means "breath of life," (Genesis 2:7).[35] The "Nishmath-Chajim" became the primary term he used to define the set of particles which linked the spiritual and the physical in man.

After acknowledging that Mather believed the Nishmath-Chajim provided the medium for conveying original sin from one generation to another, a contemporary historian has astonishingly claimed, "There is little of inherent importance, or interest, in this theory. . . . The theory and the stories . . . suggest the depths of Mather's growing anti-rationalism."[36] On the contrary, the Nishmath-Chajim theory illustrated

---

[35]William L. Holladay, *A Concise Hebrew and Aramaic Lexicon of the Old Testament* (Grand Rapids: William B. Eerdmans Pub. Co., 1971), p. 101.

[36]Robert Middlekauff, *The Mathers: Three Generations of Puritan Intellectuals, 1596-1728* (New York: Oxford University Press, 1971), pp. 318-319. Hereafter cited as Middlekauff, *The Mathers*, along with page citation. Middlekauff avoids dealing with the mystical elements in Mather's thought. I see Mather's mysticism, or "anti-rationalism," as an essential ingredient in his millennialism and his belief in the soul's immortality.

the profound consideration Mather gave to speculation concerning the soul's immortality and the physical substance contained in it. The genesis of this hypothesis stemmed not only from seventeenth-century New England's wars and pestilences answered by Mather's millennial hope in the soul's immortality, but also from his interest in classical Hebrew, dating from his days at Harvard College in 1674.

Mather's Hebrew scholarship originated at Harvard College. His Master of Arts thesis, *Puncta Hebraica sunt Originis Divinae*, argued for the divine origin of the Hebrew vowel points.[37] Scholars glorified the Hebrew language in seventeenth-century England as the language spoken by Adam and Eve in the Garden of Eden. For example, John Donne (1573-1631), an English poet and clergyman, believed that "names are to instruct us, and express natures and essences. This Adam was able to do." When Adam named God's creatures, he was exercising a divine word and utilizing the Hebrew language. Since Kabbalism, an expression of Jewish mysticism, probed the significance surrounding the Hebrew language as a symbolic structure reflecting divine revelation, it attracted a number of Christian Hebraists. Donne adequately summed up this scholastic magnetism toward Jewish mysticism when he wrote that Kabbalists "are the Anatomists of words, and have a Theologicall Alchimy to draw soveraigne tinctures and spirits from plain and grosse literall matter, and observe in every variety some great mystick signification."[30]

---

[37]*Diary*, Vol. I, p. 26.

[38]*History & Imagination: Essays in honor of H. R. Trevor-Roper*, eds. Hugh Lloyd-Jones, Valerie Pearl, and Blair Worden (New York: Holmes

To use the term "Nishmath-Chajim" to describe his perceptions concerning the soul, Mather linked himself to this Christian Hebraist tradition. More than a linguistic exercise and tool toward understanding the word of God as revealed in the Old Testament, Hebraic studies in the seventeenth century elevated the Hebrew language to a position of special divine revelation.[39] Mather linked himself to this tradition in England by utilizing the Hebrew word for "breath of life," while drawing upon primary Kabbalistic documents for interpreting the soul's form and substance. Yet, his theological scheme rested fundamentally upon scriptural exegesis and medical speculations. Mather's religious-medical explanation of the Nishmath-Chajim emphasized his familiarity with Jewish Kabbalism. In his commentary on Revelation in the "Biblia Americana," Mather's six-volume treasure of biblical interpretation essentially written between 1693 and 1712, he cited the "Cabala" remarking on the passage "I am the Alpha and the Omega," in verse eight of the first chapter. He recorded

---

& Meier Pub. Inc. 1982). See the essay by David S. Katz, "The Language of Adam in Seventeenth Century England," pp. 132-145, Donne quote on p. 133.

[39]See especially I. Baroway, "Toward Understanding Tudor-Jacobean Hebrew Studies," *Jewish Social Studies*, XVIII (1956), pp. 3-24; E. I. J. Rosenthal, "Edward Lively: Cambridge Hebraist," in D. W. Thomas (ed), *Essays . . . Presented to S. A. Cook* (London, 1950), pp. 95-112; A. C. Partridge, *English Biblical Translation* (London, 1973), pp. 33-138; C. Roth, *A History of the Jews in England* (3rd ed., Oxford, 1964), pp. 145-6. The most recent and thorough explication of the English Kabbalistic tradition which Mather would be familiar with is by G. Lloyd-Jones, *The Discovery of Hebrew in Tudor England: A Third Language* (Manchester: Manchester U. Press, 1983).

that "The Cabalists among the Jewes of the Times, did use to describe the great God after that manner. In their Book *Zohar*, and others of their ancient Books, you'll find את mystically standing for ye Name of God." He said that the letter "ath" is the first and last letter of the Hebrew alphabet, "which agrees with the alpha and omega in the Greek language."[40]

The Hebrew language allowed one, according to Mather, to "read the ORACLES of God with more pleasure," but he also understood it to be the millennial language pointed to by the ancient prophets. "It is among the prophecies of ye great and good things to be done in ye Latter Days, Zephaniah 3:4, 'I will turn to the people a pure Language:' or as it may be rendered *A Choice Language* . . ." Along with other Christian Hebraists of the seventeenth century, Mather earnestly looked "to the revival of the Hebrew tongue by God," when an exalted respect would be paid to it "in ye Days of ye New Jerusalem."[41]

Besides the classical Hebrew education Mather received at seventeenth-century Harvard College, his father, Increase, also stimulated his interest in Judaism. For Increase, a conversion of the Jewish nation was one of the primary signs indicating the last days prior to the dawn of

---

[40]C. M., "Biblia Americana," Revelation 1:8; mss. in Massachusetts Historical Society. There is no reliable pagination in this work. I will refer to the biblical chapter where Mather's commentary is found.

[41]C. M. See #60 of undated and unidentified letter fragments of Cotton Mather's at the American Antiquarian Society. See also Jones, *The Discovery, op. cit.*, pp. 266-269, for his concurrence of Mather's wishes actually being the circumstance in Tudor England.

the millennium. Such a chiliastic roadmap offered by his father influenced Cotton to initially adopt a converted Israel as a millennial sign. By 1725, after Increase's death, and during Cotton's most active millennial thinking, he dropped the Jewish national conversion as a millennial sign in his unpublished treatise, "Triparadisus," (c. 1726). But, throughout most of his career, the Jewish question aroused his chiliastic interests and simultaneously his adaptation of Hebraic concepts, particularly the "Nishmath-Chajim" for his interpretation of the soul.

His doctrine of the soul contained, primarily, an Hebraic orientation. The "mind," "soul," and "body" were not merely compartmentalized, but integrally and mystically joined to one another while retaining specific functions. Kabbalism depicted theological areas attached to physical parts of the body. For instance, the left arm is "gevura" or judgment, and the right arm is "hesed" or mercy. Kabbalism's body tree of man implied the two-way flow and interaction of the various parts of the human body to the soul. For the Kabbalist, the soul contained various lights or levels of consciousness, known from the lowest to the highest order as Nefesh (crude spirit), Ruah (spirit), Neshamah (soul), Hayyah (living) and Yehidah (individual), this last being the purest level of the lights. The "Nishmath-Chajim" formed for Mather a category which joined that which was active and perpetual in the human soul. For the Kabbalist, the "Nishmath-Chajim" formed the third and fourth levels of consciousness.[42] Mather did not concern himself to be precise in his

---

[42]For a more detailed explanation of the Kabbalistic interpretation of the soul, see the following works by Gerhard G. Scholem: "Kabbala," in *Encyclopaedia Judaica*, IX, columns 630-732; *Major Trends in Jewish*

portrayal of Jewish mystical categories. Rather, he borrowed freely from these ideas to explain the various theological and physical puzzles he wrestled with, specifically the soul's immortality during the millennium.

Among the seventeenth-century Christians perpetuating Jewish Kabbalah were the Cambridge Platonists, a group of religious philosophers among whom were Ralph Cudworth (1617-1688) and Henry More (1614-1687). They hoped to reconcile Christian ethics, Renaissance humanism, rationality, science and religion. The study of the bible and classical humanities were the poles between which the Christian interpretation of the Kabbalah arose. Biblical studies led naturally to Hebraic studies, an indispensable prerequisite for Kabbalistic understanding. The study of classical humanities led to the task of reconciling ancient thought with the Christian tradition. By an easy extension, which was also largely necessary because so many of the classical texts were transmitted through Arabic sources, Arabic studies and Hebrew texts came to be included in the program of the humanists, and, therefore, the dissemination of the Semitic languages came into prominence during the seventeenth century.[43]

Mysticism (Jerusalem, 1941); and "Philosophy and Jewish Mysticism," *The Review of Religion*, II (1937/38), pp. 385-402.

[43]See Hillel Schwartz, *The French Prophets: The History of a Millenarian Group in Eighteenth-Century England* (Los Angeles: University of California Press, 1980), p. 188, and Joseph L. Blau, *The Christian Interpretation of 'the Cabala' in the Renaissance* (Port Washington, N.Y.: Kennikat Press, 1965). On the Cambridge Platonists, see Charles Webster, *The Great Instauration: Science, Medicine and Reform 1626-1660* (London: Duckworth, 1975), and especially Margaret C. Jacob, *The*

Very little Kabbalistic material was available in Latin translations during the seventeenth century; therefore, the Semitic languages had to be learned if the Jewish mystical literature was to be read. Henry More, an English philosopher of the Cambridge Platonist group whom Mather read,[44] was representative of the Cambridge movement's mystical side. In 1662, More's work, *A Conjectural Essay of Interpreting the Mind of Moses according to a Threefold Cabbala, viz., Literal, Philosophical, Mystical, or Divinely Moral,* indicates the synthesizing effort this school attempted. Once such a doctrine as the Kabbalah was recognized by the Cambridge school, it had to be investigated and integrated as far as possible into the syntheses they were formulating. More's "conjectural essay" included an approach to Mosaic scriptural passages utilizing the layers of meaning the Kabbalah was noted for.

The Kabbalah made an excellent subject for the type of treatment given to academic areas by these synthesis seekers. It was early recognized among the Jews that some of its positions were dangerously close to Christian belief. All that had to be done by a Christian Hebraist, like Henry More, was to substitute the Messianic doctrine of the Christians' belief in a Messiah-who-had-come for the Jewish doctrine of the Messiah-who-shall-come; to substitute Jesus, a concrete redeemer who

---

Newtonians and the English Revolution 1689-1720 (Ithaca: Cornell U. Press, 1976).

[44]See "The Mather's Library Index" at the American Antiquarian Society, which includes *An Exposition* (London, 1669) by Henry More. More's *Conjectura Cabbalistica; or, a conjectural essay of interpreting the minds of Moses* was published in London, 1653.

had already been on earth, for the vague future redeemer believed in by the Jews.

Mather intercepted and applied these various currents in Jewish and Christian scholarship during the seventeenth century which investigated and propagated the Kabbalah. Initially, his hypothesis regarding the Nishmath-Chajim, or the spiritual-physical construction of man, appeared in his *Diary*, November 16, 1705. After stating a belief in the threefold empire of the body (spirit, soul, and body), he continued the description of his hypothesis by comparing the condition of a man bitten by a mad dog to the status of the soul in the human body. After a man has been bitten by a mad dog, Mather believed that the poison entered not only his body, but also the soul. When the poison has invaded the nervous system, he concluded "the Archaeus is all enraged."[45] The "Archaeus" was a term Mather borrowed from seventeenth-century natural philosophy's interest in medicine to describe the central location of physical properties in the body. It was the link which transmitted fluids or particles through the body to the soul. The "Archaeus" was synonymous with the "Nishmath-Chajim" for Mather. But the latter term was described in much more detail by Mather as his thought matured. In 1705, Mather was satisfied with a description of the soul's activity. A rabid dog passed its disease on to the man it had bitten. Although the man is physically bitten, the disease is contracted by the man's soul as well as his body, "and his Dog-bitten Soul will show him the Face of a

---

[45]*Diary* Vol. I, p. 526 (November, 1705).

Dog," as Mather concluded.[46]

But Mather's hypothesis was incomplete without an elucidation of the soul's natural condition. For Mather, the soul was depraved. Original sin had vanquished any claims to purity an individual could garnish. "The Soul of every man is Dog-bitten, or, which is as bad; Serpent-bitten, or, Divel-bitten," testified Mather. "Original Sin has depraved it; the Venom of original sin has over-run it." It was only God's spirit, he asserted, that caused a man to turn from his sinful ways and helped him to "fly Godward or Christward." Evidently, at this early stage in the development of Mather's theological hypothesis of the soul, he had not applied the mystical Jewish understanding of the soul outlined in the Kabbalah for the Nishmath-Chajim. Instead, relying heavily upon "the oracles of God," he postulated a conception of the soul which served as a beginning basis for his later, more comprehensive, medicinal-theological perception of the soul's immortality.[47]

---

[46]*Ibid.*

[47]See Otho T. Beall and Richard H. Shryock, *Cotton Mather: First Significant Figure in American Medicine* (Baltimore: Johns Hopkins Press, 1954), pp. 34-70. Also view Pershing Vartanian, "Cotton Mather and the Puritan Transition into the Enlightenment," *Early American Literature*, Vol. VII, No. 3 (Winter, 1973), pp. 218-221, and Mitchell R. Breitwieser, "Cotton Mather's Pharmacy," *Early American Literature* Vol. XVI, No. 1 (Spring, 1981), pp. 42-49. Breitwieser agrees with the interpretation expressed in this essay--that Mather's medical interests and theology go hand-in-hand--but he emphasizes Mather's medical investigations, while I stress his theological-physical understanding of the soul.

The opportunity arose for Mather to reflect more fully upon the soul's physical properties in 1712. That year he received an invitation from Richard Waller, one of the secretaries of the Royal Society of England, to send occasional communications back to that group related to scientific observations. In November of that year, Mather sent thirteen letters to the Society. Until the end of his life, he sent letters covering the whole range of his scientific interests. Astronomy, mathematics, geology, biology, meteorology, and medicine all found a place in his "Curiosa Americana," as he called them. As a direct result, in 1713, Mather was elected a member of the Royal Society, one of the first colonists to be so honored.[48]

A large number of the "Curiosa" described unusual phenomena from the natural world and medicine. Such strange titles appeared as "An Ear Strangely Molested," "A Prodigious Worm," "The Stone Mistaken," and "A Monster." In this latter communication to the Royal Society, dated October 15, 1713, Mather told a story of a woman who delivered siamese twins, "which were so united as to afford us a shocking spectacle whereof I was myself one of the spectators."[49]

While Mather was fascinated by all sorts of abnormalities and

---

[48]See his letter to Richard Waller, secretary of the Royal Society, March 10, 1715, the Harvard College Library, when he refers to himself in the second paragraph: "It was very much by your favorable recommendation that an admission into that SOCIETY has been granted unto an American, of so obscure a character. . . ."

[49]Massachusetts Historical Society, "Mather Collection," Letter to the Royal Society from Cotton Mather, October 15, 1713.

monstrosities, he usually did not witness them firsthand but recorded them from other sources, both written and oral, a common practice of the times. His own explanation of life's mysteries provided further evidence for his enthusiastic support of natural philosophy and medicine. One theme which combined his naturalistic and religious intellectual curiosity was the "Nishmath-Chajim," which appeared not only as a published "Curiosa" by the Royal Society in 1722, but also as a chapter in his unpublished "Angel of Bethesda" (1724) and as a section in his second paradise, "the place of departed souls," in "Triparadisus" (1726). From 1722-1726, there was little development in Mather's understanding of the nature and substance of the soul and the soul's activity in the millennial drama. Essentially, the three manuscripts listed above contained the same outline.[50]

Mather's concept, "the Nishmath-Chajim," unlocked the meaning of his millennialism. As a theory, it goes a long way toward explaining not only the connectedness between the body and the soul in Mather's theology, but also how death, resurrection, and the establishment of "the New Heavens and the New Earth," which are essential chiliastic aspects, composed for him a consistent millennialistic logic. His hypothesis of the Nishmath-Chajim moved him into the early Enlightenment by combining

---

[50]For a more thorough explanation of the "Curiosa Americana," see G. G. Kittredge, "Cotton Mather's Scientific Communications to the Royal Society," American Antiquarian Society, *Proceedings*, XXVI (April, 1916), 118f. The "Angel of Bethesda" was edited by Gordeon W. Jones and published by the American Antiquarian Society and Barre; Barre, Massachusetts, 1972. The unpublished manuscript "Triparadisus" is at the AAS.

his New Science rationalism and his millennialism as necessary ingredients for his intellectual growth.[51] Mather's bent toward natural philosophy, as the "Curiosa" illustrate, and particularly medicine, as his treatise "The Angel of Bethesda" exemplified, and his chiliastic opus, "Triparadisus," combined to fashion an exceptionally homogenous logic tied together by his hypothetical Nishmath-Chajim.

Like many others before him, Mather felt compelled to postulate an intermediary between the body and the soul. The Nishmath-Chajim, or the vital principle, or "Vital Ty," as Mather interchangeably referred to it, was located in various parts of the body and was composed of particles "which may be finer than those of Light itself."[52] It was not the brain, according to Mather, but "it is the Life by which the Several parts have their Faculties maintained by Exercise." It furnished such senses as seeing, hearing, and feeling, while it contributed to digestion in the body. It shaped "the Bones, and other parts, in the womb of her that is with Child" and hence had a procreative capability. Without giving any indication of being influenced by contemporary Lockean empiricism which separated sensation and reason, Mather assigned sensation to the Nishmath-Chajim and reasoning to the "rational soul" or mind. But the general rules of "Mechanism," which Mather followed up to this point in

---

[51]"Cotton Mather and the Puritan Transition into the Early 'Enlightenment,'" Pershing Vartanian, *Early American Literature*, Vol. VII, No. 3 (Winter, 1973), pp. 213-224.

[52]"Triparadisus," pp. 18, 20. (All references to "Triparadisus" are to part II.)

outlining the physical aspects of his theory, could not entirely explain "the Humane Body."[53]

Generally, the physicians of the seventeenth century conceived of disease in traditional Greek pathological terms. Illness was appointed to an imbalance or impurity in the four humors, or fluids. Various means were deduced to rid the body of such fluids; bleeding, purging, and sweating were the primary means practiced. But some physicians attempted to find a new synthesis in medicine. One school believed, as suggested by chemistry, that the body was made up of many compounds. This school believed that disease was caused by chemical disfunctioning. The treatment practiced by these physicians remedied disease by using alkalies and acids. Jean Baptiste van Helmont (1577-1644) of Brussels was a Capuchin friar who became a mystic and the founder of the "iatrochemical school" of medicine. He claimed that the body has a governing archaeus or spirit which Mather identified as his own Nishmath-Chajim. At the same time, chemical principles guided Helmont's choices of medicines when attempting a cure for a disease. For example, an undue acidity in the digestive tract was to be corrected by alkalies, and vice versa, by Helmont's iatrochemical school.[54]

---

[53]*Ibid.*

[54]R. H. Shryock. *The Development of Modern Medicine* (New York, 1947), pp. 11ff. For Mather's mechanical ideas about the body and soul, see George Cheyne, *Philosophical Principles of Religion* (London, 1715), Vols. 1, 2. As evidence of Mather's familiarity with Cheyne's work, see *Diary* II, p. 450 (May, 1717), when he writes: "The Notion of our Soul being formed with a Principle of Re-Union to God, by Him originally implanted into it, if well-cultivated, may prove of great Use, first unto my

The "iatrochemical school" opposed the "iatromechanical school." The iatromechanicalists, inspired by the writings of Rene Descartes (1596-1650), a French philosopher who conceived of the animal and human body as a machine and believed disease was a malfunction of the mechanical parts of the body, also greatly influenced Mather.[55] Mather prefaced his comments about "the Nidification of Birds" and "the Mellification of Bees" with the impression that "the Nishmath-Chajim is much like the Soul which animates the Brutal World."[56] The natural world he referred to as "Brutal" centered around instinct. But Mather was not content to explain the natural world entirely by instinct. Depending upon Descartes' iatromechanical explanation, Mather viewed the human body as a machine, but still unique from the animal world. "In every other Machin, if anything be out of Order, it will remain so till some Hand from abroad should rectify it; it can do nothing for itself," Mather observed, "But the Human Body is a Machine, wherein, if

---

own Soul, and then unto many others. Dr. Cheines [sic] Reflections on this matter, should be exquisitely considered." For the reference to this "Principle" in Cheyne's work, see *Philosophical Principles*, p. 192. Cheyne was a medical doctor and a member of the Royal Society (1671-1743). Also contributing to Mather's mechanistic ideas were the works of Rene Descartes (1596-1650), whom he read extensively. See "The Mather Library Index," the American Antiquarian Society; *Meditationes De Prima Philosophie* (Amsterdam, 1654) by Descartes is included in the list, among others. Helmont was cited by Mather in "Triparadisus," p. 19.

[55]Beall and Shryock, *Cotton Mather: First Significant Figure in American Medicine*, op. cit., pp. 12, 24, 67, n., 69n.

[56]"Triparadisus," p. 22.

anything be out of Order, presently, the whole Engine, as under an Alarum, is awakened for the helping of what is amiss, . . . Whence can this proceed but from a Nishmath-Chajim in us, with such regards for ye Law of Self-Preservation by God imprinted upon it?"[57] Here, Mather implied that an essential principle dwelt in animals as well as man, but in man this special "breath of life" accounted for some behavior in human beings otherwise mysterious to the observor and beyond instinct. The Nishmath-Chajim theory moved Mather away from the natural world and into the spiritual realm.

In the "Angel of Bethesda" Mather focused upon the medicinal values of the Nishmath-Chajim, but in "Triparadisus" he used his "breath of life" conception to go beyond a physiological explanation of the soul to posit a foundation upon which to base his millennialist interpretation of the resurrection of the soul during Christ's second coming. The Nishmath-Chajim, detailed by Mather, remained after death connected to the rational soul. To Mather, it was a "vehicle" to the rational soul and therefore, as a theory, it accounted for apparitions and "Spectres." In some mysterious fashion Mather never ventured to explain how the Nishmath transcended space and time. Yet, Mather spoke of astral projection and explained this phenomenon on the grounds of his Nishmath-Chajim. "Yea, We are certain of it That Persons before they have Died, upon Strong Desires to Visit and Behold Some Objects at a Distance from the Place to which they were now confined," he wrote, "have been thrown into a Trance, wherein they have lain some

---

[57]*Ibid*.

considerable while without Sense or Breath; and then Returning, have reported what they have Seen."[58]

Not personally familiar with astral projection, Mather relied on the witness of others which he deemed trustworthy upon which to base his account. But he was acquainted with meditation and devotional rapture which gave him a spiritual experience that paralleled and extended his sympathy toward occult matters. From the earliest years of his ministry, Mather practiced a rigorous devotional life which occasionally reached ecstatic proportions. It was not inconsequential that he argued for the continued existence of the Nishmath-Chajim into an afterlife by citing the spiritual zenith of the Apostle Paul's life. For Mather, when Paul was taken to the "Third Heaven" wherein dwelt "our Savior," he was also in paradise or the place of the departed spirits "wherein ye most Immediate and Beatific Vision of God is attain'd unto."[59] Paul's glimpse of heaven was to repay him for the extreme suffering he endured for the Christian faith and gave an indication of what paradise would be like when "he was to be Recompensed at the Resurrection of the Dead." Yet, Mather further speculated that paradise may only be an "apartment" to the third heaven, like the courtrooms are to the Holy of Holies in the Jerusalem Temple, since Jesus allowed for the prisoner crucified next to him on the cross to be in paradise on the same day as his death. Mather thought the "Holy of Holies" may be too "magnificent for the uninitiated." Citing

---

[58]"Triparadisus," pp. 24-25.

[59]*Ibid.*, p. 25.

Chrysostom, an early Christian writer of the fourth century, Mather concluded that paradise was distinct from heaven "For it contains not all the Good Things that God has promised us."[60] Mather believed that paradise existed as an "intermediate state" which housed the souls of the departed. Important for Mather's millennial outline, these spirits in paradise still comprised the vehicle of the rational soul - the Nishmath-Chajim, which became the essential link to resurrection when Jesus Christ returned. Mather's theory of the Nishmath-Chajim made it possible for the departed spirit to be joined again to his body, a body which was made imperishable and incorruptible at Christ's Second Coming.

---

[60]p. 27.

Chapter 6

"Horrible Enchantments and Possessions"

Who was Satan? To the seventeenth-century New Englander, the question rested closely upon a second query, "Who was God?" While the latter question was answered by reference to his sovereignty and covenant with his people, the former question proved to be more troublesome, if only because it posed more answers. One English best seller, *Paradise Lost*, by John Milton (1608-74), presented a portrait of the Devil which attracted not only English-speaking literati, but also the more theologically sophisticated clergy, well into the nineteenth century.[1] In the second book of *Paradise Lost*, God foretells the earth's general doom and in the third book specifies that the earth shall burn and Satan finally will be defeated. Milton's devil elicits pathos. He is doomed but not without grandeur. Such a being could be rejected but not despised; one might pity, even admire, mankind's enemy. In his tragic contest with the Absolute, he portrayed a nobility of spirit almost Promethean as he defied heaven and struggled to make God's creatures his own.

While Cotton Mather owned a copy of *Paradise Lost* and sometimes adapted its verses,[2] Milton's tragic hero received no exaltation

---

[1] See Perry Miller, "The Garden of Eden and the Deacon's Meadow," *American Heritage*, VII (December, 1955), pp. 55-61, for Milton's effect upon colonial literature and art.

[2] Massachusetts Historical Society *Proceedings* (1908-1909), Vol. 42, 3rd Series II, pp. 161-163.

from the young Boston clergyman. Mather's Satan had more the spirit of ubiquity, an eternal nuisance, "damnably dangerous" and "as little dignified as the worm that eats up the garden."[3] The arch-Adversary held power and authority second only to his heavenly opponent, according to Mather. Therefore, when the devil's wrath blew its vengeful breath upon an unsuspecting New England in the late 1680s and then whipped it into a hurricane gale by the 1690s, Mather accepted the role of God's "herald" to thwart Satan's advances. "This Day, I likewise obtained of God, that Hee would make use of mee," Mather wrote in his *Diary* April 29, 1692, "as of a John, to bee an Herald of the Lord's Kingdome now approaching, and the 'Voice crying in the Wilderness,' for Preparation thereunto." But no sooner had he put on the armor of God than his "Prayers did especially insist upon the horrible Enchantments and A good Issue to those things, and my own Direction and Protection thereabout," Mather considered, "I did especially petition for."[4] Being an "Herald" for God entailed more than Mather bargained for.

Many trials filled Cotton Mather's private and public life. Twice a widower, he had to withstand the mental derangement of his third wife; of his fifteen children, only two survived him. Yet, it was in the witchcraft outbreak of the 1690s that Cotton found his biggest trial and his most significant challenge. Two aspects composed the witchcraft challenge for Mather. On the personal level, he grappled with the

---

[3] Marion Starkey, *The Devil in Massachusetts* (New York: Alfred A. Knopf, 1949), p. 242.

[4] *Diary I*, p. 147 (April 29, 1692).

"Horrible Enchantments and Possessions" 155

meaning and purpose of his ministry. As a minister of the gospel, wasn't he called to thwart the wiles of the devil? On the public level, Mather struggled to interpret the witchcraft outbreak as theologically understandable. Could it be that the devil's activity at Salem Village, in the possession of Mercy Short, the Goodwin children, and Margaret Rule, pointed toward the grand finale of human history when the saints, led by Jesus Christ, would usher in a thousand-year reign of peace and brotherhood? Might this "Time of the Devils coming down in great Wrath upon us" be the millennial dawn?[5] At the heart of the witchcraft episode resided this fundamental faith question concerning God's nature and evil's existence, for Mather. The answer to this question rested upon his lively fascination with the great cosmic drama between God and the forces of evil led by Satan. To Mather, the drama had reached its final act. "No, the Devil was never more let loose than in Our Days," he wrote in *The Wonders of the Invisible World*, his major defense of the Salem trials, "and it is very much that any should imagine otherwise: But the same thing that proves the Thousand Years of prosperity for the Church of God, under the whole Heaven, to be not yet begun, does also prove, that it is not very far off."[6] The seeming contradiction inherent in Mather's words, that the grand millennial scheme was near, in the midst

---

[5] David Levin gestures toward this conception and outlines Mather's perception of the witchcraft outbreak through several jeremiad sermons. See his *Cotton Mather: The Young Life of the Lord's Remembrancer, 1663-1703* (Cambridge: Harvard University Press, 1978), pp. 200-203.

[6] (Boston, 1692), p. v-xii.

of Satan's most violent activity at Salem Village, is resolved when viewed as part of his chronological outline depicted in the book of Revelation and accepted by him as prophetic history.

Superimposed upon the common jeremiad framework lay a millennial historical perspective which Mather most compellingly composed in *The Wonders of the Invisible World*, his public response to the Salem Village phenomenon.[7] The entire conglomerate comprising the *Wonders*--sermon extracts, accounts of the supernatural, an 'Abstract' of William Perkins's 'way for the Discovery of Witches,' and testimonies of five of the accused Salem witches--were essentially founded on Mather's exegesis of Revelation 12:12: "Wo to the Inhabitants of the Earth, and of the Sea; for the Devil is come down unto you, having great Wrath; because he knoweth, that he hath but a short time."[8] For Mather, the prophecy of the book of Revelation illuminated contemporary demonic activity. "Ecclesiastical History has Reported unto us, That a Renowned Martyr at the Stake, seeing the Book of Revelation thrown by his no less Profane than Bloody Persecutors, to be burn'd in the same Fire himself," Mather recounted, "he cryed . . . 'How Blessed am I in this Fire, while I have Thee to bear me Company." Mather's own affection for the book was little less than the martyr's. For him, the book of Revelation

---

[7]*Ibid.*, especially pp. 15-16.

[8]p. 40. Also see his "Biblia Americana," an unpublished manuscript extending to six volumes residing at the Massachusetts Historical Society under the section on "The Book of Revelation," chapter twelve, verse twelve.

appropriately addressed the satanic circumstances New England found itself in. "As for ourselves this Day, 'tis a Fire of sore Affliction and Confusion, wherein we are Embroiled; but it is no inconsiderable Advantage unto us," Mather believed, "that we have the Company of this Glorious and Sacred Book the REVELATION to assist us in our Exercises."

Righteous New Englanders suffered from millennialism's dark side, the devil's great wrath, but they also found a "bright side." Mather was quick to point out that the Devil, "He has but a short time."[9] Mather's millennial perspective allowed him to contemplate New England's dissolution with a certain equanimity. "There is little room for hope, that the great wrath of the Devil, will not prove the present ruine of our poor New-England in particular." He realized that the identical events that portended destruction promised millennial salvation as well. While the devil wreaked havoc in Massachusetts, Mather found assurance in Christ's expected future reign. In this historical context Mather sensed New England's declension was the fulfillment of the Puritan mission. In Mather's millennial interpretation, God's chosen people would be saved, while New England would be destroyed.[10] The Day of Judgment could no longer be situated in an indefinite future, for New England was suffering for the sins of her people and the final confrontation between Satan and God was being enacted in the present diabolical activity at Salem Village.

---

[9] p. 41.

[10] pp. 52, 53-54.

Mather's millennial context for the witchcraft outbreak was not only biblically established in the book of Revelation, it was also personally experienced. From 1688 to 1693, Mather had three first-hand occasions to witness the devil's attacks upon a soul: the Goodwin children, Margaret Rule and Mercy Short.

Mather's heraldic mission began in Boston midsummer 1688 when John Goodwin's four children began to experience "strange fits, beyond those that attend epilepsy, or a catalypsy."[11] Mather made this observation. He studied medicine as a student at Harvard and carefully detailed the symptoms of the Goodwin children as meticulously as any physician. "Sometimes they would be deaf, sometimes dumb, and sometimes blind, and often, all this at once. One while their tongues would be drawn down their throats," Mather observed, "another while they would be pulled out upon their chins to a prodigious length." At other times Mather witnessed the children's jaws stretched so far apart they disjointed and then they "would clap together again with such force like that of a strong springlock." The same thing happened to the other joints of their body: shoulderblades, wrists, and elbows. Occasionally Mather viewed their extremities drawn so as to appear as if they had their neck and heels tied together. Rapidly again they would be stretched out and bent backwards to such an extent that Mather "feared the very skin of their bellies would have cracked." The children cried that they

---

[11]C. M., *Memorable Providences* (Boston, 1689), reprinted in *Narratives of the Witchcraft Cases; 1648-1706*, ed. George Lincoln Burr (New York, 1914), pp. 93-143, hereafter cited as "Burr." All quotations concerning this case are taken from this source unless otherwise noted.

were cut with knives and beaten with clubs, and their neck shifted from a limp position and suddenly again to a stiff position, so much so that "their heads would be twisted almost round."

The fits had started soon after one of the children had quarrelled with an Irish washerwoman. The servant's mother, Goodwife Glover, "a scandalous old woman" whose husband claimed she was "undoubtedly a witch," purposefully "bestowed very bad language upon the girl." The washerwoman had been doing domestic duties at the Goodwin household when one of the Goodwin daughters argued with her over linen clothes. Her mother, Goodwife Glover, had defended her daughter with severe language--a curse. The fits appeared immediately in the Goodwin daughter.[12] Goodwin, after refusing to accept the advice by his neighbors to counter the fits with white magic, accepted at first the consultation of "skillful physicians" and then ultimately the expertise of Dr. Thomas Oakes. Oakes offered his opinion that "nothing but an hellish witchcraft" could be the cause of the children's afflictions. At Oakes' request Cotton Mather and three other Boston clergymen visited the Goodwin home for intercessory prayer. The youngest Goodwin child was cured during this prayer session, but the other three remained afflicted. Dr. Oakes' final recourse was to report Goodwife Glover to the local magistrates.[13]

Goodwife Glover was convicted of witchcraft. Mather visited her

---

[12]*Ibid.*, pp. 95-96. For a more detailed account of this fascinating episode, see Levin, *op. cit.*, pp. 146-157.

[13]Chadwick Hansen, *Witchcraft at Salem* (New York: Mentor, 1969), p. 44.

twice in jail after she had been condemned and made a serious effort to convert her. Mather tried to convince her that Satan had cheated her, to which she answered "If it be so, I am sorry for that!" He proceeded to "set before her the necessity and equity of her breaking her covenant with Hell, and giving herself to the Lord Jesus Christ by an everlasting covenant." She responded that he "spoke a very reasonable thing, but she could not do it." He asked if he might pray for her, but she belligerently responded, "If prayer would do her any good, she could pray for herself." Mather persisted and prayed for her anyway, and then promptly left her rubbing a stone with spittle and mumbling to herself.[14]

Mather called on her several times while she was imprisoned, yet he unsuccessfully attempted to learn more about her pact with the Devil and her practice of witchcraft. As she entered the gallows, she claimed that the Goodwin children would continue to suffer because there had been more than just herself involved in the pact. The children's fits did not abate but persisted more violently than ever. The children barked like dogs, purred like cats, and were beaten as if by cudgels. One of the boys believed his head to be nailed to the floor. At another time the boy felt a spit run from his mouth down to his toes all the while writhing in agony and crying that he was being roasted over an invisible fire. Eventually Mather took Martha, the oldest Goodwin daughter, into his home "that I might have a full opportunity to observe the extraordinary circumstances of the children, and that I might be furnished with evidence and argument as a critical eye-witness to confute the Saducism of this

---

[14]*Ibid.*, pp. 46-47.

debauched age."[15]

Not all seventeenth-century Christians believed in the activity of what Mather called "the invisible world." A few skeptics, like John Webster in his *Displaying of Supposed Witchcraft*, confirmed the reality of devils and witches but hesitated to attribute their activity to spiritual means; rather he believed they acted through natural means to accomplish their dreadful tasks.[16] People like Webster Mather called "Sadducees" because they relegated religion to simply a mental state, not a spiritual enterprise. "We shall come to have no Christ, but a light within, and no Heaven but a frame of mind," Mather complained, if the Sadducees--the materialists--succeeded in destroying the belief in an invisible world.[17]

Martha Goodwin not only served as an example of the wonders of an invisible world by displaying symptoms identified with devil possession, she also exemplified the cosmic battle between Satan's unleashed evil in the final days before Christ's return and the Lord's desire for salvation. For Mather, observing the Goodwin daughter could enlighten him as to the manner of Satan's demonic activity and hence serve to strengthen the clergyman's own spiritual defense against the devil's tricks. As a pastor, Mather could then direct his flock as to the best method of avoiding Satan's increased activity due to the nearness of Christ's return or, at the

---

[15]C. M., *Memorable Providences* (Boston, 1689), p. 18.

[16]John Webster (London, 1677).

[17]Quoted in Hansen, *Witchcraft at Salem, op. cit.*, p. 51.

very least, prepare his congregation for the devil's onslaught. But Mather did not content himself with just observation and analysis of Martha's condition; instead he found himself directing his efforts toward healing her--an exercise in exorcism.

Martha's symptoms were extraordinary. Her stomach would expand "like a drum, and sometimes with croaking noises in it"; during one such instance Mather was praying for "mercy on a daughter vexed with a Devil," and "there came a big, but low voice from her saying, 'There's two or three of them' (or us!)."[18] One of her more unusual practices was riding an invisible horse. She went through the motions of riding in Mather's home. At the end of one episode she claimed she had been to a witch meeting and had learned the reason for her affliction. There were three of them, she believed. She named them and announced that "if they were out of the way, I should be well." Mather wisely kept the names of the accused to himself.

Mather's library proved to be the one place where she received relief from her demonic vexations. She considered Mather's study off-limits to the devils because it was a place for a man of God. The most curious symptom Martha displayed was flying. "She would be carried hither and thither, though not long from the ground," recorded Mather, "yet so long as to exceed the ordinary power of nature in our opinion of it."

The second energumen case Mather personally witnessed concerned Mercy Short, a seventeen-year-old, ex-Indian captive who in

---

[18]*Ibid.*, p. 48.

June 1692 was sent on an errand to the Boston prison by her mistress. There Sarah Good, an accused witch from Salem Village, asked her for "a little tobacco." Outraged by the forwardness of the inmate, Mercy threw a handful of shavings at her and said, "That's tobacco good enough for you." Sarah Good promptly cursed Mercy. "And poor Mercy was taken with just such, or perhaps much worse, fits as those which held the bewitched people then tormented by invisible furies in the County of Essex."[19] This reference by Mather to Essex County pointed to the notorious witchcraft outbreak in Salem Village. Mercy Short served as Mather's own personal contact to the witchcraft outbreak. Like Martha Goodwin before, Mather took Mercy under his observation to effect a cure. Ultimately he had cured Martha Goodwin through faith and prayer, and he believed that some people afflicted by the devil needed to receive in-depth Christian treatment through the means of grace, such as prayer and fasting to bring about their cure.[20]

In February 1692, Mather offered to accept the accused at Salem Village into his home, but his gesture was not acknowledged by the magistrates. At that point the witchcraft ordeal had not reached its zenith, but Mather's experience with the Goodwin children increased his curiosity over Satan's activity, especially Martha Goodwin's case. Now,

---

[19]Mather writes about his experiences with Mercy Short in "Another Brand Pluck'd Out of the Burning," Burr, pp. 259-286. The original version remained in the Mather family until 1814, when it was given to the American Antiquarian Society. It was first published by Burr in 1914.

[20]Mather's cure is most lucidly outlined in Levin, *op. cit.*, pp. 156-157.

Mercy Short became a second laboratory experiment for Mather as he continued to probe the invisible world's workings. The devils unleashed upon New England, caused by Satan's final fury before the millennium, appeared communally at Salem Village and personally in Mercy Short. Mather reasoned with himself that "If the Devils Time were above a thousand years ago, pronounced short, what may we now suppose it in our Time? Surely we are not a thousand years distant from those happy thousand years of rest and peace, and which is better? Holiness reserved for the People of God in the latter days; and if we are not a thousand years yet short of the Golden Age, there is cause to think that we are not yet an hundred." Mather's assumption rested upon his belief that Satan would be chained by Christ prior to the glorious millennium. "We do not see the Devil bound," he wrote, "No, the Devil was never more let loose than in our Days; and it is very much that any should imagine otherwise." Mather believed that the millennium must be very near due to the devil's "prodigious wrath" which currently was going to "desolate the World."[21] Mather considered Satan's wrath directed toward New England and specifically now at Mercy Short. The many hours spent with her confirmed his opinion that the afflictions were truly demonic torments.

Mercy's jaws were forced open to receive invisible poison, and her belly swelled to the point that it looked as if she had been "poisoned with a dose of rats-bane," while invisible pin pricks left bloody evidence that the pain was real and blisters formed on her when the smell of brimstone filled the room and she screamed that "Hell-hounds" scalded her. Again

---

[21] C. M., *Wonders of the Invisible World* (Boston, 1692), p. 69.

Mather applied the Christian formula he had used in the Goodwin case by employing prayer, fasting and careful observation. After several months passed, success was again enjoyed by Mather, but his victory was briefly celebrated. During the period he was occupied with Mercy Short, his wife, Abagail, was pregnant. One day, while standing on the porch, Abagail was horribly frightened by a specter. She apparently was so frightened that she felt her bowels turn inside her. Mercy told Mather that the specters had bragged about the scare they had given his wife, "in hopes . . . of doing mischief unto her infant at least, if not unto the mother."[22] Mather's infant son, born Tuesday, March 28, lived until Saturday night. The baby died of an obstruction of the bowels. An autopsy revealed that "the lower end of the rectum intestinum, instead of being musculous, as it should have been, was membranous, and altogether closed up."[23] Mather interpreted the death of his first son as the result of witchcraft. The vial of Satan's wrath had been poured over his own family. Mather had premonitions concerning the devil's torments on his own life when earlier he had recorded in the introduction of his *Wonders of the Invisible World* in the autumn of 1692: "This, as I remember, the Learned Scribonius, who reports, That one of his Acquaintance, devoutly making his Prayers on the behalf of a person molested by Evil Spirits, received from these Evil Spirits an horrible blow over the Face: And I may myself expect not few or small Buffetings from Evil Spirits, for the

---

[22]Burr, *Narratives, op. cit.*, p. 281.

[23]*Diary I*, p. 164.

Endeavors wherewith I am now going to encounter them."[24]

A third demonical conflict for Mather involved Margaret Rule of Boston. On September 10, 1693, Margaret Rule fell into a fit during worship services, whereupon her friends carried her home "where her fits in a few hours grew into a figure that satisfied the spectators of their being preternatural." Suspicion rested upon a neighbor woman practicing witchcraft. "This woman had, the evening before Margaret fell into her calamities, very bitterly treated her and threatened her." But the "people in the vicinity" decided it was better to cure Margaret of her afflictions through prayer than through another prosecution of a witch. Actually, a witchcraft trial in 1693 at Boston would not have been a real alternative due to the wary climate existing among the townspeople and magistrates toward bewitchment just after the Salem Village episode.[25]

Margaret Rule believed she was assaulted by three or four specters which she hastened to name to Mather, but he exercised restraint by not naming them to another person even though he claimed they were "a sort of wretches who for these many years have gone under as violent presumptions of witchcraft as perhaps any creatures yet living upon earth. . . ."[26] Also, it was this episode that sparked the infamous debate over

---

[24] C. M., *Wonders, op. cit.*, p. 3.

[25] Cotton Mather's account of Margaret Rule's case is in "Another Brand Pluck'd Out of the Burning," printed by Robert Calef in 1700 as the first section of *More Wonders of the Invisible World* (Boston, 1700). Also see Burr, pp. 308-323.

[26] Hansen, *op. cit.*, p. 230.

Mather's involvement with the afflicted young lady. Robert Calef, a Boston merchant, published his account of this event in *More Wonders of the Invisible World* (Boston, 1700), wherein he ridiculed both Increase and Cotton Mather for their supposed indiscretions in treating Margaret, and he therein also rejected the invisible workings of demonic activity. He did not believe bewitchment could take supernatural forms, although he did accept the fact that there was demonic activity and bewitchment. The Calef-Mather debate sharpened Cotton Mather's interest in writing and preaching apologetically on behalf of the existence of the invisible world. Margaret Rule was cured by Mather and other Boston Christians through fasting and prayer, but her afflictions illustrated for the young pastor his need for a perpetual watch against the foes of darkness as the millennium approached.[27]

Mather believed that many of the millennial prophecies pointed to earthquakes and other natural disasters. In *A Midnight Cry* (Boston, 1692), he professed his understanding that the world had entered upon a period of time where earthquakes would inaugurate the resurrection of the witnesses, understood by him to be one of the last events before Christ's return.[28] He expected the destruction and frequency of the earthquakes to increase until the end, and he was pleased by reports of

---

[27]For more information on the Calef-Mather controversy, see Levin, *op. cit.*, pp. 239-249.

[28]C. M., *A Midnight Cry* (Boston, 1692), p. 8.

the violent ones in Jamaica and Italy.[29] The earth would crumble beneath the millennial onslaught as the cosmic powers, good and evil, struggle one last time. The bewitchments and demonic afflictions Mather witnessed in Salem Village and Boston from 1688-1693 testified to the pervasiveness of evil in a world hastening toward the millennium. The evil that seemed to be prevailing was the last gasp the Lord permitted a defeated Satan until the conclusive assaults at Gog and Magog ending the thousand year reign of Christ.

Mather never relinquished his fixation upon Satan's torments. In 1696, before the General Assembly of Massachusetts during an election day, Mather preached *Things for a Distress'd People to think upon*, wherein he issued a warning to all New England to be diligent in devotion to Christ for "a Storm Raised by Wicked Spirits in High Places" had descended upon "this Land of Light."[30] Certainly, secular entertainments, such as "Modern Plays," could, in Mather's view, bring the unsuspecting observer into the demonic realm. In 1726, Mather warned young ministers to avoid reading contemporary plays. "How much do I wish that such Pestilences . . . might never crawl into your Chamber!" He quickly dispelled them as Satanic works. "The unclean Spirits that come like Frogs out of the Mouth of the Dragon, and of the Beast; which go forth unto the young people of the Earth, and expose them to be dealt withal as the enemies of God in the Battle of the Great Day of the

---

[29] C. M., *Wonders, op. cit.*, pp. 26-27.

[30] *Ibid.*, p. 27.

"Horrible Enchantments and Possessions" 169

Almighty," he wrote, "As for those wretched Scribbles of Madmen, My Son, Touch them not, Taste them not, Handle them not: Thou wilt perish in the using of them." He admonished the young minister to avoid this literature because the authors were "The Dragons whose Contagious Breath peoples the dark Retreats of Death."[31] Mather's call to be a herald of light to the world never was more energetic than after the series of events which composed his spiritual experiences of 1688-93. Even his own impending death did not quell his crusade against Satan's final fury begun in New England during the closing decade of the seventeenth century.

Writing in the final years of his life, after encouraging the faithful to sincere adherence to God's precepts, Mather cautioned against the "Special Temptations of Persecution" which believers will undergo in the last days. "All that will live Godly in CHRIST JESUS," he wrote, "shall suffer persecution Until the Second Coming of our Great GOD and SAVIOUR." The persecution's source originated in Satan. "And until Satan be bound," Mather predicted, "we cannot imagine that he will cease to give Trouble unto all that Love the Lord JESUS CHRIST in sincerity." Mather witnessed first-hand the Devil's persecutions in the Goodwin Children, Mercy Short, and Margaret Rule, as well as experiencing himself the devil's damage to the Lord's people within his own family.[32] Yet, his millennialism bolstered his theological hope in a defeated devil.

---

[31]C. M., *Manuductio ad Ministerium* (Boston, 1726), p. 43.

[32]C. M., *Agricola* (Boston, 1727), p. 46.

This age, he acknowledged, was "in the very Dawns of our Lords Coming to Destroy the Wicked one,"[33] and for him Salem Village pointed to New England as the place where the millennium would begin to display itself. Witchcraft simply illustrated for Mather New England's place in the millennial drama.

Mather's most significant comments directed toward New England's role in the devil's millennial activity came in his written defense of the Salem Witchcraft trials, *Wonders of the Invisible World*.[34] Mather believed that the witches' confessions pointed to the devil's involvement in this most recent debacle. "Now by these Confessions 'tis Agreed," he wrote, "That the Devil has made a dreadful Knot of Witches in the Country, and by the help of the Witches has dreadfully increased that Knot. . . ."[35] Mather saw that the witches' work ensured that New England temporally as well as spiritually suffered. The effects of witchcraft extended into many areas of New England life setting not only family against family, but merchant against farmer.[36] Mather recognized the increased discord

---

[33] C. M., *Winter-Meditations* (Boston, 1693), p. 51.

[34] (Boston, 1692). Also see his *The Present State of New England* (Boston, 1690). "Everything looks Black," Mather wrote, "For my own part, I freely confess what my own Thoughts are come unto: Tis, That if the Blessed God intended that the Divel shall keep America during the Happy Chiliad which His Church is now very quickly Entering into . . . A Golden Age will arrive to this place . . ." (p. 35).

[35] C. M., *Wonders*, p. 16.

[36] Boyer and Nissenbaum, *Salem Possessed*, *op. cit.*, pp. 217-221.

within his beloved home country. "But that which most of all Threatens us, in our Present Circumstances, is the misunderstanding, and so the Animosity, where into the Witchcraft now Raging, has Enchanted us."[37] He witnessed the connectedness of spiritual and secular matters for those afflicted in the Salem ordeal. Although he encouraged New England's people to respond to the crisis with prayer, he believed that the prayers were tainted due to the number and kind of quarrels among the people. "The Embroiling first of our Spirits," he purported, "and then of our Affairs, is evidently as considerable a Branch of the Hellish Intrigue which now vexes us as any one Thing whatsoever. The Devil has made us like a Troubled Sea, and the Mire and Mud begins now also to heave up apace." He concluded that "tis by our quarrels that we spoil our Prayers."[38]

While Mather considered the magistrates' actions in the court cases exemplary, he did perceive the limits to spectral evidence. Like his father, Increase, but not as adamantly so, Cotton encouraged a restraint of spectral evidence. Writing to John Richards, one of the seven judges appointed to administer the trials, but before any trial had taken place, Mather pressed Richards not to put "more stress upon pure specter testimony than it will bear." It was Mather's opinion that the devils had the ability to represent people entirely innocent and righteous; therefore,

---

[37]*Wonders*, p. 21.

[38]*Ibid.*, p. 22.

spectral evidence should not be permissible in witchtrials.[39] Mather believed this demonic experience to be natural and entirely expected during the final days before Christ's return to earth, but since the devil was a great deceiver, no one could trust whether or not a specter was a witch or an innocent person.

Demonology rested squarely within theology for Cotton Mather. To Mather, demons simply worked for Satan, a fallen archangel of God's. All devils previously occupied a place of favor before God. "A Devil is a Fallen Angel," he surmised, "an Angel Fallen from the Fear of Love of God, and from all Celestial Glories; but Fallen to all manner of Wretchedness and Cursedness." Originally, Satan and his minions were "Ministering Spirits" used by God to bring honor to the celestial kingdom and render service to the Lord. The Devil's activity played a key role in Mather's millennialism, for he conceived of an earth infiltrated with demons bent upon destroying all that was good and holy. To him devils had both a "Spiritual and Rational Substance," by which he meant that demons could take material form. Because of Satan's apostasy before God, the Prince of Darkness was confined "unto the atmosphere of this Earth, in Chains under Darkness, unto the Judgment of the Great Day."[40]

---

[39]See Levin, *op. cit.*, pp. 204-205. For Increase Mather's position against spectral evidence, see *Cases of Conscience Concerning Evil Spirits* (London, 1693). For a suggestion that Cotton and his father, Increase, differed on this matter, see David Levin's article "Did the Mathers Disagree about the Salem Witchcraft Trials?" *Proceedings of the American Antiquarian Society*, 95 (April 1985), 19-37.

[40]C. M., *Wonders*, p. 43.

Paralleling Jesus Christ's millennial reign and eventual triumphant kingdom, Satan, according to Mather, reigned supreme upon earth by leading an "Hellish Army" and going by the name "Belzbub." Basing his opinion upon Mark 5:10 where the demons of an energumen plead to be sent not from the country they were already active in by Jesus, Mather reasoned that "It is not likely that every Devil does know every language; or that every devil can do every mischief." All that Mather observed in the experience he had with Martha Goodwin, Mercy Short, and later Margaret Rule, as well as the Salem episode, pointed him toward the conclusion that all devils were not alike in their ability to wreak havoc on an individual or community. "If one may make an inference from what the Devils do," he astutely observed, "to what they are, One cannot forbear dreaming that there are degrees of Devils."[41]

Mather did not find it paradoxical for him to attribute Satan's license on earth to the Lord's judgment upon mankind. To him, a supreme God allowed Satan "to make a Descent upon the Children of Men." Citing I Peter 5:8, Mather considered the reference to the devil found therein to suggest that Satan was an "Adversary." As an adversary, Satan was fulfilling God's law, since "adversary" was a law term "it notes An Adversary at Law," as Mather interpreted the original Greek New Testament. Not only did Satan as a "destroying Angel" visit mankind with a "warrant" from God, but also Mather believed this occurrence "oftentimes must be accompany'd with a Commission from some wretches of mankind itself." The "grievous molestations" which happened in Salem

---

[41]*Ibid.*, p. 45.

Village resulted from ungodly people giving their consent to witchcraft, a witchcraft which malefically called upon the Devil to annoy neighbors and ultimately usher in the intercession of Jesus Christ as a millennial expectation.[42]

---

[42]pp. 48-49. Richard Weisman in *Witchcraft, Magic, and Religion in 17th-Century Massachusetts* (Amherst: The University of Massachusetts Press, 1984) argues that Mather believed that "the Salem witchcraft trials became the focal point of a grand cosmic drama" (p. 130). Except for the written defense in *Wonders*, Mather's own millennial construction was just as affected by his personal contact with the Goodwins, Margaret Rule, and Mercy Short as it was with the little direct experience he had with the trials. But all of these events combined to lend credence to Mather's millennial expectation for New England in 1692-93.

Chapter 7

"The Torments of Hell or Christ's Grace"

Cotton Mather, throughout his ministry, considered the millennium to begin and end with a great conflagration. God's judgment occurred when the earth's destruction by fire left all souls suspended upon the Lord's mercy. This eternal judgment, made by a victorious Christ upon each soul, placed that soul either in the confines of hell or in paradise where Christ's grace reigned supreme. Until that day, Mather believed it was the duty of Christians to witness to all of those around them, regardless of race. His Christian compassion for blacks, Indians, and Jews rested upon the premise that all people will eventually have to face Christ's judgment. Sometimes that judgment happened in one's daily life, but most certainly it would occur at the end of the millennium. The Christian, according to Mather, should encourage missions and reformation as one of many tokens of preliminary change prior to the millennium. For Mather, success or failure of the Christian evangelical enterprise rested solely upon God's judgment, but the realization of as many millennial traits as possible before its arrival fulfilled Christianity's missional call to "take the Gospel to the four corners of the Earth."

Mather viewed New England as a panoramic context for witnessing eschatological themes. To Mather, it seemed reasonable to expect "that Glorious Revolution" which would occur with Christ's return to establish the millennial kingdom at any moment; therefore, Christians were to be in constant watch and preparation. Christ would accomplish two objectives with his millennial triumph: "both disposses the Divels of our Air, making of it a New Heaven, filled with the New Jerusalem of his Raised Saints; and also by a terrible Conflagration make a New Earth, whereon the Escaped Nations are to walk in the Light of that Holy City."[1]

Christ's victory in the heavens would be followed by "a REFORMATION more Glorious, more Heavenly, more Universal far away than what was in the former Century." Anyone who opposed the establishment of this new reformation, Mather expected them to be utterly desolated. "A Wonderful STATE of External PEACE" would spread over all the world with only good and just magistrates ruling, while such rulers as Louis XIV of France, the consistory of cardinals, and the Duke of Alva, would be overthrown.[2]

Mather said that until the peace of the new reformation begins the saints should strive to obtain "as much of it Now among our selves, as may be Consistent with our present Circumstances."[3] The saints' effort set a pattern for the world which Mather believed he saw in New England. The harsh climate and demanding way of life reflected in the New England wilderness quickly broke any tendency toward a sentimental,

---

[1] C. M., *A Midnight Cry* (Boston, 1692); quoted in Thomas J. Holmes, *Cotton Mather, A Bibliography of His Works*, 3 vols. (Cambridge, Mass.: 1940), II, p. 683. Hereafter this work will be cited as "Holmes."

[2] C. M., *Things To Be Look'd For*, Holmes, III, pp. 1082-1084.

[3] *Ibid.*, p. 1084.

romantic motive. Mather considered America's church dependent upon missions - an evangelization of all people in order to fulfill the scriptural call to go out into "all the world" and preach the gospel. Mather urged New England to practice missional zeal. He did not accept the criticism that Americans had "hindered the conversion of the poor pagans." Instead, he pleaded: ". . . let not New England be the only Protestant country that shall do any notable thing 'for the propagation of the faith', unto those 'dark corners of the earth which are full of cruel habitants' . . . it is possible that the great God who 'despises not the prayer of the poor', may, by the influences of his Holy Spirit upon the hearts of some whose eyes are upon these lines, give a blessed answer thereunto."[4]

According to Mather, preparation and watchfulness were practiced by the Christian through missional endeavor.[5] In 1698, when he was appointed along with Samuel Sewall as a commissioner to the New England Company, Mather's missional interest blossomed into a significant career which linked his interest in Christian reform and evangelization to his millennialism.

The New England Company, founded in 1649, was the oldest Protestant missionary society in colonial America. It had as its purpose the conversion of the New England's Indians. Until the Revolutionary War, the New England Company financed missionaries through funds raised by investment in England. The interest was then distributed to

---

[4]*Diary I*, p. 580.

[5]See Holmes, I, pp. 50-52; and Sydney Rooy, *The Theology of Missions in the Puritan Tradition* (London, 1965), p. 249, n. 4.

American commissioners who directed the use of the funds. After the American Revolution, the New England Company continued its work in the Canadian provinces. But, throughout the colonial period it enjoyed a fine reputation for outreach into New England's backcountry bringing Christianity to Indian tribes which otherwise might not have been exposed to its precepts.[6]

For Mather, the company represented an avenue for legitimately expressing his concern for converting Indians, especially since the time for evangelizing was drawing to a close. He expressed this opinion most directly in the *Magnalia Christi Americana*,[7] a treatise which has been generally regarded as America's longest jeremiad. The *Magnalia* is a special kind of writing. It is history, but it is a history written with a religious purpose. Mather considered his work a recitation of "the WONDERS of the CHRISTIAN RELIGION, flying from the depravations of Europe, to the American Strand; and, assisted by the Holy Author of that Religion, I do . . . report the wonderful displays of His Infinite Power, Wisdom, Goodness, and Faithfulness, wherewith His Divine Providence hath irradiated an Indian Wilderness."[8] Each

---

[6]See William Kellaway, *The New England Company, 1649-1776* (London: Greenwood, 1975), and J. A. de Jong, *As the Waters Cover the Sea: Millennial Expectations in the Rise of Anglo-American Missions, 1640-1810* (Kampen, Netherlands: J. K. Kok, 1970).

[7]C. M., *Magnalia Christi Americana* (London, 1702). All citations are taken from the 1855 edition.

[8]*Ibid.*, I, p. 25.

biographical section of the *Magnalia* illustrated Mather's purpose for creating a history which not only recorded past events, but interpreted them in such a manner that each person or episode became a model for present Christian conduct. Gradually Mather's attention to preserving the church in America shifted to a more direct awareness of evangelization of all people. As his activity in the New England Company increased, his writings began to place missions in the context of revitalized Christianity, which he believed an essential endeavor because of the millennium's imminency.

In 1702, Mather published *An Advice to the Churches of the Faithful*, wherein he appealed to Christians "for regular intercession for the revival of the churches and conversion of Jews, Muslims, and pagans."[9] He saw no conflict with his millennial expectations and his zeal for evangelizing all people; instead, he joined these two strands of his thought so intimately that his millennialism was buttressed from 1698 until his death by an avid missional concern. He recorded that "all Ecclesiastical History, down from the Book of The Acts of the Apostles, to this Time, are fill'd with admirable Examples, of a Zeal flaming in the Hearts of Christians, to Christianize the rest of the World." He found that New England's zeal was absent with regards to converting black slaves. Black slaves were not being approached with the Christian gospel and its call to conversion and salvation. "Christianity, Whither art thou fled!" he exclaimed, and then prayed that it might quickly return to New England, "Return, Return, O Beautiful Daughter of Heaven, Return,

---

[9](Boston, 1702).

Return, that we may look upon thee."[10]

While occasionally his concern for Christianizing blacks seemed shallow,[11] more often it went further than mere words. Mather helped establish a black fellowship group for spiritual edification and later resolved to strengthen the Religious Society for Negroes. "I would send for the Negro's of the Flock, which form a religious Society; and entertain them at my House, with suitable Admonitions of Piety." On several occasions the baptism of blacks gave Mather an avenue to speak to other blacks about the gospel. "I baptized four Negro's;" he wrote in 1697, "and the Lord helped mee, to make this Action a special Occasion of my glorifying Him: especially with what I then spoke unto the rest of that Nation."[12] In 1702 Mather recorded the reception of two elderly blacks into the church. In 1711 two blacks were baptized and again Mather used it as an opportunity to preach the gospel. "I would make it an occasion to glorify, the Great Saviour of all men, in several Instances;" he testified, "especially in such Admonitions to that black part of the Flock, as may be needful for them."[13]

---

[10]C. M., *The Negro Christianized* (Boston, 1706), pp. 10-11.

[11]Upon seeing a black walking down the street, he said, "Lord wash that poor Soul white in the Blood of Thy Son" (Diary I, p. 83, 1681). This kind of pietistic response to a daily event Mather termed an "Ejeculation," wherewith he paralleled an everyday phenomenon to whatever Christian thought passed through his mind.

[12]*Diary I*, p. 278; Rooy, p. 245.

[13]*Diary II*, p. 43.

Also, Mather wanted to convert his own black servant, Onesimus. Mather constantly was having trouble with Onesimus. After stealing, Onesimus was forced to read, write, and recite Mather's catechism. Later, he was given leisure hours and eventually Mather gave him his liberty, after he paid the reverend five pounds. Two other servants also responded to Mather's evangelizing, one of whom was baptized in 1716.[14]

His enthusiasm for "Christianizing" blacks did not end within his own household or church. Mather founded an evening school based upon charity for the education and conversion of blacks.[15] The collection used to support this school did not always meet the expenses, so Mather financed it alone. "I have at my own single expense for many years," he wrote in 1721, "maintained a Charity-Schole for the Instruction of Negro's in Reading and Religion."[16] He also gave away books he had written for the blacks' use in directing them toward conversion and instructing them on Christian precepts. Besides appealing to the personal decision of blacks to accept Christianity, Mather also encouraged prominent people both in New England and abroad to assist him in evangelizing blacks. He used the ill-treatment of slaves as a barometer to measure a Christian's attitude toward humanity in general and God in particular. "Are they always treated according to the Rules of Humanity?" he asked, "Are they

---

[14]*Diary I*, pp. 139, 222, 271, and 383; *Diary II*, pp. 477, 547, 562, 576, 603, 672-673, 683, 698, 710; Rooy, p. 245, n. 5.

[15]*Diary II*, p. 379 (1716).

[16]*Diary II*, pp. 478, 663.

treated as those, that are of one Blood with us, and those that have Immortal Souls in them, and are not meer Beasts of Burden?" Ultimately, Mather wanted blacks to become exactly what he wished for any person to become - "the Servants of CHRIST."[17]

While Cotton Mather's interest in "Christianizing" blacks was deemed necessary by him, Indians also were considered by him to be a crucial group to bring the gospel to. Of course, his position as a commissioner for the New England Company directed his attention more toward the evangelization of the Indian than the black because of the basic premise for the company's existence, but bringing the gospel to the Indians also appeared to him to be more urgent.[18] The Commissioners of the New England Company were not paid as a rule; their services were rendered without any form of remuneration. But Cotton Mather was an exception. On April 21, 1709, the Company's Court demanded that he be paid £25 "In Consideration of his great Services in promoting the great work . . . by his writings and other ways."[19] Mather's gratitude for this special recognition came in two ways. First, he wrote to Sir William

---

[17]*Diary I*, p. 598 (1706). Also see pp. 570-71; *Diary II*, pp. 687-88. (1723).

[18]See Rooy, p. 246. Worthington C. Ford lists 16 references to blacks, 114 to the Indians, and 20 to the Jews in Mather's diary. See Index, pp. 843, 849.

[19]This quotation is from Kellaway, p. 208. For the difficulties Mather faced as a commissioner of the New England Company, see Kellaway, pp. 209-11, 235, and *passim*.

Ashurst on January 30, 1709/10 thanking the Company for "a very kind present" and explaining that he had not asked for, or expected, any kind of reward, but that the Commissioners had compelled him to accept it. Nine months later he wrote again to Sir William asking him to accept a copy of *Bonifacius. An Essay upon the Good, that is to be devised and designed by those who desire to answer the great end of life* (Boston, 1710), which was dedicated to him and his brother-in-law, Joseph Thompson, the New England Company's treasurer. *Bonifacius* contained an appendix on the Indians which had been added according to Mather, not only for the satisfaction of Lord Ashurst but also as the "Vindication from an envious passage in a Sermon of the Bishop of Chichesters. . . . It seems," Mather considered, "No Good must ever be own'd to be done, but what is done under ye Influence of the Mitre. Lett the Gentlemen of the New Society for the Propagation of the Gospel in Foreign Parts then be prevailed withal, to send a Missionary or two for the Christianizing of the Iroquois Indians. . . ." This action, Mather said, would free the Company from one of their "most uneasy Sollicitudes."[20]

One of the major difficulties when dealing with the Indians was rum. Laws were passed to prohibit the sale of alcohol to Indians, but they did not stop the less scrupulous from continuing to sell the beverage. Sermons were preached and printed to stop the scandalous trade. Cotton Mather addressed the problem in his own treatise, *A monitory and hortatory letter to those English, who debauch the Indians, by selling strong*

---

[20]*Ibid.*, p. 208.

drink unto them.[21] Therein, Mather chastised all traders involved in the nefarious practice of dealing rum to the Indians for property or trinkets. Anything, including strong drink, that stood in the way of "Christianizing" any person, Mather considered an abuse of God's precepts and a sure object for attack.

Besides the rum trade with the Indians, Mather also found membership procedures among the tribes and conversion of the natives areas of constant concern. In March 1711, Mather questioned membership practices of a local tribe, thinking that they may be too lenient in their requirements for membership. "I would procure a strict Enquiry, about the late way of Admission into the particular Church-State," he questioned, "practised among our Christian Indians; lest it should (which I hear) degenerate into a very lax Procedure." This issue prompted him to a renewed concern for converting the Indians. He wanted to "not only . . . promote Prayer for the Success of the Gospel among the Indians, every Time we hold a Meeting, but also more than ever to make it an Article of Prayer in the public Assemblies of Zion." He underlined his own laxity in evangelizing the Indians when he concluded that his "Omission of it has been blameable."[22]

While social issues, such as rum sold to the Indians, and church government issues, such as membership procedures among the Indian tribes, focused Mather's interest in Christianizing Indians, most of the

---

[21](Boston, 1700). Also see Kellaway, p. 235.

[22]*Diary I*, p. 342.

time his concern took the form of written encouragement. "I write Letters to the General Assembly at Connecticut, to Awaken their Zeal," he wrote in 1706, "to Christianize their Indians; and our Commissioners for the Indian-Affayrs do join with me, in signing them."[23] When Indian agents were to be sent to Martha's Vineyard to assist the natives there in practicing Christianity, Mather again forwarded the necessary letters to promote the endeavor. He wrote to New York's governor to encourage the work of missionaries on Long Island, and he attempted to provide a missionary for the "Eastern Indians."[24] The Indians' spiritual growth was the object of numerous writings for Mather,[25] and he maintained until his death that "The work of Gospellizing the Aboriginal Natives of this Country is one of New England's peculiar Glories."[26]

Mather also had an abiding concern for Jewish conversion throughout his ministry.[27] Even his private meditations within his study

---

[23]*Diary I*, p. 571.

[24]*Diary II*, pp. 233, 512, 531, 537, 581, 615, and 803.

[25]For example, see *An Epistle unto the Christian Indians* (Boston, 1700); *Hatchets to Hew Down the Tree of Sin, Which Brings Forth Fruit of Death* (Boston, 1705); and *Family Religion Excited and Assisted* (Boston, 1714).

[26]This quotation is taken from a letter of Mather's to Governor Dummer of Massachusetts, the American Antiquarian Society, Mather *Collection*, 1725; *Diary II*, p. 807.

[27]See Chapter 4 for his vacillation on the conversion of the Jewish nation as a necessary sign for the millennium. Also see C. M.'s

were touched by a special conviction about Jewish conversion. "This Day, from the Dust, where I lay prostrate, before the Lord, I lifted up my cries," he wrote in his diary, "For the Conversion of the Jewish Nation, and for my own having the Happiness, at some Time or other, to baptise a Jew, that should by my Ministry, bee brought home unto the Lord."[28] By 1699 he had "for diverse Tears, employ'd much Prayer for, and some Discourse with, an infidel Jew in this town; thro' a Desire to glorify my Lord Jesus Christ in the Conversion of that Infidel. . . ."[29] Vowing to direct his prayers specifically for that conversion, he hastened to write a letter to the Jew and enclose a copy of his work, *Faith of the Fathers*. He regularly prayed for his Jewish friend in Boston, but he never realized his hope that the Jew be converted to Christianity. He supported wholeheartedly the charity work done for Jewish children in Berlin, Germany, and prayed for their conversion. Besides these private wishes, Mather also publicly urged his people to be concerned for the conversion of Jews.[30]

No one fell outside Mather's purview when it came to the importance of winning souls for a Christ whose victorious return was imminent. Mather's missional interest in blacks, Indians, and Jews was

---

Expectanda (Boston, 1691) for his early view which demonstrated the necessity of a Jewish national conversion before the millennium.

[28]Rooy, p. 247.

[29]*Diary I*, p. 300 (1694); Rooy, p. 248.

[30]*Diary II*, pp. 41, 62, 219, 233, 378, 492, 494, 500, 503, 524.

prompted by his theological understanding of a millennium about to break forth. "He hoped that "Every Soul may be rescued from Eternal Miseries." The New Jerusalem established in the New Heavens would be no place for infidels or pagans, only the converted to Christ - the elect - would find a place in the millennial kingdom. No one could escape the impending judgment rendered by God. For Mather, God's judgment was both afflictive and eternal. In other words, God's judgment was witnessed in the day-to-day natural events of a person's life, like rain, snow, fire; and also it would be meted out at the conclusion of the millennium. The judgment secured each soul an eternal home ruled by Christ's grace or a place tormented by hell's fire.[31]

Three types of God's judgment can be recognized in Mather's thought: afflictive, final, and eternal. Afflictive judgment was considered by Mather to occur when a natural event or catastrophe happened. Final judgment was reasoned to be by Mather at the time of the great conflagration when the earth would be destroyed by fire. Eternal judgment occurred when God through Christ finally placed the lost sinner in hell, depriving him of God's presence, and punishing him with fire for his sins.[32]

---

[31]C. M., *The Negro Christianized* (Boston, 1706), p. 6.

[32]For a review of these three judgmental themes in colonial American thought, see James W. Davidson, *The Logic of Millennial Thought* (New Haven: Yale University Press, 1977), pp. 81-121. Contrary to what I have found in Mather, Davidson identifies the afflictive, final, and eternal judgments as primarily revealed through several ministers and their theologies. I see all three being evident in Mather's millennialism.

Afflictions such as drought, war, disease, and fire signified to Mather, and most Puritans, that divine punishment had been administered to New England and that they portended Christ's return. All events and occurrences were related to God's purpose. "These Earthquakes," one of Mather's contemporaries noted, represented "the Shaking of the Foundations of our Churches, and of our Civil State."[33] Mather seldom failed to issue a publication relating a recent natural catastrophe and the millennium's imminency. In August 1692, after the Jamaica earthquake killed more than two thousand people, Mather chose as his scriptural text Revelation 12:12: "Woe to the Inhabitants of the Earth, and of the Sea; for the Devil is come down unto to you, having great Wrath; because he knoweth, that he hath but a short time." In 1699 he considered the number of plagues and woes befalling humankind and he believed them to suggest "Further and Greater CHANGES upon the World." "Earthquakes prodigiously multiplied" underlined his eschatological expectations and supported his call for "a REVOLUTION and a REFORMATION."[34]

In Mather's most notable and thorough explanation for earthquakes as God's providence, *Boanerges*, he pleaded urgently to his listeners that they might "IMMEDIATELY" come to Christ and be "brought into, a State of Safety for Eternity." No time should be lost, for the millennium drew closer with each passing moment. God did not send

---

[33]C. M., *The Terror of the Lord* (Boston, 1727), Appendix, p. 4.

[34]C. M., *Things For A Distress'd People to Think Upon* (Boston, 1696), pp. 34-37.

his judgment so much in the earthquake as a forerunner to the final judgment; to Mather, instead, the tremors were to "Prefigure" and "therewith to Demonstrate unto Mankind, How things will be at His Coming." While the Lord had mentioned signs to be fulfilled before his coming and that the element of surprise would be present when the time came, Mather also understood that "There shall be great Earthquakes in diverse places," based upon Luke 21:11.[35]

No event in New England escaped his attempt to parallel it to biblical prophecy and the hastening of the millennium. In 1711, Boston suffered one of its worst fires. Until the fire of 1760, the fire of 1711 was called "the great fire." "Beginning at 7 o'clock in the evening and finishing before two in the morning the night between the 2 and 3 of October 1711, a terrible fire laid the heart of Boston in ashes." The old meeting house, all of Queen Street, King Street, and Pudding Lane were engulfed in flames throughout the night. Many people were killed when houses blew up or when they "ventured too far into the fire." However, even in the midst of this tragedy, Mather encouraged the people to see that "Yet in the midst of these Lamentations we may say: Tis of the Lord's mercies that we are not Consumed." His words were prompted by the fact that the winds were quiet during the evening and did not whip up the fire to enflame an even greater circle of buildings. Mather based his message of October 4 upon Jeremiah 5:3: "O Lord thou hast consumed them, but they have refused to receive correction." He realized that the "Thundering Voice" of God had been sounded through

---

[35]C. M., *Boanerges* (Boston, 1727), p. 26. Also see pp. 50-51.

the fire because "the Weekly Lecture" was not "attended as it ought to have been and God judges by fire his people."[36] Not only was afflictive judgment present, but Mather observed through the Boston fire a premonition of the final and eternal judgments.

Mather saw within the tragic fire of 1711 a demonstration of what was to occur when the final judgment was to take place. "There is a Day at Hand when, Behold the Lord will come with Fire. . . . O People of God there is a CONFLAGRATION to come."[37] For Mather, the belief in the great conflagration of the world had a scriptural base. Particularly in II Peter, chapter three, he found a biblical precedent for believing in the earth's destruction by fire when Christ returns to judge all people. "But the heavens and the earth which are now," he wrote years later in "Triparadisus," "by the same word are kept in store, reserved unto FIRE against the day of judgment and perdition of ungodly men." The scriptural reference to this conflagration was no allegorical flourish to Mather, instead he took precautions against that kind of interpretation. "Can anything be more Literal," he wrote, "than those Expressions." He argued persistently that the conflagration would be a literal judgment upon the earth, "as Literal as Water."[38]

Besides the Petrine prophecy, Mather relied upon other

---

[36]C. M., *Taberah* (Boston, 1717), pp. 21-22.

[37]*Ibid.*, p. 26.

[38]C. M., "Triparadisus," unpublished manuscript found in the American Antiquarian Society, Mather *Collection*, Pt. III, Section I.

apocalyptic sections of scripture. In Daniel 7:9, the reference to God's throne being "like a fiery flame, and his wheels as burning fire" became for Mather proof that "the Lord shall come at the end of the Fourth Monarchy and a Fiery Stream shall come forth before Him." Mather cited Psalm 50:3,4, as another reminder that the Lord will return accompanied with fire: "Our God shall come, and shall not keep Silence, a Fire shall devour before Him. . . ." In the parable of the Sower found in Matthew 13:40-42, Mather referred to Jesus' own words about his return and the end of the world: "As therefore the Tares are gathered and burned in the Fire, so shall it be at the End of the World. The Son of Man shall send forth his Angels . . . and Them which do Iniquity . . . shall be cast into a Furnace of Fire. . . ."[39]

Although Mather gave little credence to the Sibylline Oracles, a series of prophecies which tradition attributed to ten women written in Greek verse around the year 100 B.C., he cited them "meerly to show the importance of FIRE in them." Because these oracles spoke of the messiah prior to the "approach of ye REDEEMER," Mather considered them to have some authority. In the Second Book of *Oracula Sibyllina*, Mather translated from the Greek the poetic lines which verified his

---

[39]*Ibid.*, Pt. III, Section IV. Also see Mather's *Nehemiah* (Boston, 1710): Having finished the corpus of his sermon on p. 21, he continued his text in the same manner as his dedication, with consolations which may be gained from the imminence of the millennium - "Another and a Better State of the World is coming on," he said, and then cited "2 Pet. III. 13. 'According to His Promise, we Look for New Heavens and a New Earth, wherein dwelleth Righteousness.'" Also quoted in Holmes, p. 724 (vol. II).

understanding that the end of the world would be by a conflagration: "Down a vast Flood of FIRE from Heaven shall flow; and Lay all Waste upon the Earth below."⁴⁰

The Boston fire of 1711, besides illustrating for Mather afflictive judgment upon a disobedient people, and final judgment as a demonstration of the conflagration prior to Christ's judging all people at the millennium's end, it also supported his anxiousness over an eternal judgment by fire. If anyone remained a despiser of religion, Mather worried that "At your Death you will drop into an Everlasting Fire." Eternal judgment occurred when the forces of Gog and Magog had been defeated and Satan's followers had been cast into the lake of fire. Christ then judged all people at the end of the millennium to place them in their eternal resting place, either the "Third Paradise," a heaven where Christ would eternally dwell with his people, or hell, a place of separation from Christ and where existed a "Firey Oven" where "the Wrath of the Glorious God" will punish unrepentant sinners.⁴¹ Just as with other tragedies besides fires, diseases, storms or natural disasters such as earthquakes, Mather hoped that each event would lead people to look at their own salvation. "I wish you may be Saved as by Fire, in this regard,"

---

⁴⁰*Ibid.* For other references to the conflagration as a final judgment see Sections VII, VIII, IX, X. Also see the following works by Mather: *Things to Be Look'd For* (Boston, 1691); *Perswasions From the Terror of the Lord* (Boston, 1711); *The World Alarm'd* (Boston, 1721); *Terra Beata* (Boston, 1726); "Biblia," 2 Peter, and Revelation; Middlekauff, pp. 320-321.

⁴¹C. M., *Taberah* (Boston, 1711), p. 28.

he wrote hopefully, "that what has been done in the late Fire, may inflame your Agony to look after your Salvation."[42] He was afraid that people who did not heed his warning could be cast into the torments of hell after the final judgment: "O my Poor Friend, Beware, Beware, Lest all thy Affliction, be only the Prison, the Dungeon, the uneasy Fetters, of a Malefactor, to be afterwards brought forth unto an astonishing Execution; To be burnt Alive!"[43]

The last years of Mather's life did not change his chiliastic hopes. Gradually, he wished more and more for a withdrawal from the misfortunes, tragedies, and disasters of this life. He ultimately came to "look on the World with Contempt," not so much as a person disillusioned with life or as a person overwhelmed by the vicissitudes that befall all people, but instead as a Christian who considered the things of the world to be dross in comparison to the blessings of a heavenly world filled with Christ's grace. He appropriately concluded his most detailed millennial manuscript in 1726, a year before his death, with a fervent desire that "my Hope and my Joy, and my Possessions, and all my Pleasure, may be in the FUTURE WORLD."[44]

---

[42]*Ibid.*

[43]*Ibid.*, p. 15.

[44]C. M., "Triparadisus," Pt. III. This quotation is taken from the last page of the manuscript, the last sentence.

Chapter 8

"The Time is at Hand"

Cotton Mather carefully observed current events. His preoccupation with attempting to precisely date the millennium's beginning led him to examine such diverse occurrences as frontier Indian raids and the effects of a currency crisis in Massachusetts as reason to prepare for Jesus' victorious return. In *Things to Be Look'd For* (1691), a sermon for the Artillary Company of Massachusetts, Mather emphasized the possibilities for those who explored biblical prophecies. "I confess Apocalyptical Studies, are fittest for those Raised Souls," he wrote, "whose Heart-strings are made of a Little Finer Clay, than other men; and it is to them especially, that I take leave to say, There is a World of Sweetness in Diligent and Regular Studies upon the Kingdom of our Lord Jesus."[1] Since Christ would come in history, he reasoned that the Scriptures, the signs that would anticipate Jesus' coming, and the current events through which the millennium would unfold, had to be studied.

Mather found it difficult to imagine anyone believing that Christ had already begun the millennium. To him it was apparent that the Church had not enjoyed a thousand years of righteousness and peace.

---

[1] pp. 46-47. This quotation is also found in Stephen Stein's "Transatlantic Extension: Apocalyptic in Early New England," *The Apocalypse in English Renaissance Thought and Literature*, C. A. Patrides and Joseph Wittreich, eds. (Ithaca: Cornell University Press, 1984), p. 277.

He studied the prophetic signs within the bible in order to understand and anticipate Christ's second coming which, according to his millennial scheme, would usher in the final thousand years.[2] Yet, current events, even those of such magnitude as the loss of the Massachusetts charter (it was annulled in 1684) and the overthrow of Governor Edmund Andros (1688), did not entirely persuade Mather that the end he yearned for was near. The persecution of French Protestants after the revocation of the Edict of Nantes in 1685 signalled to him that the millennium approached. To Mather, France represented the tenth kingdom of the Roman Empire.[3] The slaying of the witnesses described in the book of Revelation perhaps had just occurred in Louis XIV's slaughter of Protestants. Mather based his conclusions upon a French eschatologist, Pierre Jurieu, a Professor of Divinity in France and Holland who had been ordained in the Anglican Church. Besides the French Protestant persecutions, Jurieu believed there was other evidence which indicated the

---

[2] C. M., "Biblia Americana" (hereafter cited as Biblia), The Book of Revelation, and "Coronis," an essay attached to his commentary on Revelation; *Diary II*, and *passim*. Although most recent scholars have mentioned Mather's unpublished Biblia, none have accurately dated the material. Middlekauff (p. 284) in the endnote says, "Portions of Mather's commentary were written in 1699; still others in 1702 and 1706." Levin makes no mention of the Biblia. Silverman does not date the six folio volumes, but he does tell us that Mather collected over 1000 illustrations for it in 1711 (p. 237). Apparently, the Biblia is composed of many additions which Mather wrote throughout the years 1699 until his death. Portions of Daniel and Revelation were written after 1725 due to internal evidence. Mather cited sources published after that date.

[3] C. M., Biblia, "Coronis."

millennium's nearness. Jurieu claimed the vials of wrath had already been poured upon the Antichrist; therefore, the seventh trumpet blast was all that remained. Mather pored over Jurieu's biblical exposition and endearingly embraced the contemporary events as the end times, but he hesitated when it came to accepting the fact that all the biblical prophecies were fulfilled.[4] He reasoned that the end must be near, but the question remained as to its exact date.

Mather also followed closely Joseph Mede's (1586-1638) calculations on the millennium. A Professor of Greek at Cambridge, Mede introduced for the first time some basic principles to interpret the book of Revelation. Mede believed it absolutely necessary for an interpretation of the Apocalypse to fix initially the order and collective relationships of its principal visions utilizing internal evidence. The visions' significance resided in their synchronism and succession. "By a synchronism of prophecies I mean," he defined, "when the things therein designed run along the same time or age. . . ." He continued his line of thought by suggesting the three and a half times the 1260 days of the woman in the wilderness, the 42 months of the tramping under foot of the outer court of the temple, and the 1260 days of the witnesses' prophesying in sackcloth all began at the same time and ended together, therefore synchronizing throughout their historical course, extending from the rise of the Papacy and reaching to the era of the overthrow of the

---

[4] See Pierre Jurieu's *Accomplishment of the Scriptural Prophecies* (London, 1687). For Mather's references to Jurieu as an influence upon his millennial thought, see *Things to Be Look'd For* and *A Midnight Cry* (Boston, 1692), pp. 1-9, 30-32, 63; and in the Biblia, "Revelation."

Antichrist.[5]

Mather, following Mede's suggestion, held that the Antichrist had entered the last half-time of his 1260 years at the beginning of the Protestant Reformation in 1517. A half-time equaled 180 years. This calculation was determined by the day-equal-a-year principle. Whenever the scriptures identified in prophetical language "days," they were interpreted as "years" by eschatologists. A "time" was one year; therefore, a "half-time" equaled 180 days, which, when translated into prophetical time, was equivalent to 180 years. The day-equal-a-year principle was used by Mede and accepted by Mather. Mather simply added the 180 years to 1517 and concluded that the end of the Antichrist will begin in 1697. The Antichrist's destruction would occur simultaneously with Christ's return.[6]

Mather extended his speculations especially into an examination of Turkish activity. Mede believed that the second woe trumpet began when the Turks invaded the Ottoman Empire in 1300. Some expositors assumed that the Turkish woe would last 400 years. Mather linked the half-time from the Protestant Reformation, 180 years, plus 1517 to equal his projected date for the dawn of the millennium to be 1697. The great number of commentators who agreed that the Turkish woe will last 400 years from the year 1300 added credence to his calculation of 1697 as the millennium's beginning. Turkish power, Mather ascertained, would

---

[5]This quotation is from Joseph Mede's *The Key of Revelation, . . . With A Comment Thereupon* (London, 1650), p. 1.

[6]C. M., *Things to Be Look'd For* (Boston, 1691), pp. 32, 39-40.

collapse in 1697.⁷ Actually, Mather's predictions received some verification when in 1699, eight years after his Artillery sermon, the Turks and the Austrians settled differences in the Peace of Carlowicz.

Continual revision of his computations occurred throughout his remaining years, but the projected dates for millennial activity, although suffering from inaccuracy, reflected a constant interest and belief in the millennium's imminency. During the 1690s, as noted in his Artillery sermon, he attached his millennial expectations to 1697. Mather considered earthquakes to be a good barometer to measure the millennium's nearness since Christ's first resurrection was accompanied by an earthquake as recorded in Matthew 24:54.

One of the last events before the Second Coming was the resurrection of the witnesses which would be supported by a series of earthquakes. In 1692, Mather thought the world had entered into this period of final tremors prior to the witnesses' resurrection. He focused attention upon reports about earthquakes occurring throughout the world.⁸ Other signs also indicated to Mather the end's nearness: the French Protestant persecutions under Louis XIV, the Glorious Revolution of 1688 and with it the hope that Mary would remove restrictions against nonconformity, and a few military defeats the Turks had suffered in the early 1690s. The most indicative sign apparent to Mather in the early 1690s erupted in Salem Village. The Devil, for one last time, attempted

---

⁷*Ibid.*, pp. 39-40.

⁸C. M., *A Midnight Cry* (Boston, 1692), p. 60.

through the witchcraft outbreak to torment the earth's inhabitants before his activity would be curtailed by Christ's return. In 1693, Mather remarked that, "I am verily perswaded, There are Some already Born, who shall see the most Glorious Revolutions that ever happened in any former ages. . . ." He considered his age "in the very Dawns of our Lords Coming to Destroy the Wicked one."[9]

Such prophetic forecasting as Mather engaged in carried an inherent risk - it could be wrong. But millennial computations always reflected an inexactness. Mather did not despair when 1697 arrived and Christ failed to descend from heaven. Even William Whiston (1667-1752), a noted millennial scholar whom Mather read,[10] prefaced his work on Revelation with a discourse upon the problem of translating the prophetical year into the Chaldean and Julian year. Accuracy was important to the millennialists and attempted by them, but it was not expected to be reached.

In the Spring of 1698 Mather found cause for fresh hope when he heard news about reformation in the Scottish Church, a resurgence of Protestantism in central France, and most importantly, William's Proclamation Against Profaneness, an ordinance designed to bolster

---

[9]C. M., *Winter-Meditations* (Boston, 1693), p. 51. Also see his treatise *Things to Be Look'd For, op. cit.*, pp. 32, 54-55.

[10]See Mather's Biblia, "Revelation," for his interpretation of William Whiston. Also see Middlekauff, *The Mathers, op. cit.*, pp. 340-341.

orthodoxy in England.[11] But none of these events proved to be the substantial sign needed to confirm his millennial expectations.

From 1698 to 1703, Mather continued to pore over news from Europe to find indications that the millennial prophecies neared completion. During these years he looked encouragingly to the Jews as the nation which needed to be converted prior to the Second Coming. Like his father, Increase Mather, Cotton believed the Jewish conversion would signal the millennium. For example, earlier, in 1696, Mather wrote that "The Day is at Hand, when the Vail that has been upon the Hearts of the Jewish Nation, shall be taken off, and that Nation shall Fear the Lord, and His Good Thing, the Messiah."[12] In 1699 to promote this interest in the Jewish conversion, Mather prepared a treatise, *Faith of the Fathers*. He introduced his discourse with the exclamation to the Jews to "Return, O backsliding Israel!" Several months later he learned that his book had been influential in the conversion of a Jew in the Carolinas.[13]

In 1703, writing "Problema Theologicum," an extended letter outlining his chiliastic hopes, Mather again proclaimed the importance of

---

[11]*Diary I*, p. 261-262.

[12]C. M., *Things for a Distress'd People to Think Upon* (Boston, 1696), p. 34.

[13]*Faith of the Fathers* (Boston, 1699), p. 4. The reference to the converted Jew in the Carolinas is found in Mather's *Diary I*, p. 315.

the Jewish conversion and the millennium's imminency.[14] To Mather, the Jewish nation when it rejected Jesus Christ practiced apostasy. The Hebrew people therefore needed to return to the true Messiah before the Second Coming. "Wee look for a Conversion," he wrote, "of the Jewish Nation. . . ."[15] Referring to Romans, chapter eleven, Mather was convinced that the Jewish nation "shall turn unto the Lord" prior to Christ's return. The nearest Mather could compute the millennium's beginning was 1736. According to Mather's calculations, the world would be nearly six thousand years old by the middle of the eighteenth century. "Tho indeed by the Chronology of the Samaritan Pentateuch," he exuberantly proclaimed, "it will be that age, in A.C. 1736." He underscored this calculation by relying on Joseph Mede's own reference to the end of the 1260 years of Antichrist's reign expiring in 1736.[16]

On other matters Mather did not bring himself to accept so easily Mede's position. When it came to the role America played in the millennium, Mather opposed Mede's argument. Mede believed that America would be the seat of the Devil's activity. An evil America would house all of Satan's hosts until the final outbreak of cosmic war when the Devil's minions and Jesus Christ do battle at Gog and Magog. Mather

---

[14] C. M., "Problema Theologicum." This unpublished manuscript found at the American Antiquarian Society is 91 pages long and is a letter addressed to Nicholas Noyes by Mather in Boston, December 1703. The Biblia, "Revelation," chapter 22 contains the entire letter verbatim.

[15] C. M., "Problema Theologicum," p. 24.

[16] *Ibid.*, p. 89.

vehemently disagreed with Mede on this point. "I that am an American," Mather wrote in his "Problema Theologicum," "must needs be Lothe to allow all America still unto the Devils possession, when our Lord shall possess all the rest of the world."[17] He hoped that America would, at least, be a part of the New Jerusalem. His doubts about America's millennial role wavered back and forth between optimism for the colonies as a place in the New Jerusalem and pessimism for the colonies as possibly a hell house.[18] Not until after 1706, when he read William Whiston's *Essay on Revelation*, did he begin to formulate an emphatic forecast for the earth's end and the millennium's beginning, even though his doubts about America's millennial role continued up to his death.

Mather appreciated Whiston's association with the great Sir Isaac Newton (1642-1727) and the scientific attainments Whiston relied upon to support his prophetical theories. Most of all, Mather accepted Whiston's chronology of the millennium's final events and fixed the date for the Second Coming in 1716. Whiston's argument retained a degree of flexibility. His predicted date only fixed the time for the beginning of the Antichrist's demise when the forces of God joined to overthrow the archenemy. The time actual displacement of the Antichrist took remained undetermined, but the initial steps taken for the Antichrist's destruction would begin in 1716.

---

[17]p. 68.

[18]For a positive statement concerning Mather's views on America's millennial role, see his *Theopolis Americana* (Boston, 1710). Also see "Triparadisus," Pt. III, Section X.

Mather also accepted Whiston's precision in determining the pouring of the vials. The pouring of the vials was generally accepted as an allegorical account of God's anger against the Church of Rome.[19] Whiston considered the pouring of the vials as a simultaneous event to occur along with the sounding of the Seventh Trumpet, which would sound when the Antichrist was destroyed. Previous to reading Whiston's account, Mather adhered uncritically to Mede's version of the vials. To Mede, the vials had already been poured out, except the seventh vial, which would be distributed at the time of an Antichrist's defeat. Also, Mather dropped a distinction between secular and ecclesiastical events which Mede had advocated. Instead, after reading Whiston, Mather eliminated that false separation in human affairs and looked to all news as possibly having millennial implications. To Mather, Whiston gave persuasive evidence for bringing together all of the apocalyptic symbols found in Revelation having to do with the number seven.[20] The seven thunders of Revelation, the seven seals, and the seven trumpets all combined in Whiston's thinking to point toward an imminent end to the earth. Mather agreed with Whiston and claimed that "we are just coming into ye Time of ye End."[21]

Mather adopted 1716 as the determinative year marking the millennium's outbreak. To him, all that he had studied and read

---

[19]Middlekauff, pp. 320-349.

[20]C. M., Biblia, "Coronis."

[21]*Ibid.*

indicated 1716 as the initial millennial signal ending Antichrist's reign. Two results were needed to underline this prophetic prediction: the cleansing of the temple and slaying of the witnesses. Like Whiston before him, Mather believed that the primitive Church had remained pure until 456 A.D. when Antichrist infiltrated it. After the 1260 years were added as the length of Antichrist's reign, the result was 1716. To Mather, this date would witness the cleansing of the inner temple of all Antichristian idolatries. The slaying of the witnesses Mather believed occurred before 1690 with the Edict of Nantes and the French Protestant persecutions which followed. Peter Boyer's *History of the Vaudois* and the writings of Pierre Jurieu influenced Mather's prediction. In 1692, Mather wrote that he believed that the slaying of the witnesses had already passed as a millennial event. He vacillated within the next few years as other events clouded his sureness, but after reading Whiston's *Essay*, he again considered the Vaudois' slaying the fulfillment of the prophecy. When the Duke of Savoy recalled the Vaudois, who had escaped to Switzerland in 1686 with an edict of toleration, their resurrection had been made complete according to Mather's reliance upon Whiston.[22] The grand climax came in 1716, but Mather still felt uneasy as other people and events jostled his initial sureness after having read Whiston.

Samuel Sewall, a close friend of Mather's also interested in the fulfillment of millennial prophecies, studied the prophecies and came up with a different interpretation. Sewall did not agree with Mather about

---

[22]Biblia, "Revelation"; Whiston, *Essay*, pp. 209-210; Middlekauff, pp. 344-345.

the witnesses already being slain. Until the witnesses are slain, Sewall considered the millennium a distance away.[23] A flurry of events centering upon English-French relations also brought Mather to doubt his calculations for the millennium beginning in 1716. Antichristian activity could be measured by France's involvement in world affairs if, as Mather thought, France represented the tenth and last kingdom of the Roman Empire. He followed the results of the French war in order to determine the extent of France's decline. The Treaty of Utrecht, concluded in 1713, brought an end to the fighting between Britain and France, but Mather could find no definite enjoyment over a peace which supposedly catered to French interests in English state councils.[24] Three years later, by 1716, Mather directed his anxiousness over the possible failure of the millennium's outbreak toward the union of all Christians. The Christian unity Mather proposed consisted of those Christians who could adhere to certain maxims which he outlined in *The Stone Cut Out of the Mountain*.[25] By uniting in prayer and living a life of "piety," Christians could expect the long-awaited millennium to begin soon. Mather's expectation was that the Lord would hasten the day if Christians simply would pull together

---

[23]Samuel Sewall, *Letter-Book Collections*, Massachusetts Historical Society (6th Series, Boston, 1888), II pp. 53-59, 64-65, 78, 83. Also see Sewall's work, *Phaenomena quaedam Apocalyptica Ad Aspectum Novi Orbis Configurata. Or, some few Lines towards a description of the New Heaven as it makes to those who stand upon the New Earth* (Boston, 1697).

[24]*Diary II*, pp. 171-174, 176. Also see his Biblia, "Coronis."

[25](Boston, 1716).

and practice basic Christian principles of bible reading, prayer, forgiveness, communion, and worship attendance. By August 1716, he began to focus upon Joel 2:28--"And it shall come to pass afterward, that I will pour out my spirit upon all flesh . . ."--hoping that his prayers for the millennium would introduce the millennial kingdom.[26] His prayerful exhortations, "They are coming! They are coming! They will quickly be upon us; and the World shall be shaken wonderfully!"[27] only ended with disappointment as he watched 1716 end without any angelic armies descending to initiate the millennium. Mather's millennial exuberance temporarily waned when he commented, "Doubtless, it will now be said, 'The Days are prolonged and Every Vision faileth."[28]

In *The Stone Cut Out of the Mountain*, Mather reduced Christianity to fourteen maxims upon which all Christians must adhere. By 1717, after the hopeful year of 1716 yielded no millennial fruit, Mather narrowed his maxims to three. In *Malachi*, he expressed "Real and Vital PIETY" as consisting of belief in the Trinity, love of neighbor out of respect for Christ, and total reliance upon Christ for salvation. On the one hand Mather's "Universal Religion" promoted a faith believable to a broad spectrum of people; on the other hand, his abbreviated principles encouraged people to turn to Christianity prior to the final millennial climax, thus rendering more profitable to God the final days as more

---

[26]Middlekauff, p. 346, and *passim*; *Diary II*, p. 365.

[27]*Diary II*, p. 366; Middlekauff, p. 347.

[28]C. M., "Triparadisus," Pt. III, Section XII.

souls joined the ranks added to the expected New Heavens and New Earth.[29]

Mather remained enthusiastic in his prophetic predictions during the final decade of his life. He was not disillusioned by the momentary disappointments of 1697 and 1716. Instead, he examined even more thoroughly the biblical prophecies, especially Daniel and the book of Revelation, and added his comments to his own collection, the "Biblia Americana." Also, he abandoned his earlier millennial conviction in a Jewish national conversion.

Cotton's father, Increase Mather, had publicly declared that a national Jewish conversion was one of the first events inaugurating Jesus' return. In 1695, Increase published *A Dissertation Concerning the Future Conversion of the Jewish Nation*[30] wherein he described Israel's salvation as one which had not yet occurred. Yet, he did believe it was "imminent," by which he meant that it would happen within the next few years. Israel would occupy the Promised Land and it would again flow with milk and honey. By 1710 Increase considered the Jewish national conversion under way. He observed signs which signified Antichrist's reign was ending. Wars, famine, pestilence, and revolutions were breaking out in Europe, and the Turks had fallen; 40,000 died of the plague in Danzig; and several hundred Jewish conversions happened in Hamburg. Such events

---

[29]C. M., *Malachi* (Boston, 1717); also see Kenneth Silverman's *The Life and Times of Cotton Mather* (New York: Harper and Row, 1984), pp. 300-301.

[30](Boston, 1695).

occurring simultaneously prompted him to raise the question, "May this be the first Fruits of a greater harvest shortly to follow?"[31]

Cotton followed closely his father's thoughts on a Jewish national conversion as an antecedent to the millennium until Increase's death. In 1724, a little less than a year after his father's death, Cotton rejected the Jewish national conversion as a necessary step before the millennium. More than ever Cotton expected Jesus' return to begin the millennium. Mather "daily looked for" Jesus' return and proclaimed that the signs had repeatedly been given for God's faithful.[32] Mather's assurance that all of the signs were fulfilled for the millennium left him with the familiar prophetic question, "When will the millennium occur?" Again, in these last four years of his life, Mather delved into biblical prophecy, especially Daniel and the book of Revelation, adding to his commentary the "Biblia Americana" and finishing his most thorough statement on the millennium, "Triparadisus."

The biggest influence upon Mather's prophetic predictions during these last years of his life was a work by William Burnet (1688-1729), *Essay on Scripture-Prophecy*. Written in 1724, Burnet's treatise gave more evidence for Mather to predict once more the millennium's beginning. Burnet, who was appointed the governor of New York and Jersey in 1720

---

[31] Increase Mather, *A Discourse Concerning Faith and Fervancy* (Boston, 1710). The quotation is on p. 99.

[32] *Diary II*, p. 522, 740; Middlekauff, p. 348. Mather said that a belief in a Jewish national conversion before Christ's Second Coming only produced a "Dead Sleep" (Triparadisus, Pt. III, Section XI). This quotation is also found in Middlekauff, p. 423.

and was a friend of Sir Isaac Newton, anticipated the end several years away, possibly 1790, but he did believe it had already begun with the Antichrist's decline commencing in 1715.[33]

In a letter to Mather dated April 5, 1725, Burnet responded to the Boston clergyman's query concerning the slaying of the witnesses. Mather believed that the witnesses' slaying occurred in France in the 1680s; yet the New York governor suggested that the slaying of the witnesses was recorded in II Kings within the story of Elijah and Elisha. Mather agreed with Burnet's biblical assessment; however, he held to his belief that the witnesses were already slain. Burnet also commented that he was of the same opinion as Jurieu, that the repeal of the Edict of Nantes marked the beginning of the three and a half days that the witnesses lay dead. "The Dry Bones of the Protestant Cause," Mather recorded, was revived with the other European countries taking up arms against France in April 1689, "which from October 1685 makes just Three Years & an Half." Mather found within Burnet's calculations support for his own prophetic predictions. Burnet gave Mather biblical interpretations of the prophecies which favored his own understanding of them as indicating an imminent and literal millennium.[34]

---

[33]Burnet, *Essay on Scripture-Prophecy* (New York, 1724).

[34]C. M., Biblia, "Revelation," chapter 11. Kenneth Silverman believes that Mather's last years indicate a departure from an earlier allegorical interpretation of the millennium (p. 416). Mason Lowance in *Language of Canaan* (Cambridge: Harvard University Press, 1980) also purports to present Mather as one who believed in an allegorical interpretation all through his life. James W. Davidson presents Mather as a millennialist who believed in a literal return of Christ. My own research confirms

In his commentary on Daniel, Mather pondered the consequences of Burnet's calculations. "Now the period of M. CC. XC Days," he wrote, "(if it commences at 455) expires in 1745." Believing that the "Two thousand & three hundred prophetical Days" began 553 years before "ye Incarnation of our SAVIOUR," Mather figured the time "consequently will end in 1745." Encouraged again by his own numeralogic interpretations, Mather joyously concluded his commentary on Daniel by saying that "The First Period is past; and we may happily hope That ye Kingdom of God is right at hand, even at the Door."[35]

The continuity in Mather's millennialism was much more striking than the changes. With the exception of his understanding of a Jewish national conversion as a prerequisite prior to 1724 for the millennium, and thereafter his changing his view by dropping this expectation for the millennium, Mather's millennialism gradually expanded and deepened as he aged. In the last two years of his life, he completed "Triparadisus," a compendium on millennialism, and preached numerous sermons supporting his millennial convictions. When he preached on the accession of George II in August 1727, six months before his death, he cited the recent Boston *Gazette* report that Palermo, Italy, had suffered an earthquake lasting twenty-five minutes, felling one-fourth of the houses and razing numerous churches, and killing over fifteen thousand people.

Davidson's understanding of Mather. Although Mather understood the allegorical approach to scripture, he considered it "Sadducism." Mather's millennialism portrays a literal, visible, and personal return of Christ.

[35]C. M., Biblia, "Daniel," chapter 12.

In Sicily, he recorded that people ran from their homes and fell prostrate on the ground in the commons, "shedding Floods of Tears, smiting their Breasts and saying over their Rosary with the most fervent Devotion." Inclined to view this event as a harbinger of things to come, Mather pronounced to his congregation that ". . . it may NOW, most awfully be said, His Wrath will QUICKLY Flame! - we NOW know of nothing that remains to go before the Fulfillment of that Word, The Son of Man shall come in the Clouds of Heaven. . . ."[36]

The final and most dramatic event which Mather used as an example of the millennium's nearness came on October 29, 1727, in his own hometown of Boston--an earthquake. To Mather, it sounded like a "horrid rumbling like the Noise of many Coaches together, driving on the paved Stones with the utmost Rapidity." The shock lasted only two or three minutes, but the tremendous noise coupled with the shaking of buildings, the crashing of furniture, and the fear of many people gathered in the streets created an atmosphere of tension and high anxiety. Through this natural disaster, Mather believed that the Lord had spoken and that now he must address the people and "render the Voice of the Glorious GOD in the EARTHQUAKE, while it was yet scarce over, Articulate and Intelligible unto the Hearers." Mather delivered a message based upon Micah 6:9, "The Voice of the Lord crieth unto the City."[37]

"O People Trembling before the Lord," Mather began, "Hear now

---

[36] C. M., *Christian Loyalty* (Boston, 1727); Silverman, pp. 416, 417.

[37] C. M., *The Terror of the Lord* (Boston, 1727); Silverman, pp. 417-419.

my SPEECH, and hearken to all my Words." He then quickly divulged the thrust of his message: "If I should make the Cry FIRE, FIRE! The Fire of GOD will sooner than is generally thought for, fall upon a wretched World . . . I should be as much mocked, and as little minded as Lot was in the Morning of the Day when he went out of Sodom." He reasoned that he might be mocked, but he did not care because God had spoken to him and had awakened him to the nearness of Christ's Second Coming, which would be "Literal, Personal, Visible" and accompanied with a general conflagration of the earth. For years Mather had looked at every earthquake as a portent of the earth's destruction and every blaze as an anticipation of the final great conflagration. But now the final great events ushering in the millennium had occurred in New England, in his own beloved city of Boston, where the components which made up the closing episodes of Christ's coming could be unmistakably identified. No element of the millennium's conclusion was more obvious than the end itself coming by surprise to a world asleep.[38]

Like a thief in the night, Christ would come unexpectedly to the earth. Mather knew that the element of surprise which accompanied Christ's Coming challenged his position as a prophetic predictor of millennial events. Yet, to Mather, even though Christ would appear by surprise, the circumstances surrounding the millennium would leave no

---

[38]C. M., *The Terror of the Lord*; "Triparadisus," Pt. III, Section VI, "Signs of the Conflagration Coming On;" *Things to Be Look'd For* (Cambridge, 1691); *The World Alarm'd* (Boston, 1721); *Terra Beata* (Boston, 1726); Biblia, 2 Peter, Revelation, Silverman p. 418; Middlekauff, p. 321-322.

doubt as to the meaning of the appearance. Coming on clouds of fire and smoke, accompanied with legions of angels singing his praises, he would destroy Antichrist and his minions with this final conflagration and then chain Satan for a thousand years. The saints still residing on earth would be caught up to Christ in the air, while the saints who were dead would be transformed. After the fire subsided, the earthly saints would return to a "New Earth" while the transformed saints would occupy the "New Heavens." The nations formed by the New Earth saints would live in bliss for a thousand years, building houses, planting vineyards, and reproducing themselves. The raised saints with Christ in the New Heavens would act as angels to the earthly saints. Occasionally, Christ himself would walk among the saints of the New Earth so they might worship him.[39]

At the millennium's end, Gog and Magog would rise from Hell, led by the Devil to Armageddon for a final battle. Mather believed that fire from the New Heavens would consume the Devil's legions and the last judgment would follow with a second resurrection given for sinners. The saints would live in eternal communion with Christ in the Third Heaven, while the sinners would be damned to eternal fire in Hell.[40]

Despite the millennium's surprise element, Mather considered it important to prepare for the inevitable event. Mather sent to Governor Dummer of Massachusetts on December 9, 1727, a memorial he had

---

[39]*Ibid.*

[40]C. M., "Triparadisus," Pt. X, "Where to find Gog and Magog," appended, 4 pp.

prepared for acknowledging a Day of Humiliation and Supplication that "we may be found religiously preparing for the things which may be coming." On December 14 he preached again about the earthquakes which had been terrorizing the country since the initial quake on October 29. "I again and again, declare it unto you," he passionately pleaded to his congregation, "The coming of the Son of Man on the Clouds of Heaven, 'tis what we know of Nothing to Retard it or Protract it."[41]

Ten days later, December 24, Mather preached his last sermon. Addressing his congregation on the death of the Reverend Peter Thacher, he chose the text, "Come my People, Enter thou unto thy Chambers," (Isaiah 26:20). He repeated his certainty in a place for all departed souls, prepared by God and blessed with Christ's presence, awaiting the general resurrection when the millennial trumpet shall sound and the dead in Christ arise to assist their Lord in establishing the millennial paradise. The "Chambers" of which he spoke would only be a temporary resting place. Like a railroad depot, this "Second Paradise" provided for the soul of the individual by giving shelter to it and an opportunity to wait until the final destination, represented by the Third Paradise, could be attained. But before that final destination could be reached, a thousand years of peace and goodwill would be completed.[42]

---

[41] C. M., *Boanerges* (Boston, 1727); Silverman, p. 419.

[42] C. M., *The Comfortable Chambers* (Boston, 1728).

Mather's predicted date of 1745, his final specified date for the millennium, never came for him. Six weeks after his last sermon, February 13, 1728, he died.

A BIBLIOGRAPHICAL ESSAY: COTTON MATHER'S CHANGING IMAGE

One of the outstanding developments in modern American historiography is the reappraisal of Puritanism's role in colonial culture and history. Perry Miller's weighty volumes on the New England Mind changed our understanding of Puritan thought and secured for him the venerable position as the principal scholar who ushered in this great reversal in historical research. Consequently, a host of historians have rushed to the task of restoring the reputation of the Puritans and their tradition.[1]

Despite the revisionism, however, one man's image has, until recently, defied rehabilitation--Cotton Mather. His sundry achievements in the fields of medicine and science have been acknowledged by various

---

[1] Representative works illustrating the restored reputation of the Puritans are Perry Miller's *Orthodoxy in Massachusetts* (Boston: Beacon Press, 1933); *The New England Mind: The Seventeenth Century* (Cambridge, Mass.: Harvard University Press, 1939); *The New England Mind: From Colony to Province* (Cambridge, Mass.: Harvard University Press, 1953); Edmund S. Morgan's *The Puritan Dilemma: The Story of John Winthrop* (Boston: Little Brown, 1959); *Visible Saints: The History of a Puritan Idea* (New York: New York University Press, 1963); Samuel E. Morison's *The Founding of Harvard College* (Cambridge, Mass.: Harvard University Press, 1935); *The Intellectual Life of Colonial New England* (New York: New York University Press, 1957, 2nd ed.); Norman Pettit's *The Heart Prepared: Grace and Conversion in Puritan Spiritual Life* (New Haven: Yale University Press, 1966); Darrett Rutman's *American Puritanism: Faith and Practice* (Philadelphia: J. B. Lippincott, 1970); and Alan Simpson's *Puritanism in Old and New England* (Chicago: University of Chicago Press, 1955).

A BIBLIOGRAPHICAL ESSAY: COTTON MATHER'S CHANGING IMAGE

historians. Otho T. Beall and Richard H. Shryock have gone so far as to call him "the first significant figure in American Medicine."[2] Yet, in general, such esteem has been grudging, and the man's portrait has essentially remained an unappealing enigma. This essay will trace Cotton Mather's changing image in American historiography to its present state within contemporary scholarship.

Few people's image have suffered such diverse representations at the hands of posterity than Cotton Mather (1663-1728). Member of an influential Boston family, a practicing clergyman for over four decades, and one of the most published American writers, Mather appeared destined for a positive historiographical image. For over one hundred years after his death, Mather was venerated as a Puritan saint,[3] but by the nineteenth century, colonial scholars focused upon the Salem witchcraft episode and placed him in a less favorable light. An entire series of publications which outlined his actions during the witchcraft trials peaked between 1866 and 1870, evidently prompted by the publication of

---

[2]Otho T. Beall and Richard H. Shryock, *Cotton Mather: First Significant Figure in American Medicine* (Baltimore: The Johns Hopkins Press, 1954), p. vii.

[3]Highly laudatory was the biography of Cotton Mather by William B. 0. Peabody, *Life of Cotton Mather* (Boston, 1844), which was included in Jared Spark's *Library of American Biography*. Peabody's work was largely based upon Samuel Mather's biography of 1729. For more information on Mather's image by historians, see Richard Lovelace's bibliographical essay, *op. cit.* His essay is an invaluable source for the nineteenth-century debate and one to which I am indebted.

"The Mather Papers" by the Massachusetts Historical Society in 1868.[4] W. Upham was the chief nineteenth-century proponent of the dark side of Mather's image. Originally encouraged by Mather's character in his initial investigations into the Salem ordeal, Upham became persuaded by evidence in the diary and other extant letters that the Boston clergyman was a contriver, promoter of the occult delusion in Salem Village, and the major conspirator against the lives of the sufferers.

In 1831, Upham printed his *Lectures on Salem Witchcraft*, in which he blamed the clergy of New England for fostering the excitement. Mather received more criticism than other ministers because he was considered by Upham as one of the most prominent clergymen in the colony. Between the appearance of these lectures by Upham and the second edition, printed in 1832, the accuracy of Upham's statements concerning Mather's character had been questioned. Upham, in his reply, admitted that previous to the investigation of the subject of his "Lectures," he had never entertained any doubts respecting Mather's "moral and Christian character." He added: "It was with the greatest reluctance that such a doubt was permitted to enter my mind. It seemed incredible--nay, almost impossible--that a man who had been the instrument of so many

---

[4] A series of publications on Cotton Mather and Salem witchcraft appeared between 1866 and 1870, some of the later works apparently initiated by the publication of "The Mather Papers" by the Massachusetts Historical Society in 1868. See, e.g., C. W. Upham, *Salem Witchcraft* (Boston, 1868); W. F. Poole, *The Mather Papers: Cotton Mather and Salem Witchcraft* (Boston, 1868); and his *Cotton Mather and Witchcraft: two notices of Mr. Upham, his Reply* (Boston, 1870).

A BIBLIOGRAPHICAL ESSAY: COTTON MATHER'S CHANGING IMAGE

apparent conversions, and who devoted so many hours and days and weeks of his life to fasting and prayer, could in reality be dishonest and corrupt . . . his character did actually appear in this dark and disgraceful light, a regard for truth and justice compelled me to express my convictions."[5] With the first charges made and countered over Mather's involvement in the witchcraft ordeal, William F. Poole rechallenged Upham's conclusions when the latter's *Salem Witchcraft* was published in 1867.

W. F. Poole contended that Upham's history of Salem witchcraft only repeated and defended the views presented in the "Lectures" of 1831. According to Poole, Upham portrayed Mather in his 1867 history in an even more "unfavorable light" than in the 1831 publication. Poole observed that Upham had Mather coming into the story when we should not expect him, "and always with evil purpose,--plotting and counter-plotting,--disappointed when the trials were over,--planning new excitement and other trials in Boston,--unrepentent when everybody else had taken to the confessional,--wrecked in reputation almost before his career had commenced,--and going to his grave full of remorse and disappointment." Poole revealed Upham to have played fast-and-loose with the historical records concerning Mather's role in the witchcraft proceedings. The next telling sign of counter-evidence offered by Poole to refute Upham's claim that Mather instigated the trials was summarized

---

[5]William F. Poole, "Cotton Mather and Salem Witchcraft," *North American Review*, No. CCXXIII (April 1869), pp. 338-341.

in the historical fact that "Cotton Mather never attended one of the trials at Salem in any capacity,--as advisor, witness, or spectator."[6]

While Poole tried to give a balanced account of Mather's interest in the witchcraft affair, simultaneously lifting the Boston minister's effigy from Upham's virulent handling to a more positive light, ultimately the Upham-Poole controversy had little good effect on the Puritan leader's image. Regrettably, what W. F. Poole observed in 1869 describes Mather's image in the popular mind today. "The present generation of youth is taught," writes Poole, "that nineteen persons hanged, and one pressed to death, to gratify the vanity, ambition, and stolid credulity of Mr. Cotton Mather."[7] By 1870, Mather was well on his way to becoming a stereotype of the Puritan theocrat whose stuffy theology suffocated more liberal tendencies in the American colonial past represented by free speech, separation of church and state, and democracy.

By the end of the nineteenth century a number of critics moved beyond Mather's relationship to the witchcraft trials and attacked various aspects of his work. Moses Coit Tyler, in his notable *History of American Literature* (1878), sketched Mather's personal as well as literary weaknesses. The respected Supreme Court Justice, Oliver Wendell Holmes, portrayed Mather's medicinal ideas as ridiculous and propagated

---

[6]*Ibid.*, p. 373.

[7]p. 338.

this opinion in his widely distributed *Medical Essays* (1883).[8]

Several next-generation historians held even less favorable views. Such scholars as James Truslow Adams and Vernon Louis Parrington visualized Mather as a Philistine who defended the theocracy against a majority who reflected truly-American values. Parrington, in his *Main Currents in American Thought* (1927), a book which calcified the attitude toward American Puritanism for several generations of schoolteachers, attempted a psychohistorical critique which envisaged Mather as a meddlesome, irritable, impudent, morose, scolding sexual psychopath, whose *Diary* was "the produce of a crooked and diseased mind, a treasure-trove for the abnormal psychologist which would be inconceivable if it were not in print." Mather, according to Parrington, refused to fraternize with the poor and sought high-class respectability and was "a morbid New England flagellant, a Puritan Brother of the Cross," to be compared only to that other neurotic deviant Jonathan Edwards.[9] In time, such expressions of Mather's image written chiefly in the 1920s historiography leaked into the college texts.[10] By the early decades of the

---

[8]Moses Coit Tyler, *History of American Literature* (Boston, 1878), and Oliver Wendell Holmes, *Medical Essays* (Boston, 1883), pp. 312-69.

[9]Vernon Louis Parrington, *Main Currents in American Thought* (New York: 1927, 1930), pp. 93-117.

[10]See the citations in Clifford K. Shipton, "A Plea for Puritanism," *American Historical Review*, XL (April, 1935), p. 460, and his "The New England Clergy," Colonial Society of Massachusetts, *Publications*, XXXII (December, 1933), pp. 24-54.

twentieth century, Mather's popular image had reached the stagnant abyss of historical stereotype.

This destructive historiographical trend coincided with more positive treatments. In the middle of the nineteenth century, Chandler Robbins, a Unitarian minister of Mather's Second Church at Boston, wrote that "few historical characters are less understood than COTTON MATHER." Robbins believed that Mather "paid the penalty always attached to singularity" and that "the protuberance of a few eccentricities has thrown all the elements of his character into false perspective."[11] But it was not until the end of the nineteenth century, when two biographies of Mather appeared--Barrett Wendell's *Cotton Mather, the Puritan Priest* (1891) and A. P. Marvin's *The Life and Times of Cotton Mather* (1892)-- that other than eccentric traits of his personality were presented in an extended version of his life. Both derive their accounts fundamentally from Mather's *Diary*, consequently giving a more favorable evaluation of his accomplishments and especially his motives. Marvin stridently defended the Puritan tradition represented by Mather, and Wendell also believed "it was a good man they buried on Copp's Hill one February day in the year 1728."[12] Wendell exonerated Mather from any wrong committed in the witchcraft episode and gave Mather credit for his

---

[11]Chandler Robbins, *A History of the Second Church, or Old North, in Boston* (Boston, 1852), p. 68.

[12]Barrett Wendell, *Cotton Mather, the Puritan Priest* (New York, 1891), p. 109.

A BIBLIOGRAPHICAL ESSAY: COTTON MATHER'S CHANGING IMAGE

inoculation support which culminated in the smallpox controversy in Boston during the 1720s.

Mather's image achieved partial restoration in 1926 when Kenneth Murdock focused upon the Boston minister's salient religious, literary, and scientific accomplishments. Murdock countered the negative statements Worthington C. Ford wrote in the first edition of the Mather *Diary*, namely, that this period in American history was "sterile--glacial" and that the Massachusetts community, controlled by clerical leadership, operated "under the supreme rule of orthodoxy," when he stated that Mather "sought to relieve its sterility, by bringing to it news of the advanced thought of the outside world" and that he was ultimately "no pale historical abstraction, but an intensely active individual. . . . a complex creation of flesh and blood."[13]

Within the next two decades, Perry Miller interpreted Mather's place in New England theology, while German scholars made clear the significant impact German pietism exerted on his religious perspective. Gradually, Mather's image improved as historians reviewed more carefully his accomplishments and less his personality. The capstone of this positive historiographical trend which focused upon Mather's writings emerged in 1940 with Thomas J. Holmes' exhaustive, three-volume

---

[13]Kenneth Murdock, *Selections from Cotton Mather* (New York: Hafner Pub. Co., 1926), p. xxv. The quote by W. C. Ford is found in the "Preface," Cotton Mather's *Diary*, 2 vols. (New York: Frederick Ungar, 1957), p. xi.

Bibliography.¹⁴ Holmes acknowledged the nineteenth-century historians' tendency to lean too much upon Robert Calef's (1648-1719) critique of Mather during the witchcraft trials.¹⁵ The Salem episode, Holmes believed, did not negate Mather's popularity or influence. He cited evidence of Mather's demand as a public speaker, preaching to a weekly congregation of over 1500 members, and his numerous publications to justify the Boston clergyman's continued authority in the community. Holmes also claimed that Mather's spiritual ecstasies reflected no sign of neurosis but revealed an authentic piety assisted by a profound sense of his own sin.¹⁶

Mather's image continued to rise to historical respectability with two additional building-blocks supplied by George L. Kittredge and Clifford K. Shipton. In 1929 *Witchcraft in Old and New England* appeared, preceded by several carefully researched essays by George L. Kittredge where Mather's eminence as an intellectual and scientist were supported against the negative claims of weakness and credulity. Kittredge judged that "It is easy to be wise after the fact,--especially when

---

¹⁴T. J. Holmes, *Cotton Mather: A Bibliography of his Works* (Cambridge, Mass.: Harvard University Press, 1940).

¹⁵*Ibid.*, "Introduction," and specifically "Cotton Mather and His Writings on Witchcraft," by Holmes, in *Papers of the Bibliographical Society of America*, 18:31-59, Robert Calef (1648-1719), Boston merchant who wrote *More Wonders of the Invisible World* (1700) in opposition to the Mathers on the Salem trials.

¹⁶*Ibid.*

the fact is two hundred years old."[17]

Previous Matherian historiography, according to Kittredge, relied too heavily upon subjectivism and not enough upon hard evidence. Clifford K. Shipton, in "The New England Clergy of the Glacial Age," examined the unfavorable tradition that asserted the Puritan heritage established in New England a glacial age and found that this view was contradicted by the material. The Puritan establishment, Shipton claimed, functioned on a wide basis of popular support, and the anti-Mather sentiment was situated in a small clerical party in Boston monopolized by Robert Calef. Mather had called for religious toleration and had supported the charter of 1691 which was supposed to have destroyed the theocracy. Shipton concluded that "The picture, which is built up of logic, a dislike of New England, and Calef's statements, is not supported by contemporary records." Shipton traced Mather's efforts in the witchcraft outbreak and found the clergyman to have urged moderation at the trial. To Shipton, Mather acted as a religious liberal who virtually ushered in

---

[17]George L. Kittredge, *Witchcraft in Old and New England* (Cambridge, Mass.: Harvard University Press, 1929), p. 372; preceding articles by Kittredge on Mather as a scientist and intellectual are "Cotton Mather's Election into the Royal Society," *Publications of the Colonial Society of Massachusetts*, 14 (1911), pp. 81-114; "Some Lost Works of Cotton Mather," *Proceedings of the American Antiquarian Society*, 45 (1912), pp. 418-79; "Cotton Mather's Scientific Communications to the Royal Society," *Proceedings of the American Antiquarian Society*, 26 (1916), no. 3, pp. 18-57.

advanced ideas under the scrutiny of conservative laymen.[18]

Mather's portrait as an *avant-garde* intellectual was augmented in *Cotton Mather, First Significant Figure in American Medicine*, by Otho Beall and Richard Shryock. They investigated his medicinal interests and found him to be the most important personage in American medicinal history prior to the Jeffersonian era.[19] Also, by the 1940s, Mather's scientific interests had been recognized in the works of several able scholars. Theodore Hornberger, Conway Zirkle, Samuel E. Morison, and Michael Kraus made revealing contributions, especially in relation to Mather's fascination with astronomy and genetics as well as the effects of science upon his theology.[20]

Remaining twentieth-century historiography on Mather applied essentially one of three sets of conceptual tools: psychoanalytical, literary, and intellectual. While the psychoanalytical interpretation of Mather actually began with Wendell's biography which claimed that the Puritan leader was neurotic but could not help it, Louise and Ralph Boas

---

[18] Clifford K. Shipton, "The New England Clergy of the Glacial Age," *Publications of the Colonial Society of Massachusetts*, 32 (1933), pp. 24-54.

[19] *op. cit.*, p. vii.

[20] Theodore Hornberger, "The Date, the Source, and the Significance of Cotton Mather's Interest in Science," *American Literature*, VI (January, 1935), pp. 413 ff.; Conway Zirkle, *The Beginnings of Plant Hybridization* (Philadelphia, 1935), pp. 103 ff.; Samuel E. Morison, *The Puritan Pronaos* (New York, 1936), pp. 246 ff.; and Michael Kraus, *The Atlantic Civilization* (Ithaca, N. Y., 1949), *passim*.

interpreted him even more sympathetically. In *Cotton Mather, Keeper of the Puritan Conscience* (1928), the subject as presented by Mr. and Mrs. Boas suffered from a morbid preoccupation with death, leanings toward hypochondria, a persecution complex, and a compulsive urgency which pushed him to live in a perpetual state of frenetic enthusiasm. Even the insanity of Lydia, Mather's third wife, was attributed to the effect of sexual frustration produced in her when he devoted all his time to habitual religious exercises. Assailed by an inferiority complex, Mather could give no more than "a passion for service to men . . . abasement before God."[21]

A pathetic sentimentalism drips from the pages of these psychoanalytical attempts to interpret Mather. The assumption the Boases' analysis rests upon is that we may not like Mather but at least we can understand him. The kind of understanding the psychoanalytical approach offers relies a great deal upon the older nineteenth-century critique supplied by Upham. Such an historical lens tends to distort Mather's Puritan spirituality, ignoring his acute sense of his own sinfulness and emphasizing his diary's self-revelatory nature for social and political motivations. However, most of Mather's descriptions given by the psychoanalytical school do relieve him from any guilt in the witchcraft affair, contributing to discharging that historical misnomer.

---

[21]Ralph and Louise Boas, *Cotton Mather, Keeper of the Puritan Conscience* (New York: Harper and Brothers, 1928), pp. 256-70, p. 261.

Literary estimates of Cotton Mather have emerged which continue picturing the defective or confusing aspects of his nature. In *A Loss of Mastery: Puritan Historians in Colonial America*, Peter Gay described Mather as "a pathetic Plutarch" who leaned toward liberal sentiments but utilized propaganda to pervert the past and consequently gave his own faction a mythology.[22] Mather's literary imagination derided by Gay was lauded by Sacvan Bercovitch in his book, *The Puritan Origins of the American Self*. Bercovitch believed Mather's "historicism reflects the temper of the age" and that it was significant that Mather became the first American to use the term "biography" within his ecclesiastical history of 1702, the *Magnalia Christi Americana*. Bercovitch valued Mather's bibliographical effort on the original New England founder's religious history because it displayed a "diversity of information" and represented "chronicle history." Mather's work, as Bercovitch outlined it, undermined "the current pejorative view of biographies" which beheld them as merely "an exercise in filiopietism."[23]

Kenneth Silverman exposed Mather's flaws and virtues in his *Selected Letters of Cotton Mather*. Silverman drew attention to Mather's "staggering energy issuing in specific acts of kindness: money for the poor, firewood for the sick, consolation for the griefstricken, care for the

---

[22]Peter Gay, *A Loss of Mastery: Puritan Historians in Colonial America* (Berkeley, 1966), pp. 53-87.

[23]Sacvan Bercovitch, *The Puritan Origins of the American Self* (New Haven: Yale University Press, 1975), pp. 2, 3.

orphaned, letters of recommendation or encouragement for the young, visits to the languishing" and "uplift for the degraded." He also ridiculed Mather's habits of representing his own labors with the ministry of Jesus Christ and charged him with a fluctuating personality "by turns peevish, loving, dishonest, devout, spiteful, witty, unctuous, self-sacrificing, petty, ambitious, courtly, and brilliant--by and large a charitable and holy man tainted with an overarching pride, fearful of antagonizing his elders, and temperamentally unsuited for the worldly affairs in which he felt he must play a part." Silverman negatively concluded that Mather was traditionally described as "a fascistic super-prig bloated with the kind of self-regard that results from filiopiety."[24]

William R. Manierre analyzed Mather's literary style in his unpublished doctoral dissertation, "Cotton Mather and the Plain Style." Perceptively he explained the rationale behind Mather's writings, particularly his sermons. But in his 1964 edition of Mather's *Diary* for the year 1712, Manierre yielded his literary evaluation of Mather and turned to psychoanalysis when he classified the forty-nine year old minister as neurotic.[25]

Most recently, the literary understanding of Mather has produced

---

[24]Kenneth Silverman, *Selected Letters of Cotton Mather* (Baton Rouge: Louisiana State University Press, 1971), pp. xi, xv, xiii.

[25]William R. Manierre, "Cotton Mather and the Plain Style," unpublished Ph.D. dissertation (University of Michigan, 1958); also see his introduction to *The Diary of Cotton Mather, D.D., F.R.S., for the Year 1712* (Charlottesville: University Press of Virginia, 1964).

other fruit. Mason I. Lowance, in *The Language of Canaan: Metaphor and Symbol in New England from the Puritans to the Transcendentalists*, dedicated a large portion of his work to Mather's use of biblical typology. Lowance saw Mather's biblical interpretation as epoch making. Mather's *Magnalia Christi Americana* (1702), Lowance argued, displayed the Puritan writer's "most significant use of the biblical analogy, and revealed a penchant for metaphorical construction that would give rise to Jonathan Edwards' transformation of the biblical types into images and shadows of divine things."[26] Even though Lowance raised the estimation of Mather as a biblical typologist, much remains to be done to understand the colonial clergyman's contribution to scriptural exegesis. Citing Mather's "self-acknowledged *magnum opus*," the "Biblia Americana," a several-thousand-page, six-folio, unpublished manuscript on biblical translation and interpretation, an historian succinctly states the case: "As a biblical commentator, Mather has yet to be fully revealed."[27]

Mather's image gained prestige when he was examined as a diarist. Lawrence Alan Rosenwald in "Cotton Mather as Diarist" adequately depicted the current direction of Matherian historiography when he wrote

---

[26]Mason I. Lowance, *The Language of Canaan: Metaphor and Symbol in New England from the Puritans to the Transcendalists* (Cambridge, Mass.: Harvard University Press, 1980), p. 159.

[27]Stephen J. Stein, "Transatlantic Extensions: Apocalyptic in Early New England," in C. A. Patrides and Joseph Wittreich, eds., *The Apocalypse in English Renaissance Thought and Literature* (Ithaca: Cornell University Press, 1984), p. 277.

that "the varient image is a datum, not a conclusion; it is partial, not entire; it needs to be set among the other images of Mather and reconciled to them to make a whole." When Rosenwald described Mather as a diarist, he consciously saw his result as a partial offering to the overall task of completing Mather's image.

Rosenwald's major accomplishment in this article was his emphasis upon the heterogeneity of Mather's *Diary*. He credited Mather by calling him "New England's principal editor of diaries and one who had probably read more of them than anyone else." After Rosenwald distinguished between Mather's early diary from his later diary, the former written before 1702 and the latter continuing until the clergyman's death, he observed that the *Diary* was essentially composed in two different ways. The early *Diary*, as Rosenwald defined it, developed a pattern of recording events in familiar categories, such as "spiritual experiences, particular providences, and religious experiences," while the later *Diary*, motivated by an increasingly complex and hectic lifestyle, prompted by the death of Mather's second wife, reflected a "fragmented style." To Rosenwald, the "fragmented style is Mather's normal style disintegrated, disrupted, exploded; it is explicable only if one thinks of Mather himself undergoing the same wrenching processes." The literary analysis Rosenwald gave of Mather's *Diary* has brought to the colonial clergyman's character a much needed softening. Mather's personality scale was raised in a more favorable direction through Rosenwald's positive rendition of the suffering and grief endured by the Puritan divine.[28] Even though twentieth-century literary historiography has given Mather's image a positive slant, other interpretations, like the intellectual school, has contributed ambiguous results.

The intellectual interpretation of Mather sharpened contrasts within his image. On the one hand, Mather's image gained valuable prestige by being included as a major actor in Perry Miller's *The New England Mind*. On the other hand, Miller perpetuated an image of Mather which sometimes distorted evidence. For example, within one of the most highly esteemed chapters of Miller's work, "The Augustinian Strain of Piety," he discussed the Puritan concept of an omnipotent God. With no reference to Mather's writings, Miller wrote that "Some Puritans pay no more than lip service to the doctrine, and Cotton Mather in his heart of hearts never doubted that the divine was a being remarkably like Cotton Mather."[29] Explicitly, Miller granted us no proof for such a devastating comment about Mather's theology, but implicitly, he based his comment upon the standard stereotype from nineteenth-century historiography and early twentieth-century psychoanalytical interpretations of Mather that pictured the Puritan suffering from chronic ego inflation.

---

[28]Lawrence Alan Rosenwald, "Cotton Mather as Diarist," *Prospects*, vol. 8 (Cambridge University Press, 1983), pp. 129, 136, 152.

[29]Perry Miller, *The New England Mind: The Seventeenth Century* (Cambridge, Mass.: Belknap Press, 1939), p. 10.

A BIBLIOGRAPHICAL ESSAY: COTTON MATHER'S CHANGING IMAGE

Miller's evaluation of Mather has left distinct ambiguities. Mather, according to Miller, was a "frenetic genius" loaded with false unction and egotism. Nevertheless, Mather tried to preserve the covenantal theology in the face of overwhelming social, economic, and political odds. Hence, for Miller, the Puritan leader took on a tragic-hero aura. Yet, Mather's image as a tragic-hero was tainted. To Miller, the preservation of Puritanism's intellectual substance was ultimately lost as Mather's generation gradually capitulated to the force of Enlightenment ideas and diluted the first generation's Calvinism. The theocratic leadership, of which Mather was the chief proponent, had been displaced by a "pietism of the disinherited." Miller's interpretation viewed the rise of pietism in New England Christianity as "a tired last-ditch effort of an evaporating superstition."[30]

Miller's analysis absolved Mather from strictly defending the old Puritanical regime and placed on the third-generation pietist the onus of being New England's supreme perpetrator of religious and intellectual declension. Apparently, Miller never reconciled these divergent elements he observed in Mather's activities. Miller concluded that Mather was "in a hundred respects . . . the most intransigent and impervious mind of his period, not to say the most nauseous human being, yet in others . . . the

---

[30]Miller, *The New England Mind: From Colony to Province* (Cambridge, Mass.: Belknap Press, 1953), p. 250. See also Richard Lovelace, *The American Pietism of Cotton Mather: Origins of American Evangelicalism* (Grand Rapids, Michigan: Eerdmans Publishing Company, 1979), p. 300.

most sensitive and perceptive, the clearest and most resolute."[31] Such a puzzled statement does give credence to Mather's complexity as a human being, but it does not clarify an intellectual estimate of the Boston clergyman's image.

Current historiography emphasizes the need to place Mather in his personal as well as social context by developing his theological, intellectual, and political enterprises through biography. Alan Heimert's introduction to the second republication of Barrett Wendell's biography of Mather agrees with Wendell's positive treatment of the Puritan divine's image. Heimert believes that "When all this has been said, Wendell's *Cotton Mather* is remarkable for its penetration into the inner mind of its intended subject." Wendell's elucidation of Mather rested extensively upon the clergyman's relationship to his father, Increase Mather. Heimert praises Wendell's effort and summarizes it as a triumph. "Whatever Wendell's source," writes Heimert, "he succeeded not merely in focusing on what may be an archetypal American relationship but in conveying a sense of its everlasting complexity."[32]

Robert Middlekauff's conscientious treatment of Cotton Mather within *The Mathers: Three Generations of Puritan Intellectuals, 1596-1728* deals extensively with Mather's theology while refuting the thesis that there was a decline of piety and adaptation to Enlightenment rationalism

---

[31]Miller, *op. cit.*, p. 476.

[32]Alan Heimert, "Introduction" to Barrett Wendell's *Cotton Mather, Puritan Priest* (New York: Harcourt Brace, 1963), p. xxi, xxii.

A BIBLIOGRAPHICAL ESSAY: COTTON MATHER'S CHANGING IMAGE

in the successive generations of the dynasty. Purporting to write an "intellectual history of Puritanism," Middlekauff simultaneously finds much "in the Mathers' thought and feeling . . . that was creative" and comes to appreciate "not only the larger contours of Puritanism," but also the Mathers' "inner experience as well."[33]

David Levin, after publishing several brief studies enthusiastically criticizing the conventional negative stereotypes of Mather,[34] furnishes us with the first half of a balanced and exhaustive biography in *Cotton Mather: The Young Life of the Lord's Remembrancer, 1663-1703*. Levin carefully unfolds the life of a normal and typical Puritan minister, a gifted scholar, a religious leader who was compassionate and generous. The result is a coherent picture which virtually animates Mather and brings to his image needed credibility. Levin prefaces his effort with a comment that concurs with the contemporary thrust of Matherian historiography: "I cannot claim to have learned to love Cotton Mather, but I believe I have learned to see why others loved him, and I have come to admire

---

[33]Robert Middlekauff, *The Mathers: Three Generations of Puritan Intellectuals, 1596-1728* (New York: Oxford University Press, 1971), p. vii, viii.

[34]David Levin, *Cotton Mather: The Young Life of the Lord's Remembrancer*, 1663, 1703 (Cambridge, Mass.: Harvard University Press, 1978). Earlier works of Levin's which criticize the negative stereotype of Mather's image are "The Hazing of Cotton Mather," *New England Quarterly* 36 (1963); "Piety and Intellect in Puritanism," *William and Mary Quarterly* 20 (1965), pp. 457-70; ed., *What Happened at Salem?* (New York, 1960); ed., *Bonifacius* (New Haven, 1966).

and respect him, both as a writer and as a man."[35]

Supporting this positive trend in Matherian scholarship are Richard Lovelace in *The American Pietism of Cotton Mather: Origins of American Evangelicalism* and Kenneth Silverman in *The Life and Times of Cotton Mather*. Lovelace gives a sterling account of Mather's pietism and offers a significant theological corrective to the shortcomings of Middlekauff's work on the Boston minister. Lovelace broadens the theological context within which to view Mather's work and emphasizes the correspondence between Mather and German pietism at Halle in order to "explore fully the international context of Mather's pietism" and his "relationship to the subsequent evangelical tradition." Agreeing with Alan Heimert's conclusion in the second republication of Wendell's biography of Mather, Lovelace's effort seats Mather's pietism in the evangelical tradition by affirming that "He ended his days as something of a John the Baptist to Jonathan Edwards."[36]

Silverman manages to avoid scriptural and psychoanalytical points of reference when presenting a sympathetic appraisal of Cotton Mather's life. Silverman posits the considerable opinion that Mather "is the first unmistakably American figure in the nation's history." Silverman adequately assesses the pressures incurred by Mather for his family's eminence in colonial New England, but he less ably incorporates the Puritan thinker's image as a synthesizer of Old World thought and

---

[35]*Ibid.*, p. xiii.

[36]Lovelace, *op. cit.*, p. 302.

A BIBLIOGRAPHICAL ESSAY: COTTON MATHER'S CHANGING IMAGE

redactor of scriptural scholarship apparent in the minister's unpublished works such as "Problema Theologicum" (1703), "Biblia Americana" (1696-1713), and "Triparadisus" (1726). His biography of Mather is less a study of Mather's intellectual and theological prowess than it is a study of the clergyman's humanness.

Through the biographical work of such writers as Levin, Lovelace, and Silverman, Mather's image continues to climb in the estimation of contemporary historiography. "No longer having a lampoon to kick around," one reviewer recently observes, "scholars and the wider reading public may now better apprehend what the Lord's Remembrancer actually wrought."[37]

At least two conclusions can be drawn concerning Mather's current image. First, he no longer is considered the instigator or chief persecutor in the 1692 witchcraft trials. Paul Boyer and Stephen Nissenbaum in *Salem Possessed: The Social Origins of Witchcraft* considered Mather a minor character in the whole affair and believed he recommended to the magistrates "a very critical and exquisite caution" toward the witnesses' professions.[38] Second, while Mather's image has lost the stigma attached to being a witchmonger, it still attracts a large scholarly following that presently stresses his intellectual attainments in the field of colonial

---

[37]Charles Cohen, *The Journal of American History* (Vol. 71, No. 3, December, 1984), pp. 606-607.

[38]Paul Boyer and Stephen Nissenbaum, *Salem Possessed: The Social Origins of Salem Witchcraft* (Cambridge, Mass.: Harvard University Press, 1974), p. 10.

history, theology, and early American literature. Contemporary Matherian historiography gives the Puritan divine much more credit for integrity in his character and work than earlier scholarship. Scholars from various fields will continue to be drawn to him. Mather's prodigious writings are an essential goldmine to scholars, even if his complex personality does not endear him to them. One biographer says, "For our society Mather represents a type toward which neutrality is almost inconceivable. . . ."[39] For scholarship, neutrality is not a goal; it is objectivity and objectivity is nothing more than being swayed by evidence to reach one's conclusions. For Mather's image, there continues to be a wealth of evidence to rehabilitate the "Lord's Remembrancer's" image.

---

[39]David Levin, "The Hazing of Cotton Mather," *New England Quarterly*, XXXVI (1964), p. 148.

INDEX

Adam, 15, 99, 103, 118
Ahlstrom, Sidney, 38
Andrews, William D., 127
Andros, Edmund (Governor of Massachusetts), 56, 195
Angels, 75-82, 109
Anselm of Canterbury, 69
Antichrist, 4, 23
"Archaeus", 143
Aristotle, 100
Arminianism, 39
Ashurst, Sir William, 183
astral projection, 151-152
Aulen, Gustaf, 37, 63, 65, 74

Baroway, I., 138
Barth, Karl, 37
Baxter, Richard, 20
Beall, Otho T., 144, 149, 217
Bercovitch, Sacvan, 11, 57, 60, 228
Black Period, 17
Blacks, 20, 180-182
Blake, John B., 121, 122
Blau, Joseph L., 141
Boas, Ralph, 227
Bonami, Patricia, 60
Boyer, Paul, 31, 170, 237
Boyer, Peter, 204
Breitwieser, Mitchell R., 144, 147
Bridenbaugh, Carl, 119, 121, 122
bubonic plague, 119
Bultmann, Rudolph, 6
Burnet, Thomas, 17
Burnet, William, 208-209
Burr, George L., 32, 158, 163, 165, 166

Cabala (see Kabbalah)
Calef, Robert, 9, 32-33, 166, 167, 224
Calvin, John, 100
Calvinism, 39, 50, 61
Cambridge Association, 83
Cambridge Platform, 26
Cartwright, Thomas, 120
Chardin de, Teilhard, 132
Chauncey, Charles, 34
Cheyne, George, 148, 149
Chiliasm, 1, 2, 7, 24, 75
Classical Theory, 65, 73-74
Cohen, Charles, 237
Coleman, Benjamin, 36-37, 73
conflagration, 5, 8, 13, 16, 22, 23, 97, 175, 190
Cooke, Elisha, 32
Cook, Sherburne F., 122
Cotton, John (grandfather of Cotton Mather), 27, 28, 51, 52, 121
covenant of grace, 70, 71-72
covenant of works, 70, 71
Cragg, G. R., 118
Cudworth, Ralph, 141
Cutler, Timothy, 33-34

Davenport, John, 29
Davidson, James W., 16, 54, 187
declension, 57, 59, 60
de Jong, J. A., 178
demonology, 172-174
Descartes, Rene, 117, 149
Devil (see Satan)
Donne, John, 137
Dummer (Governor of

Massachusetts), 213

earthquakes, 89-90, 167-168, 188-189, 198, 211-212
Eden (see Garden of Eden)
Edict of Nantes, 195, 204, 209
Edwards, Jonathan, 70
Eliot, John, 51, 53
Elliot, Emory, 56, 58
"Ephialtes", 130, 131
Erwin, John S., 122
eschatology, 1
Euphrates River, 93-98
Eve, 15, 99, 103, 118

Fenwick, Jeremiah, 125
Fifth Monarchy Men, 51
fire, 189-193
Ford, Worthington, 128, 182
Freud, Sigmund, 5, 117

Garden of Eden, 15, 91, 92-99, 111, 118
Gay, Peter, 228
General Convention of Ministers, 39
George, Lydia (wife of Cotton Mather), 30
Gideon, 75
Glasgow, University of, 36
Glover, Goodwife, 158
Gog, 23, 113
Good, Sarah, 163
Goodwin children, 17, 155, 158-162, 163, 169
Goodwin, John, 158

Half-Way Covenant, 27, 61
Hall, David, 60
Hansen, Van A., 4
Heaven (see New Heaven)
Heimert, Alan, 234
Hell, 23
Helmont, Jean Baptiste van, 117, 148
hermeneutical method, 6
Hobby, Richard, 126
Holladay, William L., 136
Holmes, Oliver Wendell, 221
Holmes, Thomas J., 20, 91, 92, 176, 224
Holstun, James, 53
Holy Spirit, 45-46
Hornberger, Theodore, 226
Howe, John, 83
Hubbard, Elizabeth (wife of Cotton Mather), 30

iatrochemical theory, 12, 149
iatromechanical theory, 149
Indians, 19-20, 182-185

Jacob, Margaret C., 141, 142
jeremiad, 57-58
Jesus Christ, 14, 24, 63-75, 108
Jews, 19, 185-186
judgment, 22-23; afflictive, 187; final, 187; eternal, 187
Jung, Carl, 5-6
Jurieu, Pierre, 195-196, 204, 209

Kabbalah ("Cabala"), 117, 136, 137, 138, 140-144

INDEX

Katz, David S., 138
Kedemah, 94-95
Kellaway, William, 178, 182-184
Kempis, Thomas a, 44, 57
King Philips War, 116, 122
King, Ursula, 132-133
Kittredge, George L., 35, 146, 224, 225
Kraus, Michael, 226

Laslett, Peter, 120
Leach, Edward, 122
Lee, Samuel, 92-93
Leverett, Jon (President of Harvard), 33
Levin, David, 18, 28, 31, 155, 156, 159, 163, 167, 172, 195, 235, 238
Lippincott, J. B., 216
Lloyd-Jones, G., 138
Lovelace, Richard, 26, 34, 38, 39, 50, 68, 86, 217, 233, 236
Lowance, Mason I., 57, 209, 230
Ludwig, Allan I., 129

Mackintosh, H. R., 65
Maclear, James F., 52
Magog, 23, 113
Manichaeism, 74
Manierre, William R., 229
Marvin, A. P., 222
Massachusetts Royal Charter, 31
Mather, Abagail (wife of Cotton Mather), 165
Mather, Cotton
   General:
      significance, 1
      defining millennium, 2

as pre and post millennialist, 5
family 26-27
at Harvard, 27-29
as pastor, 29
marriage to Abigail Phillips, 29-30
marriage to Elizabeth Hubbard, 30
marriage to Lydia George, 30
death of son, 30-31
spectral evidence, 31
involvement with Yale, 33
interest in science, 34-35
member of Royal Society, 35
range of writings, 35-36
conferred Doctor of Divinity, 36
theology, 38-39
defense of Calvinism, 39, 50
Arminianism, 39
predestination, 39-40
sovereignty of God, 40-41
daughter Hannah's sickness, 41
wife Abigail's sickness and death, 42
faith in Jesus, 43-44
justification by grace, 44-45
actions of Holy Spirit, 45-46
reason, 46-48
God's works of nature, 48
original sin, 49-50
doctrinal simplification, 50

millennial themes, 51
imminent return of Christ, 52
conversion of Indians, 53
conversion of Jews, 53, 54
New England's collective millennialism, 55-58, 62
New England as New Jerusalem, 55-56
individual salvation, 58-59, 62
soul's immortality, 59
Moral Influence Theory, 65-68
individual as imitation of Christ, 66-70
Penal Substitution Theory, 69-73
covenant theology, 70-73
covenant of works, 71
covenant of grace, 71-72
Classical theory, 73-74
belief in angels, 75-82
contact with angels, 77-79
ecumenism, 82-88
vital piety, 86
Christ's immediate return, 89
meaning of earthquakes, 89-90
threefold vision of paradise, 15-16, 91-115
first paradise: Garden of Eden, 92-99
"Sacred Geography," 92, 114
Garden of Eden location, 93-99
second paradise: The place of departed souls, 99-106
soul's clothing, 102-103
blessing, 103-104
visitation of Christ, 104

third paradise: Millennial kingdom, New Heaven and New Earth, 106-113
New Heaven, 106-111
New Jerusalem, 107-108
raised saints, 109
role of women, 110
New Earth, 111-113
soul's immortality, 117
smallpox epidemic, 121
death: obsession, 123-124; fear, 126-127, 131-132
dreams, 129-130
trilogy of spirit, soul, and body, 132, 143
representing death, 133-134
theory of the soul, 21, 134-135
interest in Hebrew, 137-139
Kabbalism, 138-144
"Archaeus," 143
analogy of dog bites, 143-144
body and illness, 147-148
astral projection, 151-152
personal trials, 154
response to witchcraft phenomenon, 18-19, 156
exegesis of Book of Revelation, 156-157
hope of millennial salvation, 157
observation of Goodwin children, 158-162, 163
attempted conversion of

INDEX 243

  Goodwife Glover, 160
observation of Mercy Short,
  162-165
death of first son, 165
observation of Margaret Rule,
  166-167
meaning of earthquakes and
  natural disasters 10, 167-
  168
warnings to New England,
  168-169
defense of Salem trials, 170-
  172
discouraging spectral evidence,
  171-172
demonology, 172-174
God's judgment, 22-23, 175,
  187-193
reformation, 176
activity in New England
  Company, 178-179
evangelization of all people,
  179-187
evangelization of Blacks, 20,
  180-182
evangelization of Indians, 19-
  20, 182-185
evangelization of Jews, 19,
  185-186, 207-208
earthquakes, 188-189
fires, 189-193
anticipation of millennium's
  beginning, 194-196
millennium computations, 8-
  9, 197-199
signs of millennium, 200-206
Christianity Maxims, 206
commentary on Daniel, 210
Boston earthquake, 211-212

millennium circumstances,
  212-213
last sermon, 214-215
death, 215

Writings:
*Addresses to Old Men and
  Young Men and Little
  Children*, 45, 56
*Advice from the Watch-
  Tower*, 49, 67
*Advice to the Churches of
  the Faithful, An*, 53, 179
Agricola, 86, 126, 169
Ambassadors Tears, The,
  46
Angel of Bethesda, 10, 21,
  36, 59, 146, 147, 150
Angelographia, 75
Armour of Christianity, The,
  87
Baptismal Piety, 66
*Batteries upon the Kingdom
  of the Devil*, 87
Benedictus, 68
"Biblia Americana," 23, 64,
  73, 82, 89, 90, 93, 138-
  139, 156, 195, 199, 203,
  204, 209, 210, 212
Blessed Unions, 83, 84
Boanerges, 10, 22, 89, 188,
  189, 214
Bonifacius, 71, 183
Call of the Gospel, The,
  41, 56, 57
Christianity to the Life, 45,
  67, 69, 73, 87

INDEX

Christian Loyalty, 211
Christian Philosopher, The, 36, 47
Christianus per Ignem, 76, 87
Coelestinus, 44, 46
Coheleth, 10, 134-135
Comfortable Chambers, The, 21, 133-134, 214
Comforter of the Mourners, A, 43
Curiousa, 10, 21, 59, 145, 146, 147
Death Made Easie & Happy, 123-124
Diary I, 19, 29, 30, 41, 42, 72, 76, 77, 78, 80, 130, 131, 132, 137, 143, 144, 154, 165, 177, 180, 181, 182, 184, 185, 186, 200
Diary II, 13, 15, 20, 31, 35, 37, 41, 42, 59, 70, 73, 74, 80, 82, 91, 130, 180, 181, 185, 186, 205, 206, 208
Eternal Salvation, 72
Euthanasia, 126
Everlasting Gospel, 44
Expectanda, 185
Faith of the Fathers, 19, 200
Free Grace, 39
Good Character, A, 49
Greatest Concern, The, 70, 71
Humiliations follow'd with Deliverances, 75, 76
Letters, 2
Magnalia Christi Americana, 11, 13, 14, 53, 61, 178-179
Malachi, 206, 207
Man of Reason, A, 47

Manuductio ad Ministerium, 64, 126, 169
Memorable Providences, 158, 159, 161
Midnight Cry, A, 52, 88, 167, 176, 198
Military Duties, 2, 75
Mystical Marriage, The, 126
Negro Christianized, The, 20, 180, 187
Nehemiah, 191
Oracula Sibyllina, 191
Parentator, 1, 41
Paterna, 80, 81, 82, 90
Perswasions From the Terror of the Lord, 23, 127, 192
Pia Desideri, 43
Piety & Equity, United, 85
Present State of New England, The, 69, 170
"Problema Theologicum", 16, 17, 24, 90, 201
Psalterium Americanum, 36
Reason Satisfied, 63
Salvation of the Soul, The, 76
Seasonable Testimony to the Glorious Doctrines, A, 39
Seasonable Thoughts Upon Mortality, 124, 125
Serviceable Man, The, 56
Short Life, A, 40
Signatus, 46
Small Offers Toward the Service of the Tabernacle in the Wilderness, 40, 56, 58

INDEX

Soul Upon the Wing, The, 129
Soul Well-Anchored, A, 116
Stone Cut Out of the Mountain, The, 205, 206
Taberah, 190, 192, 193
Terra Beata, 23, 192, 212
Terror of the Lord, The, 22, 23, 188, 211, 212
Theopolis Americana, 5, 54, 90, 202
Things for a Distress'd People to Think Upon, 168, 188, 200
Things to be Look'd For, 23, 176, 192, 194, 197, 198, 212
Things to be More Thought Upon, 86
Thoughts of a Dying Man, The, 123
"Triparadisus," 8, 15, 16, 21, 23, 25, 36, 59, 62, 74, 91-115, 140, 146, 147, 148, 149, 150, 151, 190, 191, 193, 206, 212, 213
Utilia, 49, 50, 64, 67
Valley of Hinnom, The, 125
Victorina, 127, 128
Winter-Meditations, 170, 199
Winter Piety, 66
Wonderful Works of God Commemorated, The, 49, 56
Wonders of the Invisible World, The, 18, 19, 32, 56, 155-156, 164, 165, 166, 168, 170, 171, 172, 173, 174
World Alarm'd, The, 23, 192, 212

Mather, Hannah (daughter of Cotton Mather), 41
Mather, Increase, Jr. (son of Cotton Mather), 13, 30-31
Mather, Increase, Sr. (father of Cotton Mather), 27, 31, 32, 51, 54-55, 75, 76, 83, 139-140, 167, 207-208
Mather, Katharin (daughter of Cotton Mather), 127-128
Mather, Richard (grandfather of Cotton Mather), 26-28
Mead, Matthew, 83
Mede, Joseph, 17, 114, 196-197, 201-202
Middlekauff, Robert, 9, 10, 17, 24, 25, 41, 43, 44, 45, 49, 86, 136, 192, 195, 199, 203, 206, 208, 212, 235
millennialism, 1; typology, 3; Christian, 11;
Miller, Perry, 12, 26, 57, 59, 60, 62, 83, 87, 114, 116, 153, 216, 232, 233, 234
Milton, John, 153
Moody, Raymond A., 105
Moorhead, James H., 11
Moral Influence Theory, 65-68
More, Henry, 117, 141, 142
Morgan, Edmund S., 216
Morrison, Samuel E., 216, 226
Moxtershed, Ralph, 125
Murdock, Kenneth B., 13-14, 34, 35, 223
mythology, 7; Christian, 5; millennial, 7;

Nebuchadnezzar, 107
New Earth, 7, 13, 16, 22, 64, 111-113
New England Company, 177-179, 182-183
New England Way, 31, 58, 59, 60-62
New Heaven, 7, 13, 16, 22, 23, 64, 88, 106-111
New Jerusalem, 54, 55-56, 88, 107-108
Newton, Isaac, 17, 202, 209
Nishmath-Chajim, 10, 21-22, 59, 1366, 138, 140, 143, 144, 146-148, 149-152
Nissenbaum, Stephen, 31, 170, 237

Oakes, Dr. Thomas, 159
Oakes, Urian (President of Harvard), 28
Onesimus (black servant of Cotton Mather), 181

paradise, 15-16; premillenialist view, 3-4; postmillennialist view, 5; first paradise, 92-99; second paradise, 99-106; third paradise, 106-113
parousia, 14
Parrington, Vernon L., 221
Partridge, A. C., 138
Peabody, William, 217
Penal Substitutionary Theory, 65, 69-73
Pequot War, 116
Perkins, Williams, 70
Person, David, 118, 119

Pettit, Norman, 216
Phillips, Abigail (also see Abagail Mather), 29-30, 42
Plato, 100
Poole, William F., 218-220
postmillennialism, 3, 4, 5
predestination, 39-40
premillennialism, 3, 4, 5
Prince, Thomas, 91
Protestant Reformation, 197
Puritanism, 11, 26, 28, 79, 120, 216

Robbins, Chandler, 222
Rooy, Sidney H., 21, 177, 182, 186
Rosenthal, E. I. J., 138
Roth, C., 138
Royal Society of England, 35, 145-146
Rule, Margaret, 18, 155, 158, 166-167, 169
Rutman, Darret, 216

Sadducism, 80, 106-107, 161
Salem witchcraft trials, 9, 163, 170-172, 217-220
"Samaritan Pentateuch", 17
Satan, 8, 9, 14, 16, 18, 23, 172-174
Scholem, Gerhard G., 140, 141
Scholem, Gershom, 102
Schwartz, Hillel, 141
"Second Wo", 16
Sewall, Samuel, 51, 54, 61, 114, 122-123, 177, 204-205
Shi, David E., 60, 62

INDEX

Shipton, Clifford K., 221, 225, 226
Short, Mercy, 17, 155, 158, 162-165, 169
Shryock, R. H., 144, 148, 149, 217
Sibylline Oracles, 191-192
Silverman, Kenneth, 1, 35, 106, 195, 207, 209, 212, 228, 229, 236
Simpson, Alan, 216
sin, 49-50, 136, 144
smallpox, 116, 121-122
soul, 117, 132-138, 144-147
Spark, Jared, 217
spectral evidence, 31, 171-172
Starkey, Marion, 154
Stavely, Keith W. F., 60
Stein, Stephen, 4, 194, 230
Sweet, Leonard, 2-3, 5

Tertullian, 107
Thatcher, Thomas, 121
Thirty-nine Articles, 39
Thomas, D. W., 138
Thomas, M. Halsey, 123
Thompson, Joseph, 183
Tigris River, 93-98
Toleration Act, 83
Tyler, Moses Coit, 221

Upham, C. W., 218

Vartanian, Pershing, 144
Venner, Thomas, 51

Walker, Williston, 28
Waller, Richard, 145

Webster, Charles, 141
Webster, John, 161
Weisman, Richard, 18, 174
Wendell, Barrett, 222, 234
Wesley, John, 66
Whiston, William, 17, 199, 202-204
Willard, Samuel, 32, 33
Winthrop, John, 61
witchcraft, 9, 18, 19, 24, 156, 170-172
Woodward, John, 34, 35

Yale, Elihu, 33

Ziff, Larzer, 52
Zirkle, Conway, 226
Zoroastrianism, 74, 75

STUDIES IN AMERICAN RELIGION

1. Suzanne Geissler, **Jonathan Edwards to Aaron Burr, Jr. : From the Great Awakening to Democratic Politics**

2. Ervin Smith, **The Ethics of Martin Luther King, Jr.**

3. Nancy Manspeaker, **Jonathan Edwards: Bibliographical Synopses**

4. Erling Jorstad, **Evangelicals in the White House: The Cultural Maturation of Born Again Christianity**

5. Anson Shupe and William A. Stacey, **Born Again Politics and the Moral Majority: What Social Surveys Really Show**

6. Edward Tabor Linenthal, **Changing Images of the Warrior Hero in America: A History of Popular Symbolism**

7. Philip Jordan, **The Evangelical Alliance for the United States of America, 1847-1900: Ecumenism, Identity and the Religion of the Republic**

8. Jon Alexander, **American Personal Religious Accounts, 1600-1980: Toward an Inner History of America's Faiths**

9. Richard Libowitz, **Mordecai M. Kaplan and the Development Development of Reconstructionism**

10. David Rausch, **Arno C. Gaebelein, 1861-1945: Irenic Fundamentalist and Scholar**

11. Ralph Luker, **A Southern Tradition in Theology and Social Criticism 1830-1930: The Religious Liberalism and Social Conservatism of James Warley Miles, William Porcher Dubose and Edgar Gardner Murphy**

12. Barry Jay Seltser, **The Principles and Practice of Political Compromise: A Case Study of the United States Senate**

13. Kathleen Margaret Dugan, **The Vision Quest of the Plains Indians: Its Spiritual Significance**

14. Peter G. Erb, **Johann Conrad Beissel and the Ephrata Community: Mystical and Historical Texts**

15. William L. Portier, **Isaac Hecker and the First Vatican Council Including Hecker's "Notes in Italy, 1869-1870"**

16. Paula M. Gooey, **Jonathan Edwards on Nature and Destiny: A Systematic Analysis**

17. Helen Westra, **The Minister's Task and Calling in the Sermons of Jonathan Edwards**

18. D. G. Paz, **The Priesthoods and Apostasies of Pierce Connelly: A Study of Victorian Conversion and Anti-Catholicism**

19. **The Agricultural Social Gospel in America:** *The Gospel of the Farm* by Jenkin Lloyd Jones, Edited with an Introduction by Thomas E. Graham

20. Jane Rasmussen, **Musical Taste as a Religious Question in Nineteenth Century America: The Development of Episcopal Church Hymnody**

21. Edward H. McKinley, **Somebody's Brother: A History of The Salvation Army Men's Social Service Department 1891-1985**

22. Stafford Poole and Douglas J. Slawson, **Church and Slave in Perry County, Missouri, 1818-1865**

23. Rebecca Moore, **The Jonestown Letters: Correspondence of the Moore Family 1970-1985**

24. Lawrence H. Williams, **Black Higher Education in Kentucky 1879-1930**

25. Erling Jorstad, **The New Christian Right, 1981- 1988: Prospects for the Post-Reagan Decade**

26. Joseph H. Hall, **Presbyterian Conflict and Resolution on the Missouri Frontier**

27. Jonathan Wells, **Charles Hodge's Critique of Darwinism: An Historical Critical Analysis of Concepts Basic to the 19th Century Debate**

28. Donald R. Tuck, **Buddhist Churches of America: Jodo Shinshu**

29. Suzanne Geissler, **Lutheranism and Anglicanism in Colonial New Jersey: An Early Ecumenical Experiment in New Sweden**

30. David Hein, **A Student's View of The College of St. James on the Eve of the Civil War: The Letters of W. Wilkins Davis (1842-1866)**

31. Char Miller, **Selected Writings of Hiram Bingham (1814-1869) Missionary To The Hawaiian Islands: To Raise The Lord's Banner**

32. Rebecca Moore, **In Defense of People's Temple**

33. Donald L. Huber, **Educating Lutheran Pastors in Ohio, 1830-1980: A History of Trinity Lutheran Seminary and its Predecessors**

34. Hugh Spurgin, **Roger Williams and Puritan Radicalism in the English Separatist Tradition**

35. Michael Meiers, **Was Jonestown a CIA Medical Experiment?: A Review of the Evidence**

36. L. Raymond Camp, **Roger Williams, God's Apostle of Advocacy: Biography and Rhetoric**

37. Rebecca Moore & Fielding M. McGehee III (eds.), **New Religious Movements, Mass Suicide, and Peoples Temple: Scholarly Perspectives on a Tragedy**

38. Anabelle S. Wenzke, **Timothy Dwight (1752-1817)**

39. Joseph R. Washington Jr., **Race and Religion in Early Nineteenth Century America 1800-1850: Constitution, Conscience, and Calvinist Compromise** (2 vols.)

40. Joseph R. Washington Jr., **Race and Religion in Mid-Nineteenth Century America 1850-1877: Protestant Parochial Philanthropists** (2 vols.)

41. Rebecca Moore & Fielding M. McGehee (eds.), **The Need For a Second Look at Jonestown: Remembering Its People**

42. Joel Fetzer, **Selective Prosecution of Religiously Motivated Offenders in America: Scrutinizing The Myth of Neutrality**

43. Charles H. Lippy, **The Christadelphians in North America**

44. N.G. Thomas, **The Millennial Impulse in Michigan, 1830-1860: The Second Coming in the Third New England**

45. John S. Erwin, **The Millennialism of Cotton Mather: An Historical and Theological Analysis**

46. William E. Ellis, **Patrick Henry Callahan (1866- 1940): Progressive Catholic Layman in the American South**

47. Virginia Peacock, **Problems in the Interpretation of Jonathan Edwards'** *The Nature of True Virtue*

48. Francis W. Sacks, C.M., **The Philadelphia Baptist Tradition of Church and Church Authority: An Ecumenical Analysis and Theological Interpretation**